Praise for *The Last Dropout*

■ ■ ■ ■ ■

"We can all agree that all students deserve an education that prepares them for college, career, and life. But with more than one million students dropping out a year, our belief in this is not enough—we need to understand the dropout problem and take the action that Bill Milliken suggests. If enough of us just do this, we can create an education system that works for all young people."

— **Patty Stonesifer**, CEO, Bill & Melinda Gates Foundation

"Bill Milliken is one of my heroes. He made a lifelong commitment to young people and always walks his talk. This book tells the truth—with facts and stories and heart and humor—about how 'the system' has failed so many of our kids, and what we can and must do about that."

— **Russell Simmons**, founder, Def Jam Music and Phat Fashions

"We must dispel the lie that our children's destinies are determined essentially by the families they're born into or the color of their skin. Comprehensive student support services that build resiliency skills in students are a key strategy to dispel that lie, and Bill Milliken has been a pioneer in this arena for many years."

— **Joel Klein**, chancellor, New York City Department of Education

"We can't possibly succeed in the hypercompetitive global economy with one-third of our young people on the bench. Additional rigor and relevance are important, but the crisis in our schools also requires all of us to pitch in. We need to mobilize an army of adult volunteers to come alongside our dedicated educators and change the dynamics of the 'Dropout Nation.' Bill Milliken is a powerful, effective advocate because he has lived the revolution he is helping to lead."

— **Governor Tim Pawlenty**,
chair of the National Governors Association

"Bill's uplifting story of his life's work shows us that every child has something to contribute, and that to achieve that potential, we must create the right environment for our children. Through better access to community services, rich connections with others, and a sense of ownership for their own success, our children can thrive in both academics and in life. In his comprehensive book, Bill engages us to envision the CIS model scaled to reach every schoolchild across the country, and he challenges all of us to work together to help our children achieve the success they deserve."

— **Pam and Pierre Omidyar**, founder and chairman of eBay; cofounders of the Omidyar Network

*"No one but Bill Milliken could have written **The Last Dropout**, because no one but Bill Milliken has been able to connect his own personal journey so powerfully to what America's students need today. This book is a well of inspiration from which one can drink again and again. If we are serious about a different vision for America—one that begins with education and runs straight through to justice for all—**The Last Dropout** shows us how to give our children the hope and promise they deserve."*

— **Billy Shore**, founder and executive director, Share Our Strength

*"Bill Milliken's book is essential reading for any businessperson who cares about the future of education in America and the importance of an educated workforce. He vividly illustrates the power of collaboration and innovation to combat the dropout epidemic that plagues our local school systems. **The Last Dropout** describes a leveraged alternative to throwing money at seemingly intractable problems; it describes a robust strategy that delivers breakthrough results—and offers a significant multiplier on our charitable dollars. America's children deserve to benefit from these insights."*

— **Thomas J. Tierney**, chairman and cofounder, the Bridgespan Group

"Bill Milliken has distilled 40 years of experience—with kids on the streets, with teachers and staff in schools, with lay and clergy in churches and temples, with corporate leaders in boardrooms, and with public leaders in halls of government—down to a few key principles with a single, compelling purpose: helping troubled students do well in school and reclaim their futures. The title

of Part 1 summarizes not only the book, but also the theme of Bill Milliken's own life and work, 'It all starts with relationships.' This is both a powerfully practical and spiritually moving book. Now there's a combination!"

— **Jim Wallis**, president of Sojourners/Call to Renewal and the author of *God's Politics: Why the Right Gets It Wrong and the Left Doesn't Get It*

"'Every child needs and deserves a one-on-one relationship with a caring adult.' I've heard Bill Milliken say this a thousand times in the 12 years I've known him—to teachers, public officials, corporate leaders—to anyone who will listen. Bill has done so much to help kids stay in school and do well in their studies. These stories are inspiring!"

— **Jim Sinegal**, president and CEO, Costco Wholesale Corporation

"The success of our students and schools is essential to the future economic well-being of our communities and our country. Bank of America has been honored to support Communities In Schools and their efforts to turn potential dropouts into student leaders for today, and our nation's leaders for tomorrow."

— **Kenneth D. Lewis**, chairman and CEO, Bank of America

"I commend my good friend Bill Milliken of Communities In Schools for sharing his vision for a future in which there are no more high school dropouts. His blueprint for change should be studied closely in communities across the country. It is imperative that we all work together to give all students the support they need to reach their potential."

— **Richard G. Lugar**, United States senator

"Education is one issue where changing policy is just the first step. In **The Last Dropout**, *Bill Milliken clearly outlines the elements necessary for lasting reform. If we don't get serious about equipping students with the knowledge and skills that they need to be successful adults, then we need to be prepared to face the economic and social consequences."*

— **Thomas J. Donohue**, president and CEO,
U.S. Chamber of Commerce

"As longtime supporters of Communities In Schools, we have seen firsthand the remarkable results that are possible when these profoundly important principles are in place. Now, other business leaders, educators, legislators, and community members can also find inspiration and a blueprint for action in **The Last Dropout.**"

— **Steve and Elaine Wynn**, Wynn Resorts

"Bill Milliken's book **The Last Dropout** *is proof that visionaries like him see the full potential in our children. These are the visionaries and leaders of our future and of our civilizations. If you want to make a difference in the world, read this book."*

— **Deepak Chopra, M.D.**, author of *The Book of Secrets*

"Great public schools are a basic right for every child. That right can only be guaranteed when communities partner with educators to assure that each student has the resources needed to succeed. In **The Last Dropout**, *Bill Milliken tells us that we can end the dropout crisis only if we get serious about working together to meet the diverse needs of students in our public schools. Milliken puts the spotlight on the crisis, and now it will take everyone sharing responsibility to correct it."*

— **Reg Weaver**, president, National Education Association

*"**The Last Dropout**, like Communities In Schools, is about hope, belief, commitment, and love: the hope for a better future for all children; the belief that certain principles, applied effectively, actually do make a positive difference in schools and communities; and the commitment, reinforced with love, to do whatever we must to ensure all kids succeed in school and prepare for life."*

— **Wally Amos**, literacy advocate and founder, Chip & Cookie, Inc.

"Bill Milliken's sensitive, out-of-the-box vision has inserted an effective and proven safety net into the enormous dropout problem."

— **Herb Alpert**, musician, producer, and cofounder of A&M Records

"This is a book about the real world: one where children are not just statistics. In it, Bill Milliken tells us how to involve the community in every school; nurture and excite each student; add a healthy dose of caring, capable educators; and truly leave no child behind. It is a recipe that works."

— **William E. Brock**, former United States senator, ambassador, and secretary of labor

"Bill Milliken is a modern-day prophet whose voice calls us to step forward and act for the common good of all our children. If you want to make a difference in the lives of children, if you want communities that work for everyone, then read this book."

— **Richard C. Harwood**, president, Harwood Institute for Public Innovation

"I have always had great admiration for Bill, right from the beginning, for his dedication and commitment to kids and education."

— **Burt Bacharach**, legendary composer

"Bill Milliken has spent a lifetime learning what the rest of us would be wise not to forget. **The Last Dropout** is a call to awareness, advocacy, and action. It is a road map for a society that has lost its way in its commitment to the next generation, and there is not grace enough in heaven for any of us who do not think about those who will come after us. I do not suggest you read this book; I suggest you take it to heart."

— **Noah benShea**, philosopher and best-selling author

"If parents, teachers and leaders make education a top priority, then our children will understand the importance of school and continue on the right path. This book clearly shows us the winning way!"

— **Jerry Rice**, NFL legend, broadcaster, and author of *Go Long! My Journey Beyond the Game and the Fame*

THE LAST DROPOUT

ALSO BY BILL MILLIKEN

Tough Love

So Long, Sweet Jesus

■ ■ ■ ■ ■

HAY HOUSE TITLES OF RELATED INTEREST

An Attitude of Gratitude: 21 Life Lessons, by Keith D. Harrell

The Covenant in Action, compiled by Tavis Smiley

Interpersonal Edge: Breakthrough Tools for Talking to Anyone, Anywhere, about Anything, by Daneen Skube

The Intuitive Spark: Bringing Intuition Home to Your Child, Your Family, and You, by Sonia Choquette

Passionate People Produce: Rekindle Your Passion and Creativity, by Charles Kovess

Saying Yes to Change: Essential Wisdom for Your Journey, by Joan Z. Borysenko, Ph.D., and Gordon F. Dveirin, Ed.D.

Who Are You? A Success Process for Building Your Life's Foundation, by Stedman Graham

■ ■ ■ ■ ■

Please visit Hay House USA: **www.hayhouse.com**®; Hay House Australia: **www.hayhouse.com.au**; Hay House UK: **www.hayhouse. co.uk**; Hay House South Africa: **www.hayhouse.co.za**; Hay House India: **www.hayhouse.co.in**

THE LAST DROPOUT

Stop the Epidemic!

BILL MILLIKEN

HAY HOUSE, INC.
Carlsbad, California • New York City
London • Sydney • Johannesburg
Vancouver • Hong Kong • New Delhi

Published and distributed in the United States by: Hay House, Inc.: www.hay-house.com • *Published and distributed in Australia by:* Hay House Australia Pty. Ltd.: www.hayhouse.com.au • *Published and distributed in the United Kingdom by:* Hay House UK, Ltd.: www.hayhouse.co.uk • *Published and distributed in the Republic of South Africa by:* Hay House SA (Pty), Ltd.: www.hayhouse.co.za • *Distributed in Canada by:* Raincoast: www.raincoast.com • *Published in India by:* Hay House Publishers India: www.hayhouse.co.in

Editorial supervision: Jill Kramer • *Design:* Jenny Richards

Library of Congress Cataloging-in-Publication Data

Milliken, Bill.
  The last dropout : stop the epidemic! / Bill Milliken.
    p. cm.
  Includes bibliographical references.
  ISBN-13: 978-1-4019-1903-0 (tradepaper)
  ISBN-13: 978-1-4019-1906-1 (hardcover) 1. Community and school--United States. 2. Dropouts--United States--Prevention. I. Title.
  LC221.M553 2007
  373.12'913--dc22   2007017544

Hardcover ISBN: 978-1-4019-1906-1
Tradepaper ISBN: 978-1-4019-1903-0

10 09 08 07   4 3 2 1
1st edition, September 2007

Printed in the United States of America

■ ■ ■ ■ ■

To my wife and best friend, Jean;
our son and daughter, Sean and Lani;
our daughter-in-law, Jill; our grandchildren, Alex and Jack;
and the wonderful extended family of Millikens, Marquises,
Kondases, and Curtises—the family I always wanted,
the reason I keep going.

■ ■ ■ ■ ■

CONTENTS

■ ■ ■ ■ ■

*"FOR THESE ARE ALL OUR CHILDREN,
AND WE SHALL ALL PROFIT BY,
OR PAY FOR, WHAT THEY BECOME."*

— JAMES BALDWIN

■ ■ ■ ■ ■

What Is *Communities In Schools?*

*This book contains information and descriptions drawn from the history of the Communities In School (CIS) organization. For readers not familiar with CIS, a brief description follows; more information is available at **www.communitiesinschools.org**.*

Communities In Schools (CIS) is the nation's leading community-based organization helping kids succeed in school and prepare for life. It's nonprofit, nonpartisan, and dedicated to ending the dropout epidemic in the United States.

For 30 years, CIS has championed the connection of needed community resources with schools. By bringing caring adults into the schools to address children's unmet needs, it provides the link between educators and the community. The result: Teachers are free to teach, and students—many in jeopardy of dropping out—finally have the opportunity to focus on learning.

CIS creates comprehensive, locally controlled nonprofit support systems around schools. In partnership with the local school system, it identifies the most critical needs of students and families—needs that are preventing children from succeeding in school . . . and in life. It then locates and coordinates community resources, dedicated volunteers, and agencies to serve in partnership with the public schools, both during the day and after school, thereby making the work of educators much more effective.

Coordination of effort and *accountability for results* are essential aspects of the service that the organization provides, because well-meaning programs often fail to focus on overall school objectives. CIS ensures that the work of these outside agencies and volunteers is interconnected and integrated to provide the support schools need most.

Each year, more than 1.2 million young people and their families in 27 states and the District of Columbia receive services through Communities In Schools.

■ ■ ■ ■ ■

FOREWORD

by President and Mrs. Jimmy Carter

We first met Bill Milliken and Neil Shorthouse more than 30 years ago when they came to us in Georgia with an innovative response to the loss of so many young people from the public school system. We supported the fledgling program, then called EXODUS, from the governor's office. Upon entering the White House in 1977, we helped Bill take his work to a national level and have continued our interest in the years since.

Having helped get Communities In Schools off to a good start, it has been a joy to watch it become an important force for change. Our affection for and commitment to Bill Milliken and Neil Shorthouse have never wavered—they are truly life companions for both of us. Bill's faithful insistence that "programs don't change people—*relationships* do" has been a constant reminder and inspiration for us in all of our endeavors.

This extraordinary account tells how Bill and Neil and their colleagues developed the insights that have meant so much to communities across the country. The publication of *The Last Dropout* couldn't be more timely. Americans are waking up to the truth about how we do—or don't—serve our children through the public school system. About one-third of all young people and 50 percent of poor and minority youth fail to graduate with their peers. This is economically disastrous for the dropout, who is crying out for social justice, not more discrimination. That poor people bear the burden of our failure to create an equitable public education system is one of the major themes of this work. Anyone who hopes to reverse the economic injustices of our society must confront this reality.

The epidemic is costing America too many children, too many tears, too many futures. *The Last Dropout* is a declaration of hope and a call to action, showing how we can change schools and communities, one student and one family at a time. It is also a book of wonderful human stories from a deeply caring and spiritual individual.

■ ■ ■ ■ ■

INTRODUCTION

Dropout Nation

"When we looked at the millions of students that our high schools are not preparing for higher education—and we looked at the damaging impact that has on their lives—we came to a painful conclusion: America's high schools are obsolete."

— **Bill Gates**, founder and CEO, Microsoft

In March 2006, the Bill & Melinda Gates Foundation issued its scathing report, *The Silent Epidemic: Perspectives of High School Dropouts*. It begins: "There is a high school dropout epidemic in America. Each year, almost one third of all public high school students—and nearly one half of all blacks, Hispanics, and Native Americans—fail to graduate from public high school with their class."[1] The report's lead author, John M. Bridgeland, a former director of the USA Freedom Corps, urged that "the nation . . . answer this wake-up call and do something significant about it."[2]

A few weeks later, *Time* magazine's cover story "Dropout Nation" brought the crisis to newsstands and supermarket check-out counters, while Oprah Winfrey brought it to millions of television viewers. Then the Economic Policy Institute released its own study suggesting that perhaps the dropout rate was "only" 18 percent.[3] The debate about the numbers was on, and will continue—as if there's some moral advantage to losing only one out of five of our students, rather than one out of three.

Thanks to this rise in media attention, millions of Americans were hearing for the first time that we do indeed have a "dropout epidemic" in this country. And they were learning about the grim real-life consequences in a new century, demanding workplace skills that most often require at least post-high-school study.

America's 3.5 million dropouts[4] ages 16 to 25 are truly have-nots: They don't have a high school diploma, and as a result they have little hope for a decent future. They're far more likely than their peers to be unemployed, live in poverty, experience chronic poor health, depend upon social services, and go to jail. Four out of every ten young-adult dropouts receive some type of government assistance. Someone who didn't graduate is more than eight times as likely to be in jail or prison as a person with at least a high school diploma. Half of all prison inmates are dropouts. In fact, on any given day, more young male dropouts are in prison than at a job.

"On my BlackBerry, I get the major crimes that happen in this city as they happen on a real-time basis. . . . When you find the suspect, you can be certain it will almost always be a high school dropout and/ or somebody who can't read or write. There is a connection, make no mistake about it, with the dropout rate."

— **Antonio Villaraigosa**, mayor of Los Angeles

The dire consequences for these young people are mirrored in the costs to American society—to you, your children, and the future of our country. Dropouts are costing us *billions* of dollars in lost wages and increased social supports, including medical care and welfare benefits. Our nation is already operating with a huge deficit. The combined income and tax losses from *a single year's dropouts* is about $192 billion—1.6 percent of the gross domestic product.

The cost of imprisoning or providing government services to these individuals is almost impossible to calculate, but one measure suggests the staggering truth: *Each youth* who drops out of school and later moves into a life of crime or drugs is costing the nation somewhere between $1.7 and $2.3 million. Just imagine what we could accomplish if this same amount were spent on education instead.[5]

Business leaders, economists, and chambers of commerce across the country agree: In a time of intense international competition, America is unable to recruit an adequate workforce while losing one-third of its youth. The opportunities that you and your children take for granted are being eroded day by day as the country is transformed into a society of haves and have-nots. In 20 years, the impact of fiscal failure and social division will be felt keenly by the haves, as U.S. global economic leadership dwindles and the nation is unable to pay its huge "bill" generated by the have-nots.

"The bottom line is that this nation cannot rightfully expect to lead the 21st century's information- and technology-driven global economy when we have upwards of 30 percent of our young people not even graduating from high school."

— **Thomas J. Donohue**, president and CEO, U.S. Chamber of Commerce

The dropout epidemic is creating a divided society whose consequences will be devastating for all Americans, not just the young people themselves. It is at once a practical disaster for our economy, a human tragedy for the children and families directly concerned, and a justice issue that confronts every citizen.

In Search of the Last Dropout

Although the challenge is enormous, we *can* stop the dropout epidemic. A growing consensus of educators and social-service providers is rallying behind *a solution that works*. The purpose of this book is to describe that solution and show how Americans at every level of society—local leaders desperate to stop the hemorrhaging of youth from their school systems, foundation heads and corporate CEOs equally determined to put their money and influence to work in this vital cause, and of course the parents and teachers of these students—can come together and *stop the epidemic*.

A million dropouts, or two million, or three, is an outrageous tragedy. But even *one* young person abandoned to a life with no future is equally tragic, equally unacceptable. Our collective goal must be a 21st-century America in which, at long last, we've seen the last dropout.

> *"Educators and policymakers have been reluctant (or unable) to make the drastic changes needed in the way schools are organized and operated. They've failed to transform the existing conventional schools into learning centers that would attract and serve the minority, immigrant, and poor students who populate our cities. . . . [They] may be starting to realize that they are not in the school business, they're in the education business; they need to value their students more than their schools and do whatever it takes to provide them the educational opportunities they need and deserve. <u>Every year of futile tinkering consigns millions of youngsters to a bleak future.</u>"*
>
> — **Ronald A. Wolk**, *Teacher* magazine, December 2006

Who will be the last dropout? The last American youth who doesn't make it through our public school system?

Will it be Marcy? She lives with her mother, her grandmother, and her three siblings in the Shaw neighborhood of Washington, D.C. Shaw has had its ups and downs over the years—the riots of 1968 took their toll on the community, as did the crack plagues and crime waves of the 1980s and '90s. Still, it's an area with a long, proud history, and Marcy's mother believes there are a lot of worse places to raise your children. She has a full-time job at the local grocery store, but it pays only minimum wage and the family income is well below the poverty level. And lately, Marcy hasn't been well—the usual childhood ailments, but also some worrisome concerns about potential asthma.

Will Marcy be the last dropout? She's only two years old now, so it's hard to say.

Will it be Jaime? His family lives in Las Vegas, but their life is a different kind of gamble. Like a surprising number of youth in the city and in Clark County, Jaime is homeless. With his parents and five siblings, he moves from shelter to shelter, relative to friend—and spends a lot of time sleeping rough under the Nevada stars. Jaime is five and ready to enroll in the public school system. I wonder where he'll be doing his homework.

Or perhaps the last dropout will be Linda, whose family has lived in the same rural North Carolina county for generations. None of them has ever graduated from high school—there's always been work on the farm and in the nearby mills as soon as a child is old enough to hold a job. Education is all very well, but every dollar is needed just to get by. In the new century, though, work opportunities for nongraduates are drying up as the county's economy changes. Seven-year-old Linda is going to need a new vision for her future—and some very practical help achieving it.

When will we see the last dropout? No one knows, of course, other than to say, "Not in this generation." But we *can* say this: Young people will stop dropping out when they receive the community support and resources they need to learn, stay in school, and graduate prepared for life.

They'll stop dropping out when we admit that our country doesn't have a "youth problem"; we have an *adult* problem. We—the grown-ups, including parents, who have a stake in the community's children—haven't succeeded in weaving a safety net of support that will keep kids safe, healthy, and motivated. The business community in particular hasn't yet committed its full energy and expertise to champion the connection of resources with schools. Nor has America modeled the kind of caring society that can serve as an inspiration and a source of hope for young people. All the "school reform" in the world won't accomplish this. It isn't only about better teachers, better schools, or more money. It is about *hope*.

My colleagues and I have spent the past 30 years developing an antidote to the dropout epidemic. **This is the good news I**

want to share with you in this book: There is a cure for the dropout epidemic. It's at work in hundreds of communities, and it will work in yours, too.

The Last Dropout is about a journey that began in Harlem in the 1960s and took us to Wall Street, to Atlanta, and ultimately to the White House. We were "street workers," trying to help young people who had already dropped out to return to school and get their diplomas. Over time, we realized it was useless to keep bailing out the basement unless we also turned off the tap, and that meant working inside the public school system. The Communities In Schools organization, originally founded in 1977 as Cities In Schools, was the result. CIS now reaches more than one million young people and their families annually, in more than 3,400 schools. These kids are chronically underserved—they fall far below the national average for every measure of student success. **Yet CIS-tracked students are staying in school and graduating prepared for life.** Why? What makes the difference?

The key principles in *The Last Dropout* weren't developed in a think tank or a graduate school. Our work with kids and families has benefited enormously from the research and documentation of the academic community, but I do want to make clear that most of the lessons in this book were learned through firsthand experience, from the ground up, by sitting down and breaking bread with families, students, teachers, and community members, as well as business and government leaders.

Similarly, my hat is off to our dedicated American educators, and this book in no way means to disparage their efforts. The school-reform movement has generated important gains for kids: Teachers have revised curricula to emphasize strategies for student success based on carefully researched models and set high standards for student achievement. Policy makers have created legislation such as No Child Left Behind, which endorses these high standards for all children, recognizing that every kid can learn, regardless of class, color, or place of origin. And we've invested a great deal of innovation and creativity into the governance of schools, holding them accountable for their students' progress.

So, both the *content* of education—the curricula, the pedagogical strategies—and the *form* of education—school management and governance—are the subject of intense reform efforts. **What's missing, though, is what I call the "third side of the triangle": the community component that will meet the nonacademic needs of children.** To put it simply, it's pretty hard to concentrate on your third-grade reading achievement test if your bedroom has no heat and you need glasses, you go to school every day scared and hungry, or you're distracted by family problems.

I've said that the dropout epidemic is also a justice issue, and I want to emphasize that again. How we respond to it will determine whether the United States becomes a permanently divided nation of those who make it and those who don't. Is that the kind of world we want our children to inherit? A place divided between gated communities and prisons, between winners and losers? I promise you, the prospect will be bleak, *no matter which side of the fence you're on.* We simply can't continue on a path that produces such drastic economic and human inequity.

About This Book

The Last Dropout offers the key principles that the Communities In Schools movement has tested over three decades, principles that lead to better schools and successful kids. Chapters 1 through 3 focus on principles for positive relationships among adults and between adults and students; Chapters 4 though 6 detail practical, organizational precepts; and Chapters 7 through 9 focus on sustainability for the long term.

You may find some of the language familiar from other contexts, but I hope that this book will help you see the words in a new light. Most certainly, I hope that you'll be inspired to apply these concepts in your own communities and to further the missions of your own organizations.

Here are the essential principles that will keep young people in school and prepare them for successful lives:

1. Programs don't change kids—*relationships* do.

2. The dropout crisis isn't just an education issue.

3. Young people need the five *real* basics, not just the three R's: a one-on-one relationship with a caring adult; a safe place to learn and grow; a healthy start and a healthy future; a marketable skill to use upon graduation; and a chance to give back to peers and community.

4. The community must weave a safety net around its children in a manner that's personal, accountable, and coordinated.

5. Every community needs a "Champion for Children": a neutral third party with "magic eyes" to see things— and people—differently, and coordinate and broker the diverse community resources into the schools on behalf of young people and families.

6. Educators and policy makers can't do it alone . . . and they'll welcome your help.

7. Curing the dropout epidemic will demand *change,* not just charity.

8. *Scalability, sustainability,* and *evidence-based strategies* are essential to creating permanent change in the way our education system combats the dropout epidemic.

9. Our children need three things from you: your *awareness,* your *advocacy,* and your *action.*

I'll clarify and expand upon each of these in the chapters that follow. However, I want first to caution you to avoid the "silver-bullet syndrome"—that is, the temptation to adopt and implement only one or two of these key principles and disregard the rest. In fact, it's precisely this fragmented approach that has doomed other community-development and school-reform efforts in the past, including some state and local Communities In Schools efforts. If there's one thing we've learned over 30 years of doing this work, it's that it takes a total commitment to *all* of these principles to yield any meaningful and lasting effect on the dropout problem.

Finally, I want to address a few words to the business and philanthropic leaders who I believe will find in *The Last Dropout* a cause for optimism and a blueprint for change. Our view is that you have a special, critical role to play in ending the dropout epidemic. Your community needs you to use the power of the private and nonprofit sectors—your connections, your knowledge, your organizational skills, your practical experience—to leverage resources for schools, children, and families and to influence how private-, public-, and nonprofit-sector institutions at all levels distribute funds for education and family services. Moreover, your *nation* needs you to champion and help spread these effective strategies for student success widely enough to meet the immense need—to "go to scale," as nonprofits now refer to it—in a way that will change, permanently and effectively, how America's schools educate their students.

We don't need you to create more charities. We need you to think and work differently. I hope this book will help. Most important, we need you to *lead*. A lot of lives are depending on you.

■ ■ ■ ■ ■

PART I

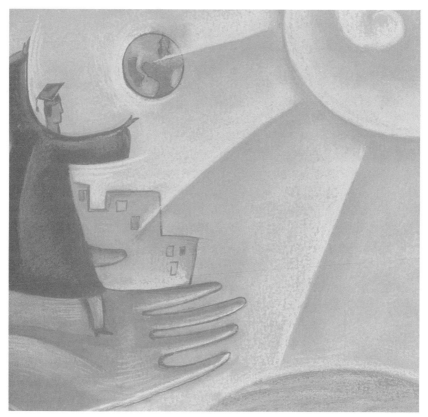

It All
Starts with
Relationships

CHAPTER ONE

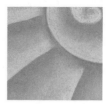

Programs Don't Change Kids— *Relationships Do*

Being Dumb

I wasn't a high school dropout. I'm sure I would have been, but I didn't get the chance—the school kicked me out before I could quit.

It was 1957, I was 17, and by most people's standards, I had it made. I was a white Anglo-Saxon Protestant. I grew up in a middle-class suburb of Pittsburgh on a quiet, shady street in a nice neighborhood. My father and his brothers had a good business, and the country club was at our disposal.

But that was just on the surface. Underneath, my home was a mess. My mother was chronically ill with emotional and physical problems, and my father was distant. I had two brothers, but they were much older and had already moved out of the house by the time I entered my teens. I'm sure my parents loved me, but they couldn't be there for me, emotionally or in any other way.

I started to rebel against all the 1950s conformist values around me as a way of hiding the loneliness and hurt I felt. And I *hated* school. I felt inferior to most of the students, and my D average reflected it. I couldn't read well and bluffed my way through most classes. Many years later, I found out that I "learned differently," but back in my day, they called it "being dumb." And so I told myself none of it mattered to me anyway—school was just a bunch of facts that I didn't need or care about.

I started getting in trouble, getting sent to detention, and hanging around with the "bad crowd" at Nobbie's Pool Hall. They called us the "Green Street Animals." Finally, the principal brought my mom into school and told her that she ought to take me out. The reason I was in so much trouble, he said, was that I "couldn't handle the work." Once again, that meant only one thing: I was dumb. No surprise, really—for three years I'd been in a special class for "slow learners." We were all labeled, and the other guys who weren't making it were my only friends.

The closest I came to feeling anything like acceptance was at that pool hall. There, hanging out with a couple dozen guys my age and older, I talked the way I liked to talk and didn't feel rejected for it. In that scruffy room with its six pool tables and dim lights, there was a sense of community that I felt nowhere else. It was real, it was honest—but also violent and purposeless. What I remember most is how the time dragged and stretched. We had all the time in the world to go . . . nowhere. I used to lie in bed at night in tears, wondering what I was doing, where I was headed, and what my life was about.

One day at Nobbie's, an older guy came in, a guy in his 30s whom I'd never seen before. He just sat there and watched us. I turned to my friend Lefty and asked, "Who is that guy?" Lefty had no idea. The man showed up each day, but we never spoke. Finally he offered to shoot a game of pool with us—"I'll pay," he said, which sounded good—and we kidded him about his lousy cue technique, and he took it and kidded us back, and eventually I got around to asking him his name and what he was doing there.

"My name is Bob, and I'm trying to start a club for kids from your high school."

"Good luck, man," I told him.

Bob was part of Young Life, a nondenominational Christian organization committed to making a positive impact on kids' lives and preparing them for the future. It was founded in 1941, and it's still going strong today in all 50 states and 45 foreign countries. You can be sure I wasn't too interested in the Christian stuff at first. The group sponsored a camp at a ranch in Colorado, and that was more to my liking. "And we'll give you a scholarship," Bob said when he told me about it. No one had ever offered me a scholarship for anything before. Even better, he told me it was a coed camp. I took a look at the photos of the girls riding horses. "Okay," I said, "I think I can make time for this."

So, along with five of my friends, I rode a bus out west; and on the bus I met Jerry Kirk, the man with whom I went on to form the most important relationship of my life so far. Jerry was the head of Young Life in Pittsburgh. The first thing I remember noticing about him was that he could fall asleep on the road in the midst of all the ruckus we were making. He even had a smile on his face while he slept!

He was a slight, wiry guy—he'd done a lot of long-distance running back in school and still had the look of an athlete. At this time he was perhaps 30 or so. I liked him right away, but he puzzled me just as much as Bob had. What was his angle? Why did this guy seem to care about me?

At the camp there was plenty of stuff to do: horseback riding, basketball, hiking. But most of all, there was time to hang out. In addition to Jerry, there were two other counselors assigned to my friends and me, and once again . . . what *was* it with those guys? I could see immediately that they wanted to know me as a person; they cared about who I was, no matter whether I "believed in God" or was willing to accept what Young Life was all about. I didn't know what to call it, but I perceived that Jerry Kirk loved me unconditionally. He believed in me as a human being, whatever I did—there were no strings attached.

It was the first time I'd ever experienced anything like this. Shouldn't I have received unconditional love from my parents? Sure—but like millions of young people, I didn't. I was desperate for a caring adult in my life.

I didn't open up to Jerry or the others right away. I was extremely distrustful, and I had to do a lot of testing, to find out if their caring was real. We had work crews at the camp, doing things like filling holes in the roads. One morning I was slacking off and Bob, who was the crew boss, said, "Milliken, you're lazy!" (Did I mention he was an ex-Marine?) *Wham!* My next shovelful of dirt just happened to catch him right in the face.

The staff had a big meeting over this incident. I knew they were going to send me home. But instead, they told me that they were going to stick it out with me. I realized that Bob wasn't being a jerk; on the contrary, he was consistent and fair, because when I did my job well, he was there to tell me so. When I didn't, he told me that, too. I was inconsistent, but he was not. And he had a sense of humor. So I apologized to him and found that I respected him even more.

The real turning point in my feelings of trust for Jerry came when I went back to Pittsburgh. Somehow I was afraid I'd never see him again. He'd gotten me to the camp and had helped me learn about God—so his job was over and he'd move on to someone else. That didn't happen. Jerry stayed with me and continued to be my friend. The unconditional love didn't disappear, and neither did he. (The trip to the Colorado camp became an annual event, too—many years later I was still going out there each summer, taking kids from the streets of New York to experience what I had as a teen.)

Something started to change within me. I was realizing that no matter how tough I thought I was, no matter how screwed up I felt my life had been, I wanted to be connected. It was the basic driving force for me, and—I understand now—for every single human being on the planet. A few years ago, I was deeply moved while watching the Tom Hanks film *Castaway.* Here's this guy all alone on a deserted island for years and he winds up establishing a personal, one-on-one relationship with a volleyball! The ball had "Wilson" written on it, so that's what the Hanks character called it. This was the best he could do, the only friend he had. He just *had* to be connected.

I firmly believe that I'm alive today because of a caring adult. Jerry, Bob, and the other Young Life counselors didn't think my friends and I were worthless. They believed we had a future, something we could give. They didn't offer us an "answer" or a "program"—they offered *themselves;* they offered the time, love, and energy it takes to form a relationship with another human being. And there's no human being harder to relate to than an alienated teenager. Jerry walked with me through "the valley of the shadow of adolescence," and, as I've learned dozens of times since, that's no easy walk. Without someone to believe in him, a teenager gets angry and he starts to take it out on other people and himself.

> PROGRAMS DON'T CHANGE KIDS— *RELATIONSHIPS* DO. EVERY CHILD NEEDS ONE ADULT WHO'S IRRATIONALLY COMMITTED TO HIS OR HER FUTURE.

Programs don't change kids—*relationships* do. This principle is the cornerstone for everything you'll ever do for children in your communities. They'll probably put it on my tombstone because I've said it so often, in so many ways. But in this increasingly high-tech "virtual" century, I believe you can't say it *too* often: It all starts with relationships. *A good program creates an environment in which healthy relationships can occur.*

"They Used to Call Me Loser"

"Don't *ever* do that to me again!" General Colin Powell was frowning at me—and believe me, the man can frown. Of course, he was only kidding . . . at least I think he was.

We were backstage at a hotel just outside of Washington, D.C., in 1997, and the general had just finished his keynote address to more than a thousand Communities In Schools network members from around the nation. It was the organization's 20th anniversary—20 years of loving kids into change, of learning how to "walk our talk" in some of the toughest neighborhoods in America.

General Powell kept glaring. I'd thought his speech was terrific. As head of the newly formed nonprofit America's Promise, he had a strong and essential message to deliver about bringing community resources to children and families. The CIS crowd loved him. Then I thought I saw the hint of a smile.

"You brought in a ringer, Milliken," he said. "Reggie Beaty gave one of the greatest talks I've ever heard."

He was referring to Lieutenant Colonel Reginald Beaty, an alumnus of the CIS affiliate in Atlanta, whom we'd asked to introduce the general and tell a little of his own story. Atlanta was where my colleagues and I started the first prototypes of what later became known as Communities In Schools. Reggie was one of the first graduates of our "Street Academy" initiative there, and he'd received a lot of honors since. Now he had a new one: the man who almost upstaged Colin Powell.

What Reggie told that audience was a story about a personal relationship. He talked about what he used to be like, what happened to him, and what he's like today. "They used to call me Loser," he said. "Now they call me Lieutenant Colonel!" It was all about how a positive bond with a caring adult made the difference.

Life of Crime

Reggie grew up in Atlanta during the 1960s, and for his first ten years, he and school got along fine. He and his four siblings were raised by his mother, who had only made it through the tenth grade herself but understood the importance of education. Then, in 1969, the Beaty family had to move to a new neighborhood: Bankhead Courts, which had the dubious distinction of being featured on *60 Minutes* as one of the worst communities in the United States. Violent crimes, murders, drugs, burglaries—Bankhead Courts had it all.

For two more years, Reggie held his ground. He was making the honor roll, studying hard, and trying to ignore the devastating poverty and insecurity that surrounded him. "We weren't short on love," he told me once, "but there was a lot of competition for a young boy's attention: drugs, sex, crime, you name it." By the eighth grade, Reggie was into it all. You didn't hear the term "gangs" too much back then, but gang activity is what it was. Reggie carried a .22 and a .38 when he was 14 years old; robbery and drug addiction were an accepted part of his world.

School was the next thing to go. In the ninth grade, he was expelled. "I started a life of crime," he'll tell you bluntly. For two years he was in and out of juvenile detention, usually for breaking and entering, sometimes for drug dealing. People in the community who knew him kept saying: "Reggie, you're too smart for this. What happened to all that potential you had?" But as far as Reggie was concerned, the normal world—especially school—had given up on him, and he had no interest in trying to find a way back in.

Then one day while he was hanging with his friends and playing basketball when he should have been at school, two older guys started hanging around too. Like Reggie, they were African American, but he'd never seen them before. They definitely weren't from Bankhead Courts. These two guys kept showing up, and after a while they explained why: They said that they were "street workers" and they were starting something called a "Street Academy" for kids who had left school. It was a way to get back inside the system and get that diploma—but in a very different environment. The academy was small (never more than 100 students at any one time), and the learning was intensive and geared to the personal pace of each young person.

At first Reggie took a pass on it, but then a couple of young women he'd grown up with—both of them now teenage mothers—said they were going to enroll in Academy T, as it was called. The "T" stood for "Transition." After a bit, they told Reggie: "You really should consider this. It's making a difference. These guys are okay." And the two street workers, Bobby Garrett and Dave Lewis, kept coming back to that basketball court. Basically, they wouldn't leave Reggie alone. They kept bugging him about giving Academy T a try.

Reggie has told me that he probably would have gone over to the storefront building that housed the academy and checked it out, just out of curiosity, even if he hadn't started to feel a connection with the men who kept encouraging him. He might even have enrolled on his own. But he never would have made it to graduation without Bobby Garrett, who became his mentor. Academy T was a great program. But, more important, Bobby gave Reggie a great *relationship,* and that was what made the difference.

Millions of American youth don't have a positive, one-on-one relationship with a caring adult. How did this happen?

In the years following World War II, millions of troops returning to the U.S. moved to small towns and cities instead of back to their farms. The economy picked up and the G.I. Bill got people through college, leading to suburbs springing up all across the country. At the same time, there was a huge migration from south to north, as poor rural blacks went looking for hope and work but ended up in ghettos. (Claude Brown's book *Manchild in the Promised Land* tells this story in the most vivid, personal terms.)

The result pulled apart what had been a fairly effective community structure, both in the agrarian states and even in some industrial sections of the country: Where I grew up in Pittsburgh, people were involved with each other around the steel mills. But over the years, the safety net—woven largely by the extended family and the faith community—slowly unraveled.

I once heard General Powell speak about the "Auntnet"; that was what they had in his neighborhood growing up, instead of the Internet. The aunts all leaned out of their windows on his street in the Bronx. If young Colin got in trouble at school, his parents knew about it *before* he got home. The word went out, neighbor to neighbor, relative to relative, right down the grapevine. That was true community, the extended family at its best. There are many neighborhoods where kids can still count on such a safety net . . . but many, many more where they can't.

Realizing that young Reggie was going to need something useful to do when he wasn't going to classes (and was no longer living the street life), Bobby helped him find a job. He introduced him to life skills—the "hidden rules" of how to get along and get ahead in society—that nobody had ever shown him before. And Bobby began acting as the male role model that the boy had never had. Reggie calls it "hard love."

Bobby Garrett decided to make Reggie his personal project, and he invested blood, sweat, and tears in the young man. Perhaps most important of all, he never judged Reggie for all the mistakes he'd made up till then. He insisted on looking at the good, and helped Reggie rediscover the talents and abilities he'd enjoyed as a small child.

And something changed. "New ways of thinking and feeling" is how Reggie puts it. I know exactly what he means. I was a white, middle-class screwup from Pittsburgh; he was a young criminal from Atlanta's worst ghetto; but we both needed the same thing—a personal relationship with a caring adult. Thank God, we both found it.

Much to his surprise, Reggie discovered that going back to school wasn't hard at all. His last school, the one that expelled him, had felt unsafe, full of fights and threats. Academy T wasn't like that. There he was secure, people cared about him, and he was shown respect. The atmosphere was serious. Even though all the students were dropouts or "push-outs" who (to use Reggie's wry phrase) had "done a lot of foolishness" before showing up at the academy, there was no trouble in class. Everyone was there to work, which was a good thing, because expectations were high, and excellence was both encouraged and expected.

"I made some stupid mistakes," Reggie says. "But I wasn't penalized with a life sentence."

When it came time for Reggie to graduate from Academy T, Bobby had another surprise for him: "You're going to college," he told the boy. The two of them sat down with Reggie's mother and a college counselor, who helped the young man navigate college admission and scholarship forms. No one in his family had ever tried *this* before. In the end, he applied to just one college and hit the bull's-eye: Stillman College accepted him for the class of 1980.

From here on, Reggie's story sounds like something I'm making up, but every word is true. He became president of the United Negro College Fund at Stillman, vice president of his fraternity, and president of his dormitory. He served on the mayor's advisory council and commanded the ROTC drill team. He received a full scholarship for the next three years as a result of his outstanding abilities in ROTC. By the end of his career at Stillman, Reggie was commander of the entire ROTC program. And he entered the Army as a commissioned officer, a second lieutenant.

Reggie's love of teaching flourished while he was in the military, with superb results: He was named the nation's best ROTC instructor in any college or university, and his work with youth in Oklahoma earned him "Man of the Year" honors. He chaired fund-raising committees for charity groups, started a mentoring program for young minority officers, and commanded a battalion of 2,000 soldiers. When he retired from the Army as a lieutenant colonel in 2000, I know he must have been asking himself: *What next? What more?*

I'll return to Reggie's story and answer that question later in this book. Right now, I just want to reemphasize what this chapter has been all about. When Reggie spoke to our Communities In Schools conference, he made it very clear how high the stakes had been for him. "The guys in my neighborhood who were getting their heads blown off, going to jail for the rest of their lives, getting strung out on drugs—these were my *friends*," he said. "These were the people I was hanging with. My relationship with a caring adult saved my life."

Hanging Out—and Hitting the Wall

Reggie Beaty and I have a lot in common, and a lot of differences, too. His road was harder than mine, for one thing. But once he rediscovered his gifts and abilities, the sky was the limit. I wish I'd had that drive and confidence when I was his age, but I didn't.

As a result of my relationship with Jerry Kirk, I was aware that I really did have something to give. But I didn't know what. I was worth something—but what? Back in Pittsburgh, I got my high school diploma after all and tried college. After my third time through the freshman year, I gave that up. I still couldn't seem to learn, and the frustration of being labeled dumb stuck with me.

Then, in the midst of all the renewed questioning about who I was and what I might do, I ran into Harv Oostdyk, a Young Life leader I'd met at the Colorado ranch on my second trip out there. He was three or four years older than I was; I'd formed a strong bond with him and with Vinnie Pasquale, a former drug addict from Newark. Harv had the vision of starting Young Life in New York City, and he got me excited about working with him among street kids. Something finally made sense for me.

· If I had a degree, it would be in "hanging out"—I'd perfected the art in all kinds of situations. And by watching Jerry Kirk and the other Young Life counselors, I'd picked up a few tricks about how to do so in a positive way—especially on the basketball court—in order to start a conversation with younger kids. I wasn't sure what gifts I had, but I knew how to go and connect with people. That's where I felt most comfortable.

A couple of months after renewing our friendship, I got a call from Harv, telling me to come to New York. It was that simple. I packed a few things and on June 17, 1960, I headed east. I met Vinnie at the Newark YMCA, where he worked part-time. We spent the night on Harv's living room floor, and the next morning we grabbed a basketball and started across the George Washington Bridge to look for some kids who wanted to shoot baskets.

We had no idea what we were getting into.

When Vinnie and I moved to the city, we had one gift between us: Like me, Vinnie could have earned a degree in hanging out. But that was exactly what was missing in the lives of those young people. Nobody was out on the streets with them, walking with them, talking with them, shooting hoops.

I wasn't very good at basketball but I could dribble more or less and at least attempt to put it through the hoop; you could maybe fit a piece of paper underneath my feet when I went for my jump shot. But I wasn't afraid to get out there and mix it up and try. *Being there* was what it was all about. Sometimes we were in the midst of some frightening situations, but Vinnie had spent a lot of his time in prison, sleeping on rooftops, and addicted to heroin. He'd seen it all, so he knew how to handle himself. He didn't look much like a kid.

We hung out in Harlem and on the Lower East Side, and needless to say, we were pretty much the only white guys around. But that didn't turn out to be important. There was so much need, and people could tell we cared—no matter what color our skin was. They knew we'd been there, too; we weren't outsiders with clean, safe offices downtown. A few of the kids thought we might be undercover cops. But the police wouldn't move in to the neighborhood and live there day and night. So they wound up deciding we were just nuts—but we had to go where the kids were.

My colleagues in Communities In Schools and I didn't invent the idea of a personal relationship with kids, and CIS is certainly not the only national organization to have figured out a way to meet this need. I'm not sure the term was even in use back in 1960, but if you had to call us anything (other than crazy), I suppose we were mentors. Today, the mentoring movement is one of the most exciting and hopeful things happening in this country, for these relationships are effective and personally rewarding for both adults and youth. CIS and similar organizations throughout the country benefit from thousands of generous, dedicated volunteers who give their time to young people. Just visit the Website of MENTOR, the National Mentoring Partnership (**www.mentoring.org**), and you'll get a sense of how large and generous a contribution mentors are making today.

Harv continued to run Young Life in New Jersey, but he came into the city almost every day to give Vinnie and me a hand. His support was critical. He was somewhere between a boss and a mentor, helping us raise funds when we needed them and also doing his share of one-on-one street work with the kids. Together, Vinnie, Harv, and I—in our own stumbling fashion—were discovering the first principle of any transformational action with young people. We just knew that positive relationships were going to get these kids off drugs, off the streets, and back to school. It had worked for us; it would work for them.

And it did work . . . sort of. We were able to convince quite a few young people to get out of gangs, get off the streets, get "clean," and start doing something with their lives. But immediately we ran into a big problem. Vinnie said it best: "How can we say we love our neighbors but let them live on rooftops? We go out there and tell them how much we care and then go back to our nice warm beds."

At this point we were living in a little $32-a-month cold-water flat in Harlem. The bathtub was right in the middle of the kitchen—but at least we *had* a bathtub, and a roof over our heads and a door with multiple locks. That was more than a lot of the street kids had. No one started talking about homelessness until the 1980s, when it became such a big "issue," but it was always a reality for the economically disenfranchised.

We were starting to realize that the first great key we'd discovered—building relationships with young people—wasn't going to unlock the door of success all by itself. We'd hit a wall. We had a lot more to learn.

■ ■ ■

Mentoring a young person is an extraordinary adventure, but this book describes a different response that community leaders can make. It's even bigger, more comprehensive, and more coordinated; and it uses these connections as just one part of a community-wide effort to turn around the lives of struggling students. Mentors, all by themselves, face the exact same challenges that Vinnie and I faced in Harlem and on the Lower East Side: Okay, you have a personal relationship, and the kids trust you—but Kenny is sleeping on the streets, Luci has a cough that won't go away, and Don is 18 and can't read. What *else* can you do?

By all means consider whether mentoring is for you *and* keep reading. There's more to come.

■ ■ ■ ■ ■

CHAPTER TWO

Why the Dropout Crisis Isn't Just an Education Issue

The Adult Problem

On April 30, 1997, along with then-President Bill Clinton, three former Presidents, and former First Lady Nancy Reagan, I was in Philadelphia for an extraordinary three-day event called The Presidents' Summit for America's Future. I'd greeted what felt like a thousand other dignitaries. I was so tired that I didn't think I could shake another hand.

Notable speakers—including Presidents Ford, Carter, Bush, and Clinton—presented their pictures of what America's youth needed and how the nation could meet those needs. General Colin Powell presided, and out of this forum was to come his America's Promise movement: a heartfelt initiative to connect youth across the land with vital resources.

I'd had the privilege of joining the general and others to help organize the April event, and the Summit team offered me the chance to be one of the speakers on the final day. I said yes, of course, although I was full of nerves and uncertainty. Day after day the speakers just got better and better. I realized that this was by far the most illustrious platform I'd ever been given. I wanted to make the most of it, but after weeks of intense effort in doing my small part to help pull the Summit together, I was several steps past exhausted. Not only that, but I'd had no time—not even 15 minutes—to sit down alone and decide what to say to this audience of national leaders.

When my turn came, I walked to the podium and realized that I *still* didn't know what to talk about. I've done a lot of public speaking and was just praying the words would come, but they didn't. I just stood there. I thought about the goodwill, the commitment, and the wealth of ideas represented in the audience. The past three days had been incredibly moving. In many ways, it was the convention I'd dreamed of attending for 30 years—and when I'm moved, I have trouble hiding it.

So I got choked up and tears began to flow. *Oh, great start, Milliken,* I thought, but then I found some words. I'm sure they were coming from a part of my brain I have no conscious control over. I said something like this: "All my life I've tried to do everything I could to be an advocate for young people and their needs. If you want to know what I've learned, here it is: We don't have a youth problem in America—we have an *adult* problem."

Even through my fatigue, I could see I'd hit a nerve. The room was silent. "I've never been trained as a teacher. I don't know how to give a course on male/female relations, or black/white/brown relations, or anything like that. But I can tell you, I've seen kids start to eat together in a school cafeteria where whites and blacks weren't sitting at the same table because they saw *adults* coming together who happened to be black and white and brown, male and female, eating together and caring about one another. Kids learn from what they see, not just what they're taught. We can talk about values, but if we're not living them out, it won't matter. You can't give away what you don't have. If *we* don't care about each other—if *we* don't have community—how can we expect young people to do any better?"

I went on to talk about some of the basic principles of Communities In Schools, and it was wonderful to see how receptive the audience was. Then, after the Summit was over and I'd rested up, I thought more about this "adult problem" idea. I decided it was another way of explaining how Communities In Schools has viewed dropouts ever since its inception.

The dropout crisis is not just an education issue. It isn't just about schools, academics, curricula, and learning. There's a crisis because we adults have failed to provide and model a community that acts as a safety net for young people, ensuring that their needs are met. We can blame it on the educational system, but that's simplistic and, in fact, irresponsible. The schools have fallen into the vacuum that was created when everything else unraveled. We expect teachers and school administrators to be mother, father, sister, brother, counselor, social worker, good cop, bad cop—and also be great teachers.

This is impossible. The needs of millions of students are simply too large and too complicated for educators to handle alone. And it isn't their responsibility to do so anyway. They need a community of concerned adults to step forward and be their partners. We have to free teachers to do their jobs again. And that means creating safe, responsive learning environments for them, for school administrators, and ultimately for the students and their families.

In his July 26, 2006, column, *Washington Post* writer Courtland Milloy quoted Johnny W. Allen, a longtime advocate for addiction treatment in Washington: "Our failure to engage and prepare our young to cope and prosper as adults is a chain of many broken promises. Most visible is our broken school system. Less visible is our health, social service, and criminal justice systems. Our businesses and churches offer little hope for these citizens of tomorrow."[1]

> KIDS LEARN FROM WHAT THEY SEE, NOT JUST WHAT THEY'RE TAUGHT. WE CAN TALK ABOUT VALUES, BUT IF WE'RE NOT LIVING THEM OUT, IT WON'T MATTER.

Allen's remark gets to the heart of the issue. It is indeed *our* failure—not just the kids', not just the parents', and not just the schools'. Many school systems are obviously in trouble, but it's the "less visible" structures that are broken as well.

I have to disagree with Allen's last point, though. It is precisely our businesses and faith communities, joining with social-service providers and volunteers, that can take the lead in offering not only hope, but real accomplishments that can help our young people become prosperous citizens of tomorrow.

School-community partnership is at the core of the Communities In Schools idea, as its name would suggest. The many helping services that young people and their families need are concentrated—or better, perhaps, to say *diffused*—in a wide array of social agencies, nonprofits, and volunteer groups throughout a typical community. The critical step is to get these services to students and families by using the school as the delivery point. Thus, the community we're building comprises partners and volunteers who can truly help; these are adults with the expertise and the mission to meet kids' needs.

> YOU'D BE AMAZED BY
> WHAT A DIFFERENCE
> IT MAKES TO SIMPLY
> GET ADULTS INTO THE
> SCHOOL BUILDING.

Partnership begins in one-on-one relationships. You'd be amazed by what a difference it makes to simply get adults into the school building. I remember taking a couple of businesspeople on a tour of a school with a CIS presence, located in a very fragmented, violent community. We always invite students to meet visitors and give their input. One young man—on the surface, a really tough type—was with us when the guests asked the principal, "Why does this place feel so calm, so safe, in the midst of this troubled community?"

The kid spoke up: "There's so many damn adults in here, we *can't* get into trouble."

And it was true: In addition to the teachers and administrators, a dozen carefully screened volunteers came each day to meet with the kids during their free periods, to help with homework or just to hang out. Social workers and health-care providers had office space they shared among themselves, and the students knew where to find them.

When the final bell sounded, the school didn't empty out. It got *more* crowded, as recreation specialists, tutors, and other caring adults arrived to supervise the various after-school programs available to students. And keeping watch over this beehive of activity was the CIS coordinator, whose unique role you'll learn more about in the pages ahead. Suffice it to say, he was the one who knew where everyone—kids and adults alike—fit into the big picture. And he was also the one who cared enough to stand outside the front door every morning and greet students by name.

The CIS coordinator at that school also brought life to a senior-citizen facility down the street. Not long ago, many of these elders would have been part of an extended family, still connected to the younger generations and playing a vital role in weaving the safety net for kids. But the trend in our society is toward fragmentation. Just as children are placed into "social institutions" such as day care and preschool at younger and younger ages, so too are older citizens often placed in isolated settings, removed from their neighborhoods and loved ones.

The elders in this particular facility were poor people, and the building they lived in and the care they received was also poor. They sat there, day after day, watching their soap operas and talking to each other with no purpose to their lives. They were literally dying because they had nothing to give themselves to. (This isn't always the case in senior-citizen homes, fortunately. The vibrant, effective ones offer many opportunities for volunteering and connection to the community.)

The CIS coordinator had the idea of asking the seniors to come down to the school and eat lunch with the students. These kids needed more "grandparenting," since their own extended families were broken down by the same forces that had placed the elders in such isolation. This program immediately made the lunchroom so much calmer. The seniors *were* like grandparents; and kids, as we all know, often respect grandparents more than their parents.

They also knew that "Grandma" was going to be tougher than anyone. She very well might say, "I'm gonna tell your momma!" The students needed guidance, and the seniors needed a reason to live and something to give to. And, like all grandparents, they could get up after lunch and leave!

This is an example of doing more than delivering services, although that is, of course, a vital part of what CIS does. The coordinator brought *life* into that school. He took two fragmented institutions and, by bringing them together, helped make them whole. He created an opportunity for adults and children to love and care for one another, not just "give things." That's the most powerful attraction in the world—whether it occurs at home with parents, with an extended family, or with an even broader community of caring adults.

Backing into Education

The dropout crisis isn't just an education issue—but our education system is the arena where the battle will be won or lost. So almost from the start, my "street work" has taken me into the world of education.

When I told the Presidents' Summit that I wasn't an educator, that was an understatement. A few years ago, a CIS site was launched at my old high school, and I was invited back to cut the ribbon. The mayor was there, and he said, "I was in Bill's class. I know God has a great sense of humor—Bill's here to talk about education!"

The truth is that my colleagues and I got into the field because the kids needed it, not because we had any calling to be teachers. Helping young people get their diplomas was simply part of helping them learn how to live; a decent foundation in learning was one component among many that they were lacking. So we backed into education, just as we improvised so much else in our early days in New York City.

You couldn't have started a "street worker" program with two less experienced people than Vinnie Pasquale and me. I was immature and in many ways emotionally unstable, and the only work Vinnie had ever done before his part-time job at the Y was to push drugs.

But it's clear to me that a higher power—the source of the spiritual journey we were both on—took a hand in what happened, and somehow we kept finding the strength to take the next step. I had to learn to deal with rejection. For every kid who was willing to listen to me, two more would give me a very cold shoulder. I'd walk up to a guy on a park bench and he'd move away to avoid me. If I stuck out my hand to shake hands, he'd look away, pretending he didn't see. If I tried to join a group for basketball, everyone else would be chosen instead of me.

It was a lesson in humility, and in a funny way it also helped teach me even more about the power of personal relationships. It was these kids' refusal to relate or acknowledge I was even there that really hurt. At least if somebody yelled at me or gave me a hard time, there was interaction, dialogue—I could get something going, start *some* kind of relationship, look each other in the eye.

During our second summer in New York City, Vinnie decided to go back to school, which he'd left in the eighth grade. I needed a new apartment mate, and I joined forces with a great guy from Young Life named Dean Borgman, an ex-paratrooper from Connecticut. Like me, he'd hung around with a bunch of suburban kids in trouble with the law both before and after his tour of duty. After hooking up with Young Life and getting a new perspective on his life, he came to New York to work toward a doctorate on the G.I. Bill, and he began teaching high school while doing graduate work at Columbia.

Dean and I found a new home, an apartment at 215 Madison Street on the Lower East Side, thanks to Dr. Eugene Callender, senior pastor of Church of the Master in Harlem. Dr. Callender had given us one of our first footholds in Harlem by "blessing" us through his church, and he also had connections at Trinity parish, a big Episcopal community on Wall Street. One of their missions was called St. Christopher's Chapel, and through the chapel's generosity, Dean and I received free rent on Madison Street. We also got free meals at the church each evening for ourselves and the young people we took in. Our little kitchen wouldn't have been able to handle a real supper, but the church gave us a place to come for sustenance and a sense of community.

It was there, at 215 Madison, that we began to create relationships, safe places, and healthy—or at least healthier—starts
for young people in 1960s New York. But the question continued to haunt us: How can we say that we care about these kids
when they've got an eighth-grade education at 18 years old? Like
it or not, we were going to have to become "educators." And if
we couldn't do that, we'd have to find some real teachers to work
with us.

Our partner Harv Oostdyk had become friendly with a retired
public school principal who asked us straight out, "Why don't you
start your own school? You could hold classes to prepare the students to pass the high school equivalency exams and get their
GED (general educational development) certification." Harv liked
the idea, and with his typical passion and brilliance, he found a
way to make it happen.

As best I can remember, no one was using the term "storefront
school" back then. Harv's inspiration was to rent a commercial
space right on the street and hold classes there to tutor the kids.
When you're young, you don't know what "won't work," so we
didn't see the difficulties, just the excitement and possibilities.
And it was such a natural extension of the logic that had motivated us ever since we began working in New York: If you care about
kids and they're sleeping on rooftops, get them a place to live. If
they're 18 years old and can't read or write . . .

So Harv started a storefront school up in Harlem, and others of
us stayed on the Lower East Side, renting an old warehouse building under a bridge. It was a "white elephant," but we painted it
blue, so it was called the Blue Elephant. Julian Robertson, one of
our earliest and most loyal business supporters, and some others
on the Young Life committee, raised money so that we could rent
it in the fall of 1965. It was two floors of decrepitude, but we fixed
it up as best we could. The neighborhood was terrible; a few years
later, Senator Richard Lugar, then mayor of Indianapolis, came as
a guest of the Lilly Endowment to check out our work and the cab
driver didn't want to take him there. The senator managed to talk
him into it, liked what he saw, and was later instrumental in helping start Communities In Schools.

The Blue Elephant needed teachers, and fortunately for us, the times were right for a whole cadre of college students from Columbia, Princeton, and New York University to volunteer their time. We welcomed them, but none of us was under any illusion that it would be easy. Our student body was exclusively composed of dropouts and street kids.

We held classes on the second floor of the Blue Elephant, but before a young person was allowed to go upstairs, he or she had to spend time with us on the ground floor, learning basic life skills and disciplines. Part of that involved a hard look at their spiritual lives, too. These kids needed to be *turned on to living* before we could *turn them on to learning.*

We had a concept called the "Steps of Life": The first step was to take responsibility for yourself, no matter how rough your situation. Then we urged the kids to look around and realize that they weren't alone—they had a community of peers and adults who were in this with them, and together they could make it happen.

We adapted a practice from our home at 215 Madison and took it to the Blue Elephant: "family meetings" to talk about our differences; discuss how to help each other rather than hurt each other; and find out who was in trouble, who was facing up to problems, and who was skirting the truth. These kids knew they were in deep trouble, that they'd taken the wrong direction. We organized the potential students into small discussion groups where the first order of business was to help them talk about the often poisonous emotions that nearly two decades of rejection and pain had created.

The most frequent question we asked was: "Why are you angry?" We confronted them about drugs: "I know you're still sneaking off and using smack. The only thing that will get you kicked out of here is lying about it. Tell us if you screwed up and we'll try to help you." Lying is the number one thing that will break down community, and all of us—teachers and students alike—had to learn this the hard way.

The next step was to replace these negative mind-sets with *hope*. We coined a slogan: "Hope is the antidote to dope," and slowly these kids came to believe it. Equally important was an emphasis on *dignity* and *respect*. We insisted that everyone who came through the door of the Blue Elephant—students, teachers, family, and street workers—be treated with respect. Those who couldn't do this (and that included some of the adults, too) were asked to come back when they were ready. These kids needed to believe in their hearts that they were accepted and afforded dignity for who they were, no matter what grade level they read at or what their home life was like. There was nothing to be ashamed of, and everyone could learn.

But we discovered that our students had almost no conception of why they ought to be back in school. "*Why* do you want to learn?" we kept asking them. We knew that we had to give them a clear grasp of the outcomes—jobs, security, a sense of self-worth, and a basis on which to raise a family—before they'd be willing to stick it out and pay the price of discipline and perseverance. We had to expose the myths of easy money on the streets: "Sure, you can make a lot dealing drugs for a year or two, but open your eyes and look at reality. The dealers you thought were so cool when you were younger are all dead or in jail. There's no hope and no future in that."

Another important tactic to help these kids answer the question "Why learn?" was to make the Blue Elephant truly *their* school. We tried to involve them in everything from painting the building and routine maintenance to decision-making about schedules and the pace of learning. Sure enough, a sense of community started to form. We called them "a gang for good," and they found they could rely on each other for encouragement. Their pride was apparent, and they began to enjoy spreading the word among their friends on the street. To our amazement, learning became the "in thing," and the storefront school became the place to go if you wanted to be hip. One of our students on the way to school would pass an idling friend, point a finger at him, and say, "Smart up!" Soon enough, our entire enrollment was word of mouth. Kids were coming to the Blue Elephant, asking to be part of it.

I don't mean to imply that we had a 100 percent success rate. It wasn't even close to that, and a lot of kids simply couldn't make it, but our successes grew as we learned to get tougher and shake off the temptation to be paternalistic. Excuses were unacceptable. Hard as it was, we had to look young people in the eye and say, "I don't care how bad you had it. A lot of people have it bad. You still have a responsibility to yourselves and to your younger brothers and sisters to succeed."

Call Them Academies

Over the next five years, Harv and his colleagues in Harlem opened more and more storefront schools there. By the end of the '60s, we had schools in Harlem and Bedford-Stuyvesant and on the Lower East Side. It was a time of amazing changes for us—and for me personally. I married my longtime Pittsburgh sweetheart, Jean. As she soon discovered, our wedding meant "marrying" all the young folks at 215 Madison, too.

But we got a place of our own, and in 1968 our son, Sean, was born. Two years later, Jean had a miscarriage, which led us both to wonder if God was pointing the way toward adoption. Almost at once, we had the great fortune to adopt a lovely six-week-old girl whom we named Lani.

Meanwhile, the storefront schools continued to evolve. At some point Harv and I realized that we probably shouldn't give our schools unorthodox names like "the Blue Elephant" or "Liberation School" (another popular choice). We asked around: What do wealthy, successful people call their schools? The answer was *academies,* so that was what we called ours.

We also needed a base in the community, since we couldn't run schools under the auspices of Young Life. Dr. Callender from Church of the Master in Harlem was now the head of the New York City Urban League. Harv approached him and he agreed to sponsor our new work as educators, so all of a sudden we could boast of Urban League Street Academies.

At the same time, Harv and I began to get to know more of the Wall Street business leaders who'd occasionally shown interest in our work. This was facilitated, sadly, by the riots that hit New York City in the mid-'60s. These events were a wake-up call to many business leaders. They realized that the larger world out there beyond Wall Street was in big trouble, and—sometimes out of enlightened self-interest but more often out of genuine concern and desire to contribute—they were very open to finding ways to partner with "street workers" like us.

Young Life supporters such as Julian Robertson, who'd helped us get financing for the Blue Elephant, were willing to build bridges for us. At the time, Julian was working at Kidder, Peabody (the securities and investment-banking firm), and he and several of his colleagues were involved at Trinity Parish, which supported us at 215 Madison . . . so gradually the connections were made. This was a big realization for me: Relationships are the key *everywhere*. Wall Street is a street like any other, and what I'd learned on the streets of the Lower East Side worked here as well. Our hanging-out skills remained our biggest asset.

> THIS WAS A BIG
> REALIZATION FOR ME:
> RELATIONSHIPS ARE
> THE KEY *EVERYWHERE*.
> WALL STREET IS A
> STREET LIKE ANY
> OTHER.

Once we were established with the Urban League thanks to Harv and Dr. Callender, there was an additional incentive for the business community to take part. It was one of those moments of synchronicity—you had major corporations looking for ways to help the community, and here we were with a program that was in place and achieving success.

By 1968, 16 corporations—including American Express, Time, Morgan Guaranty, Chase Manhattan, Union Carbide, and Burlington Mills—were convinced that business needed to build bridges to its neighbors, and each funded one of the Academies.

We also developed four "prep schools": Lower East Side Prep, Harambe Prep, Newark Prep, and Harlem Prep, which became known as places where everyone was expected to go on to college. The whole prep-school idea was again borrowed from our sense of what wealthy people called their elite institutions. Well, these were for *our* elite—students who'd shown exceptional promise in the academies and could clearly do well in a college environment if they had a regular high school diploma. So the prep schools were accredited by the school system and our graduates, armed with a "normal" diploma, found acceptance at colleges around the country. It was a wonderful evolution for the Street Academies, which had no accreditation and worked to prepare students to take the GED exam.

I continued to stay in touch with Vinnie Pasquale, by the way. He'd gotten his degree, married, and gone on to work with kids through the YMCA. Tragically, he died just a few years later, suffering a heart attack on a basketball court while doing what he loved best: hanging out with, and giving hope to, young people.

The "Street Academy movement," as it came to be known, has since been called "the most imitated social program of the 1960s" by the Ford Foundation. And it's true that outside-the-system academies (started both by us and by others) sprang up in many cities during the period from the mid-'60s to the early '70s. In fact, the small- or alternative-school movement has never really stopped. Today the country has thousands of such initiatives, with sponsors and support from groups such as the Bill & Melinda Gates Foundation, the Center for Collaborative Education's Small Schools Network, the Alternative High School Initiative, the Coalition for Community Schools, and many others.

Proud as we were of our successes back then, we saw two things with increasing clarity:

- Dropouts had already been scarred by the failures of the system; their road back was tough.

- For all our accomplishments, more and more kids kept quitting school. Our storefront academies couldn't begin to handle the flood of young people who needed a second chance.

So the answer was obvious, although incredibly difficult to implement: We had to find a way to move our operation *inside* the public schools and reach potential dropouts *before* they quit.

There was another benefit to this approach. When you get right down to it, school is where most of the kids are. It's a lot easier to reach them there than on the streets—although it took us more than a decade to admit this. Being "anti-establishment" was a high value in the '60s. We were reluctant to become part of a system we perceived as negligent and unjust. But we had to acknowledge that it was crucial to find a way to stop the wave of dropouts before they overwhelmed our—or anyone else's—ability to respond. We wanted to inoculate kids against the dropout epidemic rather than try to cure them after they'd fallen victim to the disease.

> This is a lot of ground to cover. Let me pause to repeat three key points here:
>
> 1. The dropout crisis isn't just an education issue. It reflects a failure of adult community.
>
> 2. Students at risk of dropping out have needs that are too pressing and too complicated for educators to handle alone. Again, a group of concerned adults must join forces with schools to meet these needs.
>
> 3. Delivering services *at the school* is the critical step that adults can take, forming a community that can provide the resources kids and families need.

I've tried to make it clear that my colleagues and I didn't sit down and think up these insights. We learned them through experience, slowly and painfully. So, rather than offer more theory, I want to tell you about a living example of the principles I'm discussing.

It's taking place in Los Angeles, and no movie studio could have dreamed up such a story. It begins in tragedy and grows into an odyssey of redemption and hope for thousands of the most despised young people in America: the violent gangs of the San Fernando Valley.

Peace in the Valley?

The news came to Blinky Rodriguez and his wife, Lilly, at 12:15 A.M. on a Saturday morning in 1990. The phone rang, and when Blinky answered, a young man said, "I'm at the hospital. Something happened to Sonny."

The Rodriguezes found themselves in a car driving down to a hospital in Mission Hills. When they arrived, a priest came to meet them. "Mr. and Mrs. Rodriguez," he said, "we have a body in Room 2, and we need you to identify it."

Their 16-year-old son was dead, murdered in a drive-by shooting by Pacoima gangbangers.

"It dug a deep, deep trench in our lives," Blinky says. Community violence, which the Rodriguezes had tried so hard to channel in productive ways through their commitment to sports in the San Fernando Valley, had shattered their family.

Blinky is a man of faith, and he knew that he had to make a response that would honor his son and—somehow—bring good out of evil. He resolved to do the impossible: bring peace to the Valley's 75 gangs.

The San Fernando Valley has three million inhabitants. Were it an independent city (an initiative rejected by voters a few years ago), it would be the sixth largest in the U.S. It's an astonishingly diverse and complex world.

It's also a very different place from the Valley that William "Blinky" Rodriguez grew up in during the 1960s. ("Blinky," by the way, is an Anglicization of an affectionate name given to him as a toddler by his grandmother.) Back then there were clubs, not gangs—car clubs, mostly, with guys competing to see whose ride could outpace the rest. Guns on the street were almost unheard of, and school was a smaller and more personal place.

One day when he was 16, Blinky was sent to the vice principal's office for refusing to strip down for gym class. "I'd heard that this guy, Jack Jacobson, swung a mean paddle, so when I walked into his office, I immediately assumed the position. 'What are you doing?' he asked. I looked back over my shoulder at him and replied, 'Aren't you going to give me a swat?' 'No, sit down,' he told me."

It turned out that the dean of discipline was more interested in finding out *why* Blinky was in trouble than administering punishment. He finally got the youngster to admit that he was ashamed to take off his shoes and socks because he had a raging case of athlete's foot. Jacobson immediately took him off campus to the nearest drugstore and bought him a new pair of sneakers, a pair of white socks, and his first can of Desenex.

After this demonstration of concern, it was no wonder that Blinky bonded with Jacobson. He learned that the vice principal's extracurricular passion was martial arts, so the teen began taking classes.

He was a natural. Focusing on kickboxing as his sport of choice, in a matter of years he became one of the great U.S. champions, and the foremost pioneer to introduce the pastime to millions of new fans. He met his wife, Lilly (also a world-champion boxer and kickboxer), and they became the first husband and wife ever to perform on a professional boxing show. Their son, Sonny, was born in 1974, the first of five children.

Blinky's kickboxing gym was state of the art, and a stone's throw from the neighborhood of his youth. He made sure to offer scholarships to neighborhood kids and preach the message that the discipline of sports was a priceless way to learn values such as integrity, perseverance, and fairness.

"I had a heartbeat for working with this population," he says. "You can't just incarcerate them when they do wrong."

Then Sonny was shot dead.

The story, as Blinky eventually pieced it together, was both ridiculous and tragic. Sonny and his girlfriend were riding in her car; she was teaching him how to drive. Busy with the lesson, neither noticed that they'd driven into an off-limits neighborhood. It was the wrong turf, "belonging" to a Pacoima gang. This sign of disrespect ignited tempers, and a young life ended.

Blinky made his vow to end the violence in a community that saw a gang-on-gang killing nearly every day. But there was a step that needed to come first. "Lilly and I had to forgive the three men who murdered our son," he says matter-of-factly. His faith gave him the strength to do this, publicly, at their trial. "Father Offers Forgiveness," the headlines read, and it triggered a reaction in the community that further strengthened Blinky's new mission.

He began helping gang members leave their violent lifestyles behind, walking the streets and preaching "to anyone who would listen, trying to speak some sense to all the nonsense." Aided by Donald "Big D" Garcia, a friend who'd spent 31 years behind bars and understood the culture, Blinky made his kickboxing gym a safe place for youths to come for counseling and support. He opened his home to Bible study groups and soon had more than 100 young people from six gangs.

He also began acting as a moderator between rival gangs. The Pacoima ones knew Blinky had publicly forgiven their "homies" for gunning down his son, and it added immeasurably to his credibility as a spokesperson for peace. Others, of course, knew him as a legendary figure in the martial arts.

> "SPEAK THE TRUTH, SPEAK TO THEIR HEARTS AND MINDS, AND BREATHE HOPE AND VISION. WE'RE A COMMUNITY FOR YOUTH."
>
> — WILLIAM "BLINKY" RODRIGUEZ

Eventually, gang members formed a Peace Treaty Council and, with Blinky's help, began their peacemaking efforts. On October 31, 1993, representatives of all 75 gangs—with a population of more than 1,000—signed the treaty at a huge gathering at a local church. Celebrities such as Jane Goodall and Stevie Wonder were there, and community members covered the stage with roses.

The treaty called for leaders to bring any divisive issues to a weekly facilitation meeting before resorting to violence. Gang representatives also exchanged phone numbers and pledged to call each other to inquire about perceived insults or signs of disrespect before assuming the worst.

The truce was inaugurated with a football game in February 1994 between rival gangs, attended by city officials and hosted by Blinky and Donald Garcia. Big D was dubious at first: "Come on, Blinky, these guys are gangbangers. They don't want to play football!" Just watch, Blinky told him—and he was right. Everyone wanted in. YMCA officials were recruited to wear the "zebra" shirts, a business supporter sprang for jerseys for the players, and a city councilman presided at the kickoff. All told, more than 600 people participated.

During the year that followed, the number of Latino gang-on-gang killings dropped from 52 to 2. Members turned to football to release aggression and attended intense group meetings to air grievances. As Blinky put it, "A game is more than a one-time event—it creates a forum for relationships and dialogue."

Blinky came up with a phrase to celebrate the treaty. It touches my heart every time I hear it, and it became a rallying cry for hundreds of other anti-gang-violence efforts across the country: "No mothers crying and no babies dying."

You may be thinking, *This guy is amazing, but what exactly does his story have to do with schools?* In fact, Blinky wondered the same thing. He was having an experience very similar to mine back in New York. It was all well and good to work solo, trying to stop gang members from killing each other, but wasn't there a way to reach more kids earlier—to stop gang membership before it started, before lives were lost?

Blinky knew a guy named Robert "Bobby" Arias who happened to be the Southwest Regional Director for Communities In Schools. Bobby was based in L.A., and his daughter was a cheerleader for the Pop Warner football league one of Blinky's children played in. One day when both fathers were attending a game, Blinky challenged Bobby Arias: You're doing this great work for kids in California—what about your own backyard? What about the Valley? And Bobby threw back the challenge: Your mission is great, too, but you need to get organized, become a registered nonprofit, and get some funding. You and Big D can't keep doing this all by yourselves.

It was a true meeting of the minds. Before he knew it, Blinky found himself the executive director of the newly formed CIS of the San Fernando Valley. It was his first exposure to the principles of CIS, but in a sense he already knew them. Pull together a caring community of adults (just as he'd done at that first football game and dozens of times since), show them working together for something they care about, and young people would want to be part of it.

Gang members weren't monsters; they weren't evil, no matter how much harm they did and however much the community reviled them. So many times I've heard Blinky tell an audience: "They're *kids*, man! Do you realize the bullcrap they have to navigate, growing up? The violence in movies, music, video games? The disrespect and immorality of society? It's not 'the way it used to be' anymore—it's not even close. Think about that before you demonize these kids."

Blinky's karate and kickboxing students were a good place to start building the community of adults he needed. Many were judges, attorneys, and businesspeople; and their respect for Blinky was high. They were willing to listen to this new thing called Communities In Schools. Two influential churches—one affluent, the other a street ministry—also lent critical support.

"It's not just one punch that's going to do it," Blinky says. "It's the setup, the combination of punches." Perhaps the most important pieces of the fledgling CIS community were the Los Angeles Police Department and the county's gang-prevention and probation agencies, which recognized a natural ally in Blinky and lent their wholehearted support to CIS's work in schools.

Today, the CIS effort in the Valley has expanded to become CIS of Greater Los Angeles, with Blinky continuing to serve as executive director and Bobby Arias as its president. This affiliate works in 101 schools. Community partners are in place to provide youth the resources they'll need to get out and stay out of gangs, remain in school, and find their place as productive citizens. These resources include tutoring and mentoring programs, "life-readiness" programs ("getting the gang tattoos off their foreheads," Blinky calls it), job-readiness training, parenting classes and family counseling, one-on-one counseling, anger management, and conflict resolution. An after-school program provides a comprehensive range of services to youth at high risk of dropping out, along with services for their families.

CIS functions as the lead agency in this collaboration with other community-based organizations. A job-development program provides an array of work-related services in partnership with local educational agencies, businesses, and community-based organizations. Key partners include the Los Angeles County probation department, City of Los Angeles prevention and intervention programs, the mayor's gang-youth program, and several local unions. The emphasis is on encouraging kids to complete their high school diploma or GED.

Community building through sports has continued to be a centerpiece of Blinky's work with CIS. In 2003, he sponsored a softball tournament featuring six gang teams, a team of LAPD officers, and a team fielded from the Los Angeles County Gang Probation Unit. That tournament has become an annual event. And Blinky has kicked off 170 gang-versus-gang football games since the first one in 1994.

The heart of his work remains his commitment to stop the plague of gang violence, keep kids in school, and prepare them for life. The state of California has named CIS of Greater Los Angeles a model gang-prevention program. In 1999, Blinky and Lilly flew to Geneva, Switzerland, to receive the Medaille d'Excellence at the 50th anniversary of the United Nations' Universal Declaration of Human Rights.

I can't improve on Blinky's eloquent description of how he connects with the kids society has demonized: "Speak the truth, speak to their hearts and minds, and breathe hope and vision. We're a community for youth."

Before the Three R's

Blinky Rodriguez is one of the most extraordinary people I know, and his story moves me every time I hear it. But there's another reason I wanted to introduce you to him and his work.

I've said that the dropout crisis isn't just an education issue. I can't think of a clearer illustration of this than the story you've just read. Can anyone really believe that the thousands of Los Angeles gang-involved or gang-threatened youth who leave school every year are quitting because they "don't like school" or are "challenged academically"? **They are dropping out because of gangs.**

The gangs got there first, offering a community (however flawed) that many young people deeply crave. And for many others, it is simply unsafe to go to school while such groups own the streets. Getting from home to school may involve crossing hostile turf; and as Sonny Rodriguez found out, that's a mortal danger. To keep these kids in school, you're going to have to provide a viable alternative to the terrible dilemma they face. *Then* you can work on academic success. Blinky began by intervening on the streets; now he and Bobby Arias are doing prevention in the schools (where gangs often do their recruiting), but it's all part of the same big picture.

Not every community is victimized by gang violence, but this basic model is true for virtually any other roadblock to graduation you can name. We learned it back at the Blue Elephant: *Kids need to be turned on to living before you can turn them on to learning.* Whether it's drug addiction, family dysfunction, lack of health care, homelessness, joblessness, or plain poverty, the strategy must be the same: Meet these pressing needs *first,* and then young people can concentrate on the three R's.

Communities In Schools has a name for the nonacademic needs of students. We call them the Five Basics, and they're the subject of the next chapter.

■ ■ ■ ■ ■

CHAPTER THREE

Before
the Three
R's . . .
the *Real*
Basics

What Every Child Needs

If you're a parent, you're probably far too busy ever to sit down with a pencil and paper and make a list of what your children need. It isn't really necessary, anyway. You address your kids' needs as they come, day by day. Parenting is complicated and demanding enough without trying to write it all down.

But imagine what such a list might look like: Nutritious food, regular checkups, recreation . . . affirmation of your children's gifts and abilities . . . clear rules to keep them safe ("Don't cross the street in the middle of the block") . . . strong ethical guidance ("Be kind to people and animals") . . . constant reassurance that they're secure and cared about ("I love you and you can always trust me to have your best interests at heart"). . . .

These are the sorts of things our children need; they're what *all* children need. If you combined the dozens of daily needs into a few key groups, you might come up with this:

Every young person needs and deserves:

1. A one-on-one relationship with a caring adult
2. A safe place to learn and grow
3. A healthy start and a healthy future
4. A marketable skill to use upon graduation
5. A chance to give back to peers and community

Communities In Schools calls these "the Five Basics." Our experience has shown us that if these things aren't addressed, kids are going to have a hard time succeeding in school. The first three in particular need attention *early*—the seeds of dropping out are sown long before students reach their teen years. Children can't begin to learn if they're convinced that nobody cares about them, that they're worthless and unsafe physically and emotionally. Nor can they concentrate on schoolwork if their most basic needs—nutrition, shelter, health care, and the like—aren't being met.

It's certainly true that most of the kids we reach through CIS are from poor families, often victimized by multigenerational poverty. And low-income families equal "bad" neighborhoods and underfunded schools, so they're also frequently bearing the burden of decrepit, dangerous school buildings; outdated textbooks; and sometimes, unqualified teachers.

But when we say that every child needs the Five Basics, we really mean *every* child. Suburban kids from middle-class homes are also at risk of quitting school if they don't get the essentials. My own example shows that clearly enough. I grew up in a nice house but it wasn't a home. My parents didn't or couldn't discover what I needed; alcoholism and emotional dysfunction wrecked my home. I seldom had an evening meal with my family—they were too busy. That's true for many families who are running around so much that they don't have time to create a genuine sense of home.

Pain-filled, dysfunctional households send kids to school in bad shape. It doesn't matter how much money a family has. Poverty can create dreadful childhoods, but so can abusive, uncaring parenting in $500,000 "starter castles."

So I strongly believe that the Five Basics are what *every* child needs and deserves. At the same time, I'm not trying to say that poor families and those who are well-off are starting at "Go" with the same chance for success. That's not so, and the well-being of children is perhaps the number one justice issue in America today. You can argue back and forth, depending on your politics, about what kind of assistance, if any, poor adults may need. The debate usually hinges on questions of personal responsibility. But children are a different story. A five-year-old girl who goes to school hungry isn't going to learn anything about "personal responsibility" (let alone anything about the three R's) if she continues to go unfed. It won't be good for her character; it won't do anything except hurt her. Denying her what she needs is, quite simply, unjust. She has done nothing wrong—other than to be born in a ghetto, on a failing farm, or in a former mining community with no more work to offer adults. And blaming her parents won't help either.

I applaud the school-reform movement for insisting that "no child should be left behind." But to believe that every boy and girl comes to school with the same resources and support is wishful thinking. It flies in the face of the grim reality: Millions of American children are uninsured, underfed, and unprepared to take that walk to school.

The First Basic

As I've said, I wouldn't be here today without a positive relationship with a caring adult. The First Basic, "a one-on-one relationship with a caring adult," remains the cornerstone and the most directly experiential of all Five Basics. Think about your own life. There was *someone*—a parent, an uncle, a teacher, a coach, or perhaps a faith community leader—who cared enough about you to hang in with you and be real.

Today, **mentors** are the most common and successful means for providing the First Basic to students. Programs in schools, in particular, have repeatedly shown their effectiveness. Dr. Jean Rhodes's article "School Based Mentoring" (written for MENTOR, formerly the National Mentoring Partnership, an organization CIS is proud to partner with) reviews the literature and provides clear evidence to supplement the intuitive sense we all have that positive relationships with adults make a big difference:

- School-based mentoring programs sponsored by Big Brothers Big Sisters show "substantial improvements in students' school performance, attendance, confidence, attitudes, expression, trust, respect and relationships with adults. Because they correlated with report card data, these impressions appeared to be grounded in actual progress. Youth in longer-lasting relationships enjoyed additional academic benefits."

- A research study by Public/Private Ventures found that school-based mentoring produced "improvements in the students' behavior (particularly academic), attitudes and self-confidence. About half of the parents interviewed reported that their children had made significant academic improvements subsequent to being involved in the program. Teachers noted that children improved in a range of subjects, including math, reading, social studies and citizenship. Three of the four teachers also mentioned increased confidence as a common area of improvement."[1]

The Second Basic

The Second Basic, "a safe place to learn and grow," also developed out of personal experience. The kids we worked with in New York City lacked that most basic of needs: a roof over their heads. And that's often true of young people today, too. The National Coalition for the Homeless estimates that, on any given night, 1.35 million U.S. children 18 and younger are homeless.[2]

Even more children, however, need safe places in addition to their homes. While the issue of violence inside schools has been, in my opinion, exaggerated and sensationalized, it's true that too many of them pose physical and emotional dangers to students, and a climate of hostility and threat must be faced directly. The best solution, as I noted earlier, is to bring so many caring adults into the building that kids *can't* get into trouble. It's also extremely important not to let schools grow so large that individual students get lost and become potential victims of cliques and bullies.

Equally important, though, is the question of safe neighborhoods and communities. When children are afraid to walk to school and have nowhere to go and nothing to do after school hours, the Second Basic isn't being met.

There are many positive and successful responses to this situation. One of the best is the new enthusiasm for using schools as true community centers and creating before- and after-school programs that give kids—and their families—a safe and productive place to spend time. The Afterschool Alliance offers these encouraging results from its research:

Evaluations of the Los Angeles County after-school program LA's BEST, which includes both academic and recreational activities offered in low-achieving high schools, show that "students' regular school-day attendance improved once they began participating in the after-school program. Improved attendance in turn led to higher academic achievement on standardized tests of math, reading and language arts."

A five-site evaluation of the Boys & Girls Clubs' national Project Learn program found that "as program involvement increased, engagement in reading, use of verbal skills, writing, tutoring, and the study of geography all significantly increased . . . There was also a direct and statistically significant relationship between program involvement and enjoyment of reading, use of verbal skills, writing, and geography." Further, average grade increases over the 30-month study period were greatest for youth who participated in Project Learn.[3]

One of the themes we'll look at in the next chapter is the critical importance of coordinating and interweaving all of the Five Basics, rather than regarding them as isolated "fixes" for students' issues. With that in mind, consider this reminder from MENTOR:

Although not fully appreciated, after-school settings provide wonderful opportunities for the formation of informal mentoring relationships. Faced with fewer curricular demands than teachers, the staff who work in after-school programs have unique opportunities to engage in the sorts of informal conversations and activities that give rise to close bonds with youth. Similarly, working parents, who are often stretched to their limits by job and family, rarely have the luxury of spending hours of quality "downtime" with their children each afternoon. In fact, there is growing consensus that caring youth-staff relationships may be a key determinant of both retention and success in after-school programming.[4]

The Third Basic

Children need to be healthy—physically, emotionally, spiritually. My understanding of the Third Basic, "a healthy start and a healthy future," was born out of the catastrophe of drug addiction among the young people of Harlem and the Lower East Side. Vinnie, Dean, and I could often get kids out of the street gangs. But, ironically, at that time those very groups offered a kind of community that had kept the members clean. Drugs and gangs didn't mix back then. You couldn't be a reliable member if you were getting high. So the downside of breaking up gangs was that the kids, now isolated, turned to heroin to relieve their pain.

Drugs were everywhere, starting with pot and alcohol for the little kids—eight-, nine-, and ten-year-old addicts were commonplace. The ruined lives are almost impossible to comprehend unless you've seen it yourself. If you want to destroy a community, a nation, this is the way. There were few treatment options back then, no fancy rehab clinics and no Narcotics Anonymous. Sometimes I could persuade a kid to check into a hospital, where the medical staff might or might not know how to help him, or care whether he got help.

More often it was "cold turkey." I never want to sit through that again, watching helplessly for hours while a young person shivered and screamed and wept in our apartment at 215 Madison. You can't insulate yourself from that kind of pain—it changes you forever. And the worst of it was, a kid might come out of the hospital or leave the apartment, hit the street, and a few hours later be high again. The pressure of reality, of the life he or she was faced with, was too much.

Over the years I saw a lot of young people die. I spoke at a lot of funerals. Kids would do their best but then start lying about it and get back on drugs. This is when the whole concept of "tough love" began emerging, and *Tough Love* was the title of my first book, published in 1968. I knew it was the only kind of caring that would work under those conditions. Dean and I had to find the courage to say what a good father would tell his children: "I don't care how this makes you feel toward me. You may hate my guts, but I love you, and I'm doing this because I love you. I don't expect you to understand right now, but I have to do it anyway. Either tell the truth about whether you're getting high, or move out."

When we were too afraid to be tough, we usually lost the kid. At the same time, we had to learn when to take on the traditional "mothering" roles as well, doing our best to provide emotional nurturing and hot meals.

Drugs and alcohol are still a huge challenge to growing up healthy, but so are the less dramatic dangers: poor eyesight, asthma, lack of proper nutrition, and teeth that hurt so much that a kid bangs his head against the wall. (I saw this happen.) As we launched the first Communities In Schools sites, we knew we'd have to take this on in a very direct way. It was another major impetus for us to create *partnerships:* If we weren't educators, we certainly weren't doctors either. It was vital that community health centers, along with volunteer nurses, physicians, dentists, ophthalmologists, and therapists, be linked through the school site with their young patients.

One eight-year-old girl's statement says more about the value of the Third Basic than any words of mine. She was asked why her grades had improved so much in the second semester of the school year. Touching her new eyeglasses, she said happily, "I can see the blackboard!"

The Fourth Basic

The Fourth Basic, "a marketable skill to use upon graduation," sprang directly from our early experiences as "educators." We knew that young people needed a high school diploma to become part of mainstream American society. We also discovered that kids needed a *reason* to get that certification—they had to be given reasons to hope, to believe in themselves. It isn't enough to say, "Well, reading, writing, and math are good things, and people expect you to know them, so please spend the next five years studying." We had to help create concrete goals for our students, and usually that involved helping them think about career paths. If we could get them to see that education led to skills that would earn them money and give them a way out of poverty, it was a big motivational step.

I've known some people who are skeptical about this. They believe that poor kids, especially those from urban environments, are all about the easy allure of drug money and crime-based lifestyles. While it's true that those role models need to be explicitly debunked, the idea that "inner-city youth would rather deal drugs than work" is a middle-class myth. Most of these kids are just like you and me: They don't want to feel their heart going 50 miles an hour, desperately afraid that they might be shot down in a drug deal. They want to live. They'd much rather learn the skills that qualify them for legitimate work and a path to a future, even if the jobs pay less money than illegal activity.

> IT ISN'T ENOUGH TO SAY, "WELL, READING, WRITING, AND MATH ARE GOOD THINGS, AND PEOPLE EXPECT YOU TO KNOW THEM, SO PLEASE SPEND THE NEXT FIVE YEARS STUDYING."

Forty years ago, graduating from high school with a marketable skill represented an excellent start. Even dropouts could find work, with luck. Today, the world is different. Our Fourth Basic is about careers, and that means it has to be about higher education, too. Fewer and fewer options are available without a college degree; dropouts are three times more likely to be unemployed than are college graduates.[5]

Another way of stating this principle might be: "Every child needs and deserves a clear career path to follow upon graduation from high school." Naturally enough, the majority of our CIS sites around the country are concentrating on helping kids get into college as part of providing this basic. They're also connecting students with high-quality career-preparation programs to train them for future employment markets.

The Fifth Basic

Of all the Five Basics, it's the last one, "a chance to give back to peers and community," that surprises many people. Once you accept the idea that kids need some nonacademic bedrock on which to stand before they can succeed in school, the first four ideas are pretty intuitive. As I said, it's no different from what you'd want for your own children. But the Fifth Basic, while equally critical, isn't always so obvious. Yet receiving young people's gifts is the key to helping them find their own identity, meaning, and self-worth.

Many years ago I was part of a panel invited to testify at a government hearing about the plight of the education system. Sometimes I feel that these gatherings are totally irrelevant; they call them "hearings" because nobody's listening. This one was the usual scene: people making speeches, talking past each other, and looking good for the cameras. Finally, in the last minute or so, I was asked: "What's the difference between the kids you've seen make it and those who haven't?"

I spent the first 30 of the 60 seconds I'd been allotted dealing with my anger and pain. Somehow it just seemed outrageous that a politician wanted me to sum up decades of one-on-one successes and failures in a tidy sound bite. Then I said, "The ones who made it did so because we *allowed* them to make it."

"What do you mean?"

"I mean that **the greatest gift you can give someone is to allow them to give something to *you*.**"

That's what the Fifth Basic is.

> "Giving back" is more than encouraging volunteerism, service-learning, or peer mentoring, although those things are extremely important. Our nation must vigorously expand programs like AmeriCorps that hold up community service as a great American value.

One on one, there's an incredible, precious thing that happens to young people when they find out they have a gift that somebody else values. They may be feeling all this hatred, hostility, and anger; and then suddenly they see that a grown-up wants to *receive* something from them. An adult *values* an ability or talent or gift of theirs. This, by the way, is one of the reasons why it's such a mistake to cut funding for arts programs in schools. You're eliminating so many opportunities for students to discover a talent they'd never dreamed of.

If you don't think kids have anything to give you—if you think you're better off than they are in this area, with all *your* gifts—then you'd better stay away from young people, because you'll do them more harm than good. You do have things to contribute, but children have plenty to share with you, too. It's a two-way street.

One-way help isn't always beneficial. You can destroy people and keep them in poverty by "helping" them, especially if your attitude screams out: *Here I am sharing my abilities with you, who have none!* And consider the effect of this kind of belief on communities that, for generations, have been on the receiving end of impersonal, paternalistic "help" from various governmental sources. By emphasizing the *value* of giving back, we also emphasize the *responsibility* to do so.

We have to learn how to receive as well as give. I'm still working on it. I like the image of myself as "someone who helps others." It's a lot harder to identify and accept my own vulnerabilities and limitations and admit that I need to receive something from you. But to help, to give, is a profound spiritual need, and an eight-year-old boy in Appalachia feels it just as strongly as any of the rest of us do.

It's not always easy. You have to start by believing in that young person and finding the patience and love to get beyond his hostility, pain, or shame—whatever may be keeping him from embracing his gifts. When a kid discovers that he or she has something valuable to give, it can open so many doors.

Kodak once donated some cameras to the young people in our Los Angeles affiliate, and a number of students found out they were naturals at photography. Their pictures were published in the *Los Angeles Times* magazine, and they were encouraged to consider turning their talents into careers. But to do so, they had to "smart up" and find out more about how photography worked. They had to learn math, English, and some practical science. Suddenly school was no longer remote from life; it was a clear path to doing what they loved. The experience of having their gift valued made them appreciate, in turn, the value of education. They'd found their passion, and they couldn't wait to learn more.

Every child wants to give—even those who literally have nothing to give you. I no longer remember where I first heard this story, but I've never forgotten it: A young boy from an extremely poor family formed a close relationship with his fourth-grade teacher. At the end of the school year, he handed her something wrapped in newspaper. She opened it; inside was an old Sears Roebuck catalog. "I wanted to give you a present, but I don't have money to buy you anything," the boy told her. "So I found this old book in our closet. Look through it and pick whatever you want most. Then pretend that's what I gave you."

Spreading the Word

The Five Basics were all born out of personal experience—my own, my colleagues', and the thousands of kids we've known—

coupled with a collective discussion within the CIS network that occurred over many years.

I don't think the ideas themselves are startling or revolutionary. We didn't invent each one of them, and in a sense every parent already knows them. But we were able to frame and articulate them in a way that struck a chord with many people. This too occurred over time—I wouldn't want to give the impression that we always thought of them as "the Five Basics," or indeed that we even considered them as discrete principles at all. That came later, as we tried to create a replicable process that communities across the country could use to fight their own dropout problem. By the mid-1990s, though, I'd come to refer to Four Basics—minus the "healthy start" one—and most of the Communities In Schools network had adopted them as a cornerstone of their strategies.

As I mentioned in Chapter 2, I was asked to help organize the Presidents' Summit for America's Future in 1997. General Powell wanted to harness the energy that came out of that event to launch a new movement called America's Promise, dedicated to providing children with the resources they need to succeed. The organization's symbol would be the "little red wagon" so beloved by children everywhere—an excellent image for an organization pledged to resource delivery. One of our CIS board members, Ray Chambers, was the driving force behind the summit and in the formation of America's Promise. Not long after the event, he called me to say that General Powell and his advisors felt that CIS's Four Basics would make a perfect framework around which to organize the goals of America's Promise.

I was overjoyed. Here was an incredible opportunity to disseminate our principles to what I hoped would be hundreds of new communities. It felt appropriate and humbling to be able to share the fruits of our many decades of work with this new organization. We were honored that America's Promise embraced our Basics.

A few days later, Ray called again. How would I feel about adding a Fifth Basic? The United Way of America and Marian Wright Edelman, head of the Children's Defense Fund, wanted to include something about a healthy start for kids. Ray had heard me speak about this many times, and he knew that our CIS affiliates put a great deal of stress on it. I told him that was fine—it struck me as an excellent improvement.

So CIS now had Five Basics, and the new group had its Five Promises. These critically important principles were part of the "little red wagon" mission, advocated for by America's Promise affiliates in all 50 states.

Getting It Together

Let's imagine, once again, that you've made a list of all the things your children need. You've grouped them according to the Five Basics. What do you do next?

Here's one thing you *don't* do: You don't draw a map of your house and start dividing it up into little "help stations." You don't say to your spouse, "Okay, you deal with the caring relationship here in the living room. I'll be downstairs in the rec room waiting to assess the kids' health situation. When we're both done with that, you go up to the attic and do some math tutoring and then send everybody down to the porch so that I can talk to them about community service."

This would be insane. A caring home is an integrated, one-stop shop. Parents and extended family members, with help from others in the adult community when appropriate, work together to find out what the children need and figure out how to coordinate the necessary resources in the most efficient way.

But this safety net—woven by parents, extended families, faith communities, and tightly knit neighborhoods—no longer exists in the lives of millions of kids. The public schools have fallen into that vacuum. So schools, we realized, are the ideal place to deliver all those missing components that prevent students from succeeding academically—what we later came to call the Five Basics. Just as important, we discovered that the *way* these resources are delivered is also critical. To understand why, we'll take a look at the hurdles families face in a typical community.

▓ ▓ ▓ ▓ ▓

PART II

In Search
of Community

CHAPTER FOUR

Bureaucratic, Fragmented, and Duplicative— or Personal, Accountable, and Coordinated?

"What Should I Do?"

Tara Larson isn't feeling well. The pretty, shy 11-year-old has begun her first semester at Van Buren Middle School, a large urban facility that's seen better days. Classes are crowded; textbooks are in short supply; and even after eight weeks of classes, Tara's teachers seem to have trouble remembering her name.

Her mother, Ruth, is starting to worry about her. The girl is losing weight, often picking at her food or skipping meals altogether. She's tired and listless. At least once a week, she asks to stay home from school because she has a bad headache.

Ruth Larson is a divorced mother of three, working a full-time job as a veterinary assistant plus an additional 18 hours three nights a week at the local Blockbuster. It's hard enough to arrange day care for Tara's two little sisters, ages three and four. If Tara is too sick to go to school, her mom doesn't have many options. She can call in sick herself or ask her nice neighbor, a retired public-school teacher named Mrs. Hartshorne, if she'd mind helping out.

Clearly, something must be done. And now she's been called to the school to meet with Tara's guidance counselor. The counselor seems kind enough, but harassed and rushed. After quickly reading through the girl's folder (Ruth suspects that the counselor needs to remind herself which parent this is), she informs Ruth that her daughter's grades are plummeting. Tara has been inattentive in class, has failed to turn in homework, and has done poorly on tests. If this keeps up, she'll likely be held back a grade.

"What should I do?" Ruth asks. "What's the matter with her?"

Well, the counselor replies, it could be so many things. A physical checkup is a must, and the doctor might recommend some counseling. Of course, 11 is a very difficult age for girls—there are so many social and maturational changes going on. And speaking of changes, yes, going to middle school is a big shift in and of itself. A lot of new sixth graders have difficulty adjusting. Some of the older students are involved with drugs, sexual activity, and even gangs.

The counselor says, sighing, that she knows this isn't good, but what can the school do? The entire community has changed, hasn't it? Or maybe Tara just needs some tutoring, something to snap her out of her academic doldrums. The counselor gives Ruth a recommendation for a private tutoring service.

Ruth Larson leaves the meeting feeling overwhelmed. She's tried talking to her daughter about what's wrong, of course, but Tara doesn't appear to know. "I just don't feel good," she repeats. So it's up to her mother, who loves her children very much, to find the help the girl needs.

Where to begin? Health insurance will pay for a visit to the HMO—which is across town and not particularly near public transportation. But Ruth doesn't have a car.

She calls the HMO, and the only available appointment that isn't weeks off is on a Monday morning at ten o'clock. To keep it, Ruth will have to take yet another sick day from work. Her boss, Ms. Brown, the vet's office manager, has been understanding about all these days off, but this time Ruth can tell from the expression on her face that she's run out of patience.

Getting to the HMO involves two buses and five blocks on foot in a part of town Ruth would rather not have to take her daughter through. It doesn't feel safe, but they walk quickly and try not to meet the stares of the idling young men on the street corners.

At the HMO, Dr. Edwards gives Tara a thorough exam. Nothing is obviously wrong, he tells Ruth, although the girl is clearly underweight and tired. He recommends several more tests. Will the insurance cover it? He looks away and says, "I think so. Probably. But you need to talk to the folks out front about that." He also recommends that an adolescent mental health counselor evaluate Tara. He writes a referral—to a different building in another part of the city. "And be sure to check with the folks out front about that, too," he says. "Mental health coverage varies from policy to policy, you know."

"The folks out front" are polite and helpful, but Ruth gets the feeling they've given up on the health-care system. Their answers to her questions are tentative and full of a resigned, half-humorous tone that seems to say: *This crazy system—who knows how it works? Everything will probably be okay. Just make sure you do the paperwork right! Gotta do that paperwork right.*

Even after three pregnancies, Ruth has never mastered the paperwork of the health-care system. She doesn't know anyone who has. She can feel her stomach tensing as she makes the appointments for Tara's tests and a visit to the mental health counselor. All the appointments are—of course—during working hours. What will she say to her boss *this* time?

Back home, Ruth calls the tutoring service recommended by the guidance counselor. It's located near the city line in a rather affluent neighborhood Ruth doesn't often visit. Her phone call is discouraging: Yes, they'd be happy to meet Ruth and Tara—in three weeks, their first opening. No, there are no reductions in the hefty tutoring fees for people of moderate income—and no, it's not something health insurance would cover. Public transportation to the office? "Oh, I think you should take your car, dear," says the woman on the phone.

Ruth says nothing. As the call is concluding, she asks, "Do you know if there are any volunteer tutoring organizations? We just don't have a lot of funds right now." The woman on the phone has no problem answering this question. She provides the names of five different nonprofit tutoring groups. Ruth writes down the names and numbers, wondering how she can possibly manage to contact them all and figure out which one would be best for Tara.

The visit to the HMO and the call to the tutoring service have taken, all told, five hours of Ruth's day. At this rate, she realizes despondently, meeting her daughter's needs will be another part-time job, one that she'll somehow have to fit in without losing either of her other jobs.

A Name on a Form

The adolescent mental health specialist is named Gwendolyn Smith. She's warm and funny. Ruth likes her immediately, and she can tell that Tara does, too. Hopefully, it will be worth the half-day leave Ruth took from work. Ms. Brown, the office manager, didn't even try to be nice about it this time. She said that this was the last "sick day" she could authorize—from now on any more leave would be without pay. And, she said firmly, we need to have a talk about your situation. Dr. Hagen can't keep doing without you like this.

Tara is in Gwendolyn Smith's office (which looks more like a cheerful recreation room) for nearly an hour and a half while her mother leafs through magazines and tries to find a balance between worry and hope. When the appointment is over, the counselor speaks to Ruth alone.

To begin with, Gwendolyn says, we have to rule out some possible physical issues. She then proceeds to recommend the same three tests Dr. Edwards called for. When Ruth says that she has already scheduled them, the other woman looks abashed.

"I'm so sorry," she says. "They didn't put that in the referral." She shakes her head. "With every client, it's like starting over. And if I call over there and ask for more information about the physical workup, they'll either refuse to talk to me or put me through so many holds and loops that it might be weeks before I get anyone who knows who Tara Larson is. . . . I'm sorry to sound so discouraging."

It's all right, Ruth assures her. This mother has already begun to see how the system "works"—or doesn't. Tara, her precious daughter, is just a name on a form, on many forms scattered throughout the agencies of this big city. It's not the *people* who don't care. On the contrary, people like Gwendolyn Smith, Dr. Edwards, and even the "folks out front" at the HMO care very much. They're good and decent.

Rather, it's the *system* that doesn't care, Ruth is realizing. All this separation of people and resources seems designed to ensure that no single individual sees Tara as a whole person. Each specialist is brought to bear on his or her area of expertise.

She tries to convey some of this to Gwendolyn, who nods sadly. "I know," she says. "It's so hard to find anyone who sees the whole picture—except you, of course."

"And I already *have* a job," Ruth says, trying to laugh.

Anyway, Gwendolyn goes on, Tara could probably use some counseling, no matter what the tests show. As the school guidance counselor had said, sixth grade is a big challenge and so is being an 11-year-old girl. She'd be glad to take Tara on as a client. Will insurance cover the sessions?

Ruth is now pretty sure she has the answer to this. Yes, 85 percent of the first 12 sessions are taken care of, and then 50 percent of the next 12, but in between she has to get her HMO to approve the DSM-IV diagnosis sent to them by Gwendolyn, and then . . . "I *think* the percentages are right," she ends. "And I *think* I can pay my part of it, although I'll have to dip into my savings."

Gwendolyn talks a bit about what to expect from counseling—and what not to expect. "Part of the problem," she says, "is the school itself, I'm sorry to say. For instance, Tara talked to me for quite some time about what she feels walking the halls between classes. She says the older girls are mean to her and the older boys make her feel 'dirty.' She's always afraid somebody's going to bully her."

"She should tell a teacher about that!" Ruth exclaims indignantly.

"Tara says she doesn't know any of the teachers, and they don't seem to know her. She's afraid she'll 'get in trouble' if she talks about what's bothering her. Then there's the problem of making friends. There are a couple of girls she really likes, but they've already asked her if she wants to get high. When she told them no, they stopped talking to her."

"I didn't know that," Ruth murmurs.

"It would probably be a good idea for Tara to have something to do after school, too," Gwendolyn continues. "She told me that she gets bored and lonely in the apartment by herself, but there's nothing going on at school either. I know of a great program called AfterHours that the city runs, and it's free for kids her age. They have sports, games, and study time. In fact, that might be just the thing to help Tara get her grades up. It's held at the community center on Garver Avenue."

Ruth has been smiling at the description of the program, but the smile fades as she says, "But that's more than a mile from the school. How do they expect the kids to get there?"

"I'm not sure," Gwendolyn admits. "It was started to serve the kids in a different neighborhood from yours. But we can find out."

And, a few days later, they do find out: There's no regular transportation for the kids from Van Buren Middle School. AfterHours primarily caters to its own neighborhood.

The same day Ruth Larson learns this, her office manager, Ms. Brown, calls her in for that promised—or threatened—talk about the situation. It's more of a monologue, and the message is clear: Ruth needs to start showing up for work consistently or she can look for another job.

"It's just that . . . well, my daughter is having difficulties right now," Ruth pleads. "She really needs me to be there, to take her places . . ." She trails off, realizing that the story of her daughter's needs is long and complicated.

She looks up and sees that Ms. Brown's eyes are tired and gentle. "I know, Ruth," she says softly. "But everyone still has to do their jobs—you, me, and Dr. Hagen. Isn't there somebody who can help you with your daughter?"

No, Ruth thinks, *there isn't. That doesn't appear to be anyone's job.*

When she arrives home after picking up the younger girls from day care, she finds her oldest daughter on the couch, staring at the TV with the sound turned off. "What's wrong, sweetie?" her mother asks.

"I just don't feel good," Tara says.

What's Wrong with This Picture?

Ruth Larson is a loving mother. She couldn't be more committed to the well-being of her children.

Tara Larson's school is large, underresourced, and full of the potential for ugly trouble, but in one important sense, it's doing the right thing. The guidance counselor has become aware that Tara is in danger of academic failure and has taken action. The girl's mother has been notified; suggestions for help have been made. Moreover, the helping resources are available: physical and mental health care, tutoring, and some healthy after-school activities. It's not the impossible dream.

And certainly there are no villains here. The individuals Ruth has encountered in her quest to meet her daughter's needs have been polite, professional, and willing to help.

So what's going wrong? Why, after nearly a month of concentrated effort, is there still no plan for helping Tara Larson? Why is her mother on the verge of giving up?

The resources are in place, but they're in the *wrong* place. They're scattered all over town, difficult to access, and open for business during—what else?—business hours. They don't talk to each other. Each encounter involves a barrage of paperwork that even the professionals are often unclear about. Ruth would need a Ph.D. in systems to figure it all out.

It's as if, in order to write a report, you had 26 keyboards in different parts of the office. To type an A, you have to use the "A keyboard," because that's the only letter it will type. To type a B, you set off on your journey to find the "B keyboard" . . . and on and on.

When resources are scattered and isolated like this, an already faulty system starts to experience even more strains and dysfunctions. The natural tendency, if you work in one particular area, is to concentrate on what you do best—what you get paid for—and pass on the rest of the responsibility. If Tara Larson needs a tutor, that's hardly the problem of the guidance counselor. Her job is demanding enough. Who could expect her to be on the phone on her own time, trying to line up a tutor for one girl out of the dozens she sees every week?

So good people get tunnel vision. They hold themselves accountable only for their particular piece of the problem. It's really self-protection. Teachers face the same dilemma. They're not being paid to be counselors, advocates, and experts in social systems. Just teaching is hard enough.

As for Ruth, how in the world is she supposed to find the time to master the "system"—to get that Ph.D.—while she's already working nearly 60 hours a week?

And remember, Tara Larson isn't some special, unusual case. There are Taras in most schools. If teachers, recreation counselors, tutors, and therapists had to spend the time and effort on each one of these children that would be needed to see them holistically, to really coordinate a response to their issues, no one would ever go home. There aren't enough hours in the week.

THE RESOURCES ARE IN PLACE, BUT THEY'RE IN THE *WRONG* PLACE.

So each person does his or her job. There's nothing wrong with that, but it means that Tara and the thousands like her in schools across the country are falling through the cracks because *no one* has the most crucial job of all. Nobody gets paid to make sure the whole system works.

Reversing the Arrows

The solution to this sad, all-too-common situation is simple . . . but not easy. Look at the following diagram. It shows the typical "flow" of energy when students need assistance. All the arrows point out from the schoolhouse in every direction of the compass.

Now imagine the diagram looked like this.

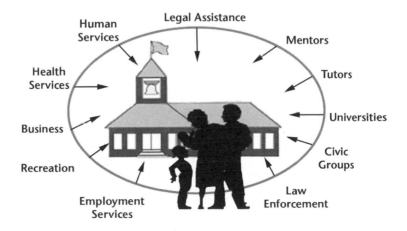

All we've done is reverse the direction of the arrows, but what an enormous change that makes! Now the various outside agencies are bringing their services *to* the school instead of waiting for students and parents to come to them. The school has become the delivery point. Not only are families better able to find the help they need, but the agencies can also find their "customers." We've been looking at the problem from a parent's point of view, but social workers, health-care specialists, and all the other community resource providers are also frustrated by the typical fragmented situation.

With one stroke, we've ended the nerve-racking back and forth from office to office that Ruth and Tara experienced. Now the "offices" are down the hall from the girl's homeroom. The after-school program is held at the school, too, instead of at the community center.

Take a look at the following illustration. It's a snapshot showing how all Five Basics can come together at the school. A mentor is meeting one of "his" children and providing the First Basic, a positive, one-on-one relationship with a caring adult. An after-school drug-education program helps with the Second Basic, a safe place to learn and grow. The nurse's office hosts an array of visiting health-care specialists providing the Third Basic, a healthy start and a healthy future. Business volunteers join kids in the computer room for employment training to give them the Fourth Basic, a marketable skill. Community service and service-learning opportunities form a regular part of classroom instruction, thanks to partnerships with neighborhood volunteer groups that are eager to provide the Fifth Basic, a chance to give back to peers and community.

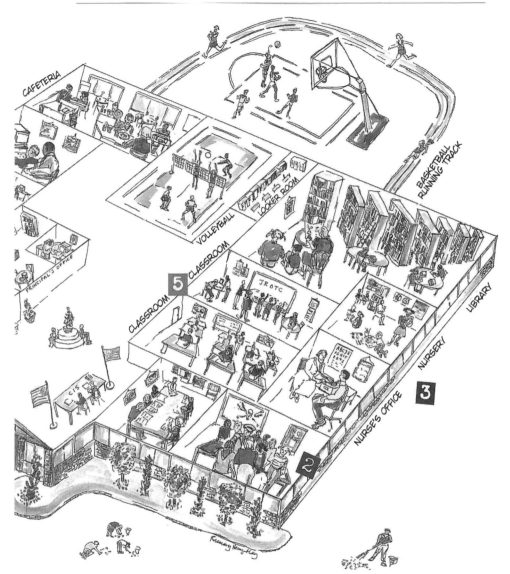

It's a wonderful, vibrant place, and a big improvement over the way it used to be. But all the problems aren't solved yet. The resources are in the schools, but we still need someone whose job it is to ensure that they're delivered to the students who need them in a manner that's personal, accountable, and coordinated. Such an individual—Communities In Schools calls him or her the *site coordinator*—is on-site, in touch with the students and the resources, and expert at the one job no one else has the time or training to do: *connecting the students with the people who care and can back it up with expertise.*

As I said, it's simple, but not easy. It requires a long-term commitment by the school system and a slow but steady change in the way the community allocates its helping resources.

When it works, it's the best antidote I know to the dropout epidemic.

The Case of Wichita, Kansas

The four school districts comprising the greater Wichita/ Sedgwick County area are in many ways typical of urban school systems throughout the country. Poverty rates are going up, resources are strained, and talented and committed educators are challenged every day by problems they can't solve by themselves. The county graduation rate is pegged at 78 percent, but the Wichita school district's is closer to 67 percent.

Communities In Schools has operated in Wichita/Sedgwick County since 1991. Dan Glickman, a former Wichita Board of Education member, was at that time Wichita's congressman. He later became secretary of agriculture in the Clinton administration, and now heads the Motion Picture Association of America. Dan and his wife, Rhoda, were instrumental in helping CIS get off the ground in Wichita. They went to community meetings with me, met all the stakeholders, and gave tireless support and encouragement. Dan was just the sort of political leader that our schools need, and I'm happy to say he shortly joined the national CIS board of directors, where he continues his superb advocacy for children and families.

Judy Frick has headed the CIS effort in Wichita since day one. She's an incredible person—smart, energetic, and compassionate. Her credo is: "We do whatever it takes to help a child and family be successful. Quite honestly, the sky's the limit. Tell me what *doesn't* fit into those Five Basics."

A quick look at the services Wichita CIS provides reveals that all Five Basics are amply represented. The organization began its work in the district in January 1991 in one elementary school, expanding to seven more schools the following fall. The community needs assessment revealed that poor health care was the single greatest challenge to student success, and thus the Third Basic, "a healthy start," needed immediate attention. The solution? A *school-based* health center on the grounds of the elementary school.

Judy hosted a conference involving health-care providers, legislators, foundations, and social-service providers to demonstrate the need for such a center and to consider how it might be supported. As a result, Kansas Health Foundation invited her to submit a proposal and wound up providing major funding, along with the United Methodist Health Ministry Fund. All told, 22 other partners significantly supported the development of the Healthy Children Center, which opened in 1996. Now the facility, run by a local health-care provider, is open to all students in the school district and offers Medicaid reimbursement to the families who qualify for free or reduced-price lunches (a reliable marker of low economic status).

CIS acts as the conduit, making sure that students with probable medical issues are referred to the health center and followed up to ensure their needs are met. As the result of a new health-promotion project, CIS elementary site coordinators arrange personal health inventories and physicals for the kids and provide "health tip" cards for mentors and tutors.

In fact, mentoring is the bedrock here, as is usually the case when CIS enters a community. Judy Frick has collaborated with Big Brothers Big Sisters since 1997, facilitating school-based matches between students and mentors to ensure the First Basic, "a one-on-one relationship with a caring adult." Another program, Compeer, sponsored by the Mental Health Association, matches firefighters and police officers with emotionally troubled children. Yet another brings Foster Grandparents to the schools as tutors. Local university students also get credit for tutoring and mentoring.

As valuable as all these mentoring efforts are, it's the *way* they're done that makes the difference. The matches are made *at the school* and, under the auspices of CIS, are part of *a coordinated, personalized response to children's specific needs.*

The Second Basic, "a safe place to learn and grow," finds expression in a partnership between CIS and the YMCA, which sends buses to schools to pick children up for an after-school recreational program, then takes them back to the school. Second Step, a violence-prevention program, has been implemented in several schools to ensure that they are safe places. In another direct response to keeping kids safe and in class, a truancy-prevention grant from Sedgwick County recently allowed CIS to expand to eight new middle school sites. Their focus is on sixth graders, based on research showing that this year is the most valuable time to intervene when kids start skipping school.

The Kansas Department of Social and Rehabilitation Services (SRS) also collaborates with CIS to help students and families stay safe. SRS provides a liaison in each school with a CIS presence to serve as a resource in areas such as truancy, abuse and neglect, health care, basic needs, and custody cases. The representative is an expert in connecting the school with the right person at SRS to solve an issue quickly. In addition to meeting with the school support team, this person also conducts training for faculty and staff on relevant issues. The collaborative effort results in better services for children and families, healthier lives for all, and more effective relationships between the schools and the county's support services.

One of my favorite examples of how to help young people learn about marketable skills (our Fourth Basic) is Wichita CIS's "Reality Store." I like it because it approaches the whole issue of money and responsible planning in a fresh, creative way. It doesn't deal directly with jobs or careers, yet it most certainly teaches a powerful lesson about their importance and has the added bonus of building a significant volunteer/partnership base for CIS.

The Reality Store is a 60-minute exercise that has helped more than 7,000 Wichita eighth graders and high school students understand some of the tough truths involved in preparing for an employable future and adulthood. Students are assigned an "occupation" based on specific educational plans after high school—or after dropping out. Each student "earns" a salary equivalent to the average monthly wage in that job at the age of 26.

The students proceed to the school's gym, where they meet with volunteers representing the housing industry, utilities, grocery stores, and child-care centers; their challenge is to spend their monthly after-taxes salary on the necessities and luxuries they envision to be part of their adult lifestyle. In short order, the kids gain a new appreciation for their parents' efforts to provide for them, as well as the difficulties they could face when a budget problem turns into a crisis.

Some students are given computerized dolls to represent their families. The "babies" cry throughout the exercise, convincing many of the young people to rethink their choice to start families early or to reconsider the number of children they want to have. Funny—and not-so-funny—things happen. One young father left his "baby" at the grocery store and was fined for his negligence.

The young Reality Store shoppers discover that their salaries as dropouts can hardly meet even the most thrifty budget. And no matter how carefully they plan, there are the "Chance" cards. They're required to take these periodically in order to learn about the unexpected things that affect daily life, both the good and the bad. One student plops her head down on the table when she reads: "You've fallen off a ladder and broken your arm." The medical bills and loss of income weren't in her budget, and she had no savings.

As a companion to the harsh lessons of the Reality Store, Wichita CIS offers job-shadowing opportunities at local hospitals, department stores, and law firms. In partnership with the Simon Youth Foundation, CIS also collaborated with the Wichita school district to establish two unusual "Mall Academies" at the Towne East and Towne West shopping centers. I had to smile when I first visited them because they reminded me so much of the "storefront school" days when we first started out, except here the storefront was part of a row of classy clothing boutiques and audio shops.

But the idea is amazingly similar. The Mall Academies (form-ally known as Education Resource Centers) target young people ages 17 and older who have already dropped out and want a chance to turn their lives around. The emphasis is on individualized, self-paced study. The majority of the students are between 17 and 24 years old. They don't want to complete their high school diploma at a traditional school where they'd feel out of place; for example, a girl who was taunted by her high school classmates due to a learning disability is thriving here. The highly personalized environment created by the caring academy staff helps students successfully pursue their dreams: A teen mom is now college bound and young Hispanic parents want to obtain their diplomas to be positive role models for their children.

Job shadowing is a big part of the experience at the Mall Academies. They've followed teachers at two elementary schools and accompanied police officers in their squad cars to see what that career is like. One student worked with a TV news broadcaster, and several others have spent their time with the mall management's marketing person. A young man performed community service for a local football team, which resulted in a job for him: acting as the "guard" for the cheerleading team to protect them from unruly fans!

Wichita CIS has been introducing students to the Fifth Basic, "a chance to give back to peers and community," from its earliest days in the district. Started during the organization's first full academic year, the HUGSS program (Helping Us Grow through Service and Smiles) links kids with community-service opportunities. The Giraffe Program teaches students about local heroes who "stick their necks out" for others, and then assists the young people to develop a creative plan of their own.

The culmination of CIS's commitment to the community is CIS (Children In Service) Day, an annual event that brings hundreds of elementary, middle, and high school students together for several hours of volunteering. Some students work on intergenerational projects with seniors; some pick up trash and plant trees; some deliver "meals on wheels" to elder-care facilities.

No Miracle Workers

To my mind, Judy Frick and CIS of Wichita/Sedgwick County have one of the most thorough and varied responses to the Five Basics that I can imagine. What's so critical, however, is that all these services (and I've just mentioned the ones I admire most; there are many others) are delivered in a *personal, accountable, and coordinated* manner. These three values have been long-standing tenets of the CIS movement and have special meaning in relation to how services are provided at a school site.

Personalism is the keystone of this kind of integrated service delivery. Building and maintaining one-on-one connections among a caring adult, a student, and the student's family brings dignity and respect to the service relationship by acknowledging the worth of all concerned. Resources are tailored to students' and families' unique needs; it can't be "one size fits all."

Accountability means showing up and doing the job with integrity, and it's a direct outgrowth of personalism. When you have ongoing, caring relationships with the people you work with and for, when you look them in the eye each day and ask "How are you doing?" it's hard to hear the answer and then say, "It's not my problem." Accountability means not passing the buck, and it guarantees that goals are met consistently and responsibly. When parents ask why something has or hasn't happened to their child, "the system" won't be blamed or credited. An individual project team member accepts responsibility. CIS staff are accountable to school personnel, partner agencies and volunteers, students and families, the community at large, and each other.

Coordination ensures that previously fragmented approaches to service delivery are connected into a comprehensive, holistic plan. At the school site, assigned agency staff and volunteers function as an integrated team in providing services to students and families.

The CIS coordinator at each school is the key to making all of this happen. This individual is always available at his or her site to answer questions, provide information, assist teachers and staff, and develop a holistic picture of the needs of children. The CIS of Wichita main office finds resources through partnership agreements with more than 200 agencies, businesses, and civic and religious groups, as well as colleges, universities, and National Honor Society high school groups throughout the city.

The main office notifies the CIS coordinators about these resources as they become available. The coordinators then match needs with resources. Fortunately, as the value of this work has become widely known, the coordinators can now count on assistance from part-time cooperative-education students from Wichita State University, as well as social-work practicum students from area colleges.

In the end, how much of a difference does all this work really make? The answer is: a huge one.

In the 2005–06 school year, CIS of Wichita provided direct, intensive services to 2,759 students at its 31 school sites. An additional 8,311 students had access to services on a one-time or as-needed basis. Tutors or mentors were linked to 92 percent of the kids, and 99 percent were connected with needed agency resources. Average daily attendance for elementary students was 92 percent; for secondary students, 89 percent.

These are pretty good numbers, and for CIS of Wichita's high-poverty schools, they're *very* good and will get even better. Remember, CIS works with young people who are referred because they're already experiencing the kinds of challenges that will affect their academic success. In that context, the achievements of these students are extraordinary.

They may even seem miraculous. If there's one belief I want you to take from this chapter, however—indeed, from this entire book—it's that there is nothing miraculous about it at all. There are no miracle workers in Wichita, no saints, and no one is acting in the "hero" role. They're *all* heroes and saints as far as I'm concerned. They're changing children's lives and those of their families because the *system* is now school based, personal, accountable, and coordinated.

Furthermore, there's nothing miraculous about Communities In Schools, nothing we do that any community organization based on these principles can't achieve. I'm proud of CIS, my colleagues, and their years of dedication to kids, but I would hate it if this book came off as an infomercial for the movement I helped found. I care about the principles, and I want you to care about them, too, because I'm counting on *you* to help make them a reality in dozens of communities CIS will never reach.

As Judy Frick says, "What we do is a combination of providing services and improving how the system operates. Our role is not only to offer direct services, but to connect kids with the right resources. This makes them go the furthest and be most efficient.

"The school district," she points out, "has significantly increased their contribution to CIS out of their general allocation fund. This says to me that they recognize that the services and resources we provide are essential to student success. I feel like we've arrived."

Susan Hussey, former principal of Wichita's Lincoln Elementary School, put it this way: "My job and the job of each and every staff member at Lincoln is made easier just knowing we have CIS to support us on our journey to assure our students achieve academic success. It would be extremely difficult to work in a high-poverty school without the support of CIS. It's wonderful to know we have this continual support that we rely on to help us meet the needs of our students and families. Because of our great community support, we can also teach our students to 'pay it forward.' In other words, we remind them: 'When you are adults, give back to your community. Remember, someone helped you!'"

A Community That Cares

It's not hard to picture how a middle school in Wichita with a CIS presence might respond to Tara Larson's situation.

Her pattern of academic difficulty and absences brings her to the attention of the CIS coordinator. The coordinator makes a home visit—another hallmark of the CIS approach—and Ruth Larson learns about the resources available for her daughter. A CIS volunteer brings Tara to the Healthy Children Center, where she receives a thorough physical exam. The necessary tests are performed, and to everyone's relief, they reveal no serious illnesses. They do indicate, though, that her headaches may result from low blood sugar. Sure enough, once the recommended remedies are in place, that problem disappears.

The coordinator arranges for tutoring at home for Tara. (I like to imagine that her tutor might be the Larsons' nice retired-schoolteacher neighbor, Mrs. Hartshorne, who now has a place to volunteer thanks to CIS). Tara is enrolled in the CIS/YMCA after-school program, too.

What about a mentor? Ruth Larson is an excellent mother, but she'd be the first to admit that, working so many hours, she doesn't get to spend as much time as she'd like with her children. She welcomes the mentor match that CIS arranges with a young university student. And this person is able to give Tara a ride once a week to meet with Gwendolyn Smith at the adolescent mental health facility.

Of course, all of Tara's problems don't vanish. But a CIS school site is a different place from the one we first described. Yes, there are safety issues around drugs and sex and bullying, but here there *are* grown-ups whom she can talk to. The entire school climate is different. She doesn't feel as if she's alone, facing the challenges of being a new sixth grader all by herself. And Tara can see that the many adult volunteers at her school are making a difference. Other students are more respectful; there's a general sense of higher standards, higher expectations for the young people. The school is part of a community that cares.

Furthermore, as a "CIS student," Tara isn't viewed as a collection of separate, isolated problems and referrals. The CIS coordinator knows her well, is familiar with her issues, and understands what has been done to deal with them. This person has the knowledge necessary to work with agencies and systems. She gets regular reports from all the volunteers and service providers; she can see the big picture. *Case manager* is the term that social workers use for this role, and many CIS affiliates use it as well. But it's a more successful—you might say "purer"—type of case management because the coordinator truly has access to the necessary resources. She's able to back up her accountability with action.

The coordinator continues to make home visits, and Tara's mother is very much part of the big picture, too. Ruth Larson realizes that she has more friends and resources at her disposal than she'd ever thought possible. She has found an accountable, coordinated team of caring adults—a true "community in school."

Hurricane

Wichita CIS, and the many affiliates like it around the nation, was launched to deal with recognizable community issues that affect the well-being and success of students. Poor health, peer pressure, lack of academic assistance, and an unsafe environment—sadly, these are the common or garden-variety problems that plague hundreds of thousands of American students.

Sometimes, though, a challenge that no one could have anticipated will arise, rather like one of those unlucky "Chance" cards at the Reality Store. In August and September 2005, the Gulf Coast endured the fury of two devastating hurricanes. In the aftermath of Katrina and Rita, a massive displacement of students and their families occurred during the first week of the school year. Communities In Schools affiliates in nearby areas were among the many groups who rallied to help school systems meet the needs of the displaced students and families: About 30,000 young people, along with 6,000 parents and guardians, received services through 61 CIS affiliates.

Houston, like many other communities in Texas, welcomed the evacuees. By December, Houston-area school districts had absorbed more than 21,000 newly enrolled students. CIS of Houston is one of our oldest and most successful affiliates, and the four districts in which it has programs were serving 12,000 of those children, along with many of their families.

Cynthia Briggs, executive director of the Houston CIS affiliate, got a call from the mayor in the midst of this crisis, asking her to take on an impossible project. "He said that hundreds of teachers had been displaced by Katrina, too, and he really needed us to be the lead agency to place them in schools in 11 counties. He told me: 'I know you don't have CIS programs in all those counties, but if anyone can do it, you can. This way it won't be an issue in terms of school districts taking the lead. You bring the best of the community.'"

It was an important moment for all of us in CIS—and an enormous challenge. Houston's mayor needed exactly what CIS could provide: a way of responding to an unprecedented disaster that was personal, accountable, and coordinated. I often wonder how differently things might have gone in New Orleans and the rest of the Gulf Coast if the *original* response to the storms had displayed even a little bit of those three qualities. What the entire nation saw instead was a round-robin of finger pointing and endless explanations of why such a thing was so difficult to achieve.

Cynthia Briggs has spent more than 20 years building confidence and success in Houston's schools, and that experience paid off. In an incredibly short period of time, Houston CIS placed 145 teachers.

"It was really a work of the heart," Cynthia told me. "Those folks had been on the phone with FEMA, trying to understand what was going on. It was awful for them. And suddenly they had a number to call to reach us. Our phones were ringing off the hook with people trying to find jobs. We responded to everyone personally. I answered the phone myself one day and said, 'Hold on, we'll get to you, just hold on,' and the woman on the phone said, 'Ma'am, if you'll just promise me you'll come back to the phone, I'll hold as long as I need to. Just promise me you'll come back.'"

With financial assistance from the Gulf Coast Work Force Board, CIS of Houston launched Operation School Work, placing the teachers as tutors and mentors in Houston-area schools that had received a large number of evacuees. Not only did the educators receive regular paychecks and full benefits, they also provided invaluable guidance and mentoring to students who, like them, were suddenly uprooted and forced into unfamiliar and often stressful situations.

Although the official project ended at the close of the 2005–06 school year, Operation School Work laid the foundation for continuing success among adults and kids alike. Many tutors have gone on to find permanent, long-term teaching positions in the districts they served.

And what about the displaced students themselves? With the generosity typical of this country following such a tragedy, monetary and in-kind donations poured into CIS of Houston and many other helping agencies. When the Michael & Susan Dell Foundation asked how it could help, the CIS of Texas state office, under the leadership of Nellie Reyes, responded by coordinating the efforts of the dozens of local CIS affiliates throughout the state that were absorbing large numbers of evacuees from the Gulf Coast. They created a program that addressed not only the unique set of needs facing the students and their families, but also the need for community building between these new arrivals and local residents.

CIS was able to place social-service coordinators at the school campuses that had absorbed large concentrations of evacuee students and didn't already have a CIS presence. The coordinators provided direct support to hurricane evacuees at the school sites, including individual and group counseling sessions to assist students with transition issues, grief, and peer relationships.

"We wanted to make sure to address not only the individual needs of the evacuees, but the stress on the school as a whole as students adjusted to the new circumstances," said Sylvia Teague, CIS of Houston's director of field operations. Again, this kind of coordinated, farsighted response is possible if you're fortunate enough to have a *system* already in place that rewards such efforts.

"The Glue That Held Them Together"

Our CIS affiliate in Houston's Bay Area (comprising the Clear Creek and Dickinson school districts) received a visit during this time from Pulitzer Prize–winning author Jed Horne, who subsequently wrote about his experience in his book *Breach of Faith: Hurricane Katrina and the Near Death of a Great American City.*

Horne went to McWhirter Elementary School to see how displaced New Orleans students were being assimilated into the school's activities. He then wrote:

> About two-thirds of McWhirter kids were low-income, and most of them were Latino. Mostly African Americans, the New Orleans kids were immediately identifiable and somewhat exotic. Outside the classroom, a woman named Glenda Rice was the glue that held many of them together. She was the program coordinator for an outfit called Communities In Schools (CIS), a national nonprofit that had set up shop at nine schools within the Clear Creek district, McWhirter being one of them. (CIS had also been a presence in New Orleans.) In essence, Rice hooked up newly arrived low-income families with the services they needed. Someone had a toothache? Rice would scrounge for a dentist willing to pull the tooth for free. Blankets? She'd track down a donor. She leaned a lot on a women's group called ALBA that was good for a pair of quality tennis shoes and two or three outfits per needy child. At the sight of a likely prospect, Rice would whip out a tape and measure the child.
>
> "I walk around the school and look," Rice said. "I'll casually ask a new kid, 'You got a coat?'" She got a school in a rich Clear Creek neighborhood to do a coat drive and came up with 60. Book bags? Rice got Home Depot to kick in 400. She was also known for her signature "birthday boxes," soup-to-nuts party kits that contained candles, cake mix, party favors, and the like.
>
> Rice was also good at thinking well outside the birthday box. One afternoon she was visited in her office by a New Orleanian named Yavana Johnson. Johnson had dropped off her kids at school, except for the baby in her arms. As much as anything she just needed to reminisce. She needed to talk about what it was like growing up in a city that seemed no longer to exist. . . .

Rice [learned] that Johnson, a woman of fashion, had dreamed of becoming a beautician. Rice urged her to pursue her dream and found a beauty school not only prepared to admit Johnson but to offer her a $4,000 scholarship. Johnson held back. She would need day care. Rice hit the phone again and lined up day care. Johnson began to realize she might have a future in Webster. . . .[1]

Systemic change, once begun, is hard to stop. Epidemics spread, but so do the forces for good. When a community carries out its commitment to help children succeed, it also builds the relationships and trust that can take on *any challenge*.

■ ■ ■ ■ ■

CHAPTER FIVE

The "Magic Eyes" of a Champion for Children

Leading the Orchestra

Let's consider the picture we've painted so far of the situation facing a typical school system as it tries to stop the dropout epidemic. We have talented and committed educators who are stretched far beyond their resources. They'd like to help every student succeed, but the needs of so many children are simply beyond what a teacher, principal, or guidance counselor can handle.

Parents, too, however much they love their children, are overwhelmed by the confusion of "helping agencies" scattered throughout the community.

These organizations, their staff, and their volunteers are by no means unhelpful. In fact, altogether they may well have the solutions to most of the problems children face—but they *aren't* all together. They work in a way that's often fragmented, impersonal, and hard to access.

Now we imagine that concerned community leaders—perhaps from the business community or leaders of the volunteer, faith-based, or philanthropic sectors—have a new idea: Bring this important work *to* the schools in a manner that's personal, accountable, and coordinated so that each child can be viewed holistically and matched with the services that he or she needs to succeed in school and in life.

The superintendent of schools listens, and likes the idea. What's the next step? What's the effective way to get the resources where they belong?

Every community needs a "Champion for Children," a neutral third party to coordinate and broker the diverse community resources into the schools on behalf of young people and their families. Like the router for a computer, this person is an expert "relational router" who can get individuals working *together* instead of on separate paths. Or we can borrow an image suggested to me by Quincy Jones, a longtime supporter of CIS: "It's like an orchestra," he said when I first described our work. "CIS is the conductor who makes sure all the individual musicians are playing from the same score and coming in when they're needed."

In practice, a successful local CIS affiliate has Champions on at least two levels. The executive director's job is to identify the most pressing needs of students and families and then create partnerships among helping agencies to bring their resources, talents, and volunteers into the public schools to address those needs. Then, at the various school sites, we've seen how the coordinators implement the executive director's vision for their schools, translating system-wide assets and needs into a one-on-one, student- and family-centered approach.

I've described the Champion for Children as a neutral third party. What does this mean in practice? The best and most effective way to put this person to work is to make him or her responsible to the board of directors of an independent nonprofit corporation.

The Champion's board should be composed of a wide cross section of local leaders. I hope that many readers of this book will be excellent candidates to lead such a board. The active support of the private sector is absolutely critical to effective management and advocacy. So is the participation of the superintendent of schools—ideally, as a board member. Beyond this, different places will have different leaders, but the same overall framework applies: The dropout epidemic is a *community-wide* crisis that affects everyone, so all the key sectors of the community must join together to combat it. After all, an orchestra with nothing but, say, percussion and woodwinds would be awfully limited in what it could play.

The Champion's neutrality is critical. He or she mustn't be perceived as having a competitive bias toward one of the partnering agencies. Instead, the Champion's task is to ensure that *all* stakeholders are fairly represented so that their ideas and concerns are made part of the new community/school partnership. It's hard enough to convince potential partners that this collaborative approach will be worth the effort and that giving up a certain degree of independence and recognition will further their mission in the long run. We don't want to make it even harder by creating the suspicion that the Champion harbors a hidden agenda, whether political or structural. Again, think of the orchestra: If the conductor keeps favoring loud passages for the horn section, people are

THE CHAMPION'S NEUTRALITY IS CRITICAL.

going to figure out that this guy used to be a horn player. Rather, the Champion's sole job should be to create the best outcomes, the best music, for children and families.

Another important aspect of neutrality reflects the grassroots, homegrown nature of the initiative. Positive change can't be led or managed from the outside. Without the support of local leaders who know everyone's interests, any process of collaboration is doomed. Groups that just show up to do something "for the community" are often rightly perceived as disempowering, paternalistic, and arrogant. This was a lesson I had to learn in the early days of my street work in New York. Until my colleagues and I were perceived as being *part* of the neighborhood, we couldn't be part of the solution.

These considerations hold true for the entire collaborative board, and most particularly for the Champion. He or she needs to be—and to be perceived as—a homegrown advocate for families and schools.

If you're a businessperson, you've already realized that our Champion must be a fine manager. It's no easy task to wield a small budget against the big problems faced by overburdened school systems and families. The challenges of hands-on, day-to-day coordination of resources are considerable. Management skills are essential to the job, and if you want to start a CIS-like initiative in your community, your Champion had better come equipped with an excellent management résumé.

POSITIVE CHANGE CAN'T BE LED OR MANAGED FROM OUTSIDE THE COMMUNITY.

People skills are obviously critical as well. The Champion has to be comfortable and effective with a wide assortment of individuals and cultures. She's the kind of person who can meet for breakfast with the mayor, have lunch with the school superintendent, talk with union representatives in the afternoon, join the Junior League for dinner, and hang out with the kids in the evening.

But (as this demanding schedule suggests) there's even more to it than administrative ability and a knack for getting along with people. In taking on the dropout epidemic, we're taking on a world of trouble. The challenges that schools, families, and students face didn't arise overnight, and they won't be turned around in a semester or a year. Moreover, we're not talking about manufacturing widgets. Our "customers," if you will, are children. We care about them. We *have* to care, or we wouldn't be taking on this challenge, and every failure hurts. It's like the old metaphor about how much time it takes to turn around an ocean liner—except that in this case children and families are inevitably falling overboard and drowning while we make the agonizingly slow adjustments of the rudder that are necessary to redirect the way our community assists them.

It requires a special sort of person to stay positive in the face of these daily human tragedies. Hanging out is a great skill when you're working with kids—but *hanging in* is just as important.

How's Your Vision?

While leafing through the reading material in a dentist's waiting room years ago, I saw a children's book called *Magic Eyes*. I no longer recall the story, but the title has always stuck with me. It's a perfect name for that special quality that a Champion for Children must have in order to get the job done for kids.

When you have magic eyes, you see things differently. You notice solutions and assets, not problems and liabilities. *Every* situation children face in your community is an opportunity; and you discover the possibilities, not the drawbacks. It's like trying to start a campfire: You see those little sparks, and instead of focusing on all the wood that's not catching, you blow carefully on the glowing specks. Pretty soon you have a flame, and then the fire overcomes the coldness.

This kind of leadership, in my opinion, starts with the heart, not the head. It's about "care providing," not caretaking, and caring isn't a job but a way of life. It's a calling, and it comes from an acute perception of the brokenness all around us, the damaged lives, the broken dreams. Often it comes from the brokenness in ourselves, too—all the ways we've had to learn to go on despite our wounds.

I'm reminded of the time that a friend of mine was in the hospital and quite despondent about it. While I sat with him, a nurse came in and did all the things a nurse does: check the chart, monitor his vital signs and medications, and so on. She was very skillful and very cold. You could tell that she was "doing her job," but she didn't want any interaction with my friend. Her goal was to be efficient, to do what had to be done, and then move on to the next patient.

The next time I visited, a different nurse came in. From the moment he entered the room, he was talking and laughing, making eye contact, touching my friend's shoulder, and asking him how he was—you could tell that he really wanted to know the answer and wasn't just going through the motions. This nurse not only performed all the same tasks the first one had, but he brought joy and healing to that room, and to me, too. There's no way to eliminate all the tension and fear that a sickroom breeds, but he did his best. My friend, who was very ill, was *excited* about the nurse's visit—that's the only word to describe it. His despondency was lifted.

Now both these professionals were "being good nurses," but for one it was a job and for the other it was a calling. That second one needed the salary—I'm sure he had a family to take care of and bills to pay just like anyone else. But that wasn't why he was doing it. You could tell he loved his patients. There's no substitute for skill, but if you're working with and for people, technique isn't enough.

A good pair of magic eyes will keep you focused on what you *can* do, not what you can't. It will also help you see others differently. When I first began trying to reach out to kids, I didn't know how to build community. I was highly suspicious of the "Establishment" and all its works. If you'd asked me what to do about the public school system, I would have said in frustration, "Get rid of it."

But gradually, through the example of others and through my own painful lessons, I came to understand that everybody has a place at the table—and that most definitely includes professional educators and administrators. Once I started hanging out with teachers, I saw their viewpoint and felt *their* frustration. People like me had been pointing fingers at them and lecturing them: "You have to change, and we'll tell you how." I was beginning to realize how arrogant that position was. The teachers I met understood very well that schools had to change and were more than willing to be a part of that change. But they wanted to be *included* as partners with an equal say, not told how to do their jobs.

Arrogance and anger have no place in community building. Do you want to fail as quickly as possible, trying to build a coalition around kids? Just walk into that first meeting and treat your potential partners—especially the ones with resources and standing—as if they aren't as good as you or the kids you serve. As if they've "sold out" or they "owe the community" something. On the contrary, you are *giving* them a precious gift by inviting their help. You're allowing them to be part of something bigger than themselves.

There are times, too, when magic eyes help you see the most basic and obvious realities—simple truths that get lost in the complications of our daily struggles. I remember being part of a team that President George H. W. Bush pulled together to advise him on an upcoming Governors' Education Summit. I heard some wonderful ideas from this group of national leaders in the field. In fact, I was starting to feel a little out of place since I was the only noneducator in the room.

I kept silent for a long while, but finally my turn came to speak. I complimented everyone on the depth of their insights and told them how moved I was by their concern, which was absolutely true. Then I mentioned what seemed obvious: "The only word I haven't heard is *children*. Shouldn't we be starting with them instead of theories and strategies? How do we connect with them so they'll get turned on to learning?" And—for a while, at least—the conversation changed.

THE TEACHERS I MET UNDERSTOOD VERY WELL THAT SCHOOLS HAD TO CHANGE AND WERE MORE THAN WILLING TO BE A PART OF THAT CHANGE. BUT THEY WANTED TO BE *INCLUDED* AS PARTNERS WITH AN EQUAL SAY, NOT TOLD HOW TO DO THEIR JOBS.

Seeing things differently leads to *thinking* differently, which in turn leads to *acting* differently. Simply trying harder is no longer enough. This doesn't mean, however, that persistence and dedication in the face of sometimes overwhelming challenges can be bypassed or replaced with "new thinking." Over the years as I've watched successful community leaders both inside and outside the CIS movement, the common denominator is always persistence.

Atlanta businessman George Johnson, one of our first board members and one of my closest friends, once told me about a visit he made right after college to one of his city's legendary lawyers and most prominent bankers. As a new graduate, George asked him, "What's the key to success?"

"There are three basic ingredients," the attorney said.

"Do I need to write them down?" George asked.

"No, you'll remember them. Number one, above everything else, is 'stick-ability.' It's not about who you know or what you know—it's perseverance. Number two is perseverance. And number three is perseverance. George, you've just got to keep showing up!"

This story means a lot to me because of how George himself has lived it out. He has been one of our most faithful supporters, "showing up" for kids and for CIS for more than 30 years.

Perseverance is an old-fashioned notion. But it's just as essential as seeing and thinking differently. We have to declare collectively that we're completely committed to these kids, that we want to see a broken world knit together and made whole. We're not going to give up, no matter how many defeats we suffer, because love never quits. Love is for a lifetime.

"This is a very important lesson. You must never confuse faith that you will prevail in the end—which you can never afford to lose—with the discipline to confront the most brutal facts of your current reality, whatever they might be."

— **Admiral James Stockdale**[1]

No Cheap Grace

My friend Neil Shorthouse has magic eyes. We've been colleagues for 40 years, and he's helped me see so many things that I would have missed without his 20/20 vision. There wouldn't be any Communities In Schools without Neil. Here's how it happened:

You may recall from Chapter 2 that our New York Street Academy movement was facing some tough questions by the end of the 1960s. Increasingly, we were wondering how we could reach potential dropouts *before* they left school. We couldn't address this quandary, however, until we confronted some immediate and serious practical problems. We'd received federal funding for a number of the Academies, but by the early 1970s that was withdrawn. Many of our private supporters were also backing off. I don't mean to sound cynical, but there are trends in causes just like in everything else, and "street work" was no longer as fashionable as it had been. The urban riots were over, the fires were out, and a lot of people had moved on to different social issues.

Our long-range question was: *How do we keep this thing going?* In the short term, the question was even more immediate: Which of our struggling prototypes—by that point launched in five cities in addition to New York—could we use as a new beachhead, a restarting point?

I'd known Neil Shorthouse since we were both teenagers in Pittsburgh. Unlike me, however, he was a star in everything he attempted. He went through the University of Pittsburgh in three years on a golf scholarship. He was involved with an organization called the Fellowship of Christian Athletes, a group that fit in well with the theology of his upbringing; but he also joined Young Life, the same youth organization that had turned me around.

Neil graduated from college in 1963, while I was deep into street work with Vinnie and Harv in New York City. He'd considered a career in law, picturing himself doing Christian advocacy work, but soon decided it wouldn't suit his person-to-person temperament. Instead, he became a Young Life staffer, running youth clubs in Pittsburgh and later becoming the program director in Philadelphia. At first he was based in the Delaware County suburbs, but soon expanded into the tough ghetto of West Philly. It changed his life.

Neil saw that his version of Christianity—which he now calls an "Everything's all right!" viewpoint—couldn't make sense of the poverty and hopelessness that surrounded him in West Philly. "I had a kind of 'Everything's all wrong!' conversion," he says. "The world is wrong, there's no justice, churches are missing the point, and the schools are terrible." It was a necessary swing in the other direction, but a long way from magic eyes.

Then in 1968 Neil learned about a community in Georgia called Koinonia. An IBM executive who was a supporter of ours told him about it. The man suggested that Neil, Dean Borgman, and I might want to learn more about this remarkable Christian agrarian commune that was led by a man named Clarence Jordan.

It turned out that Clarence was going to be spending the weekend at a boys' school in New York State, so a number of us, including Neil, went up there to hang out with him.

I'd kept in touch with my friend over the years, but this was the first time we'd really spent time together since boyhood. Both of us were amazed by Clarence Jordan. He had a Ph.D. in New Testament Greek and a high level of sophistication as a peanut farmer—an unusual combination for a Southern Baptist minister. His take on spiritual matters was unique and so down-to-earth, so focused on social justice and personal transformation, that it was like hearing the Christian message for the first time.

"Fear is the polio of the soul—it prevents you from walking by faith."

— Clarence Jordan

Clarence had been active in the civil rights movement in Georgia, putting his life in danger to help his brothers and sisters. Koinonia itself was the target of continual violence from those who were opposed to the commune's commitment to civil rights. But Clarence believed that "fear is the polio of the soul—it prevents you from walking by faith." He also introduced us to the German theologian Dietrich Bonhoeffer's concept of "cheap grace": You get saved but there's no cost, no transformation, and you keep right on as before. That wasn't Clarence's way, and Neil, Dean, and I realized it could never be our way either.

Neil and his family visited Koinonia a few months later, and he was even more impressed with the way the community was living out its spiritual values. He returned to Philadelphia with renewed energy but still angry and frustrated about the failure of the school system and the indifference of society toward its children. Inevitably, he found himself being alienated by Young Life. "They thought I was heavy baggage," he recalls. He and the organization parted ways in 1970, six months after Neil and I had mourned another parting as we learned of Clarence Jordan's death at the age of 57.

What next? Neil and I and our families made one of the most difficult decisions of our lives: We would relocate from New York City and Philadelphia, respectively, to Atlanta, and begin living communally in a way that would reflect the Christian values of peace, brotherhood, and sharing espoused by Clarence Jordan. We chose Atlanta for two reasons: It was close to Koinonia, and our Street Academies were still active in that city.

We decided to incorporate as a nonprofit organization to run the schools. We called our new project EXODUS, Inc. Our first "office" consisted of two desks, one phone, and one file cabinet in the 10' x 10' dugout basement of the communal house where 16 of us were living. It was a modest beginning, but seemingly all we needed.

The Street Academies in Atlanta had received funding from the U.S. Postal Service and used mail carriers as teachers, mentors, and administrators. An ex–postal worker named David Lewis had been vital in creating the schools in Atlanta, and we were fortunate to be able to team up with him and his partners in our new endeavor.

Dave was another guy with magic eyes. I've never known anyone who could make a connection with kids—any kids—the way he did. (You may remember that he was one of the street workers mentioned in Chapter 1 who helped Reginald Beaty decide to believe in himself and go back to school, beginning his transformation from "loser" to lieutenant colonel.) An African American, Dave could overcome barriers of race and class in a truly extraordinary way. Along with Neil and me, he was the third cofounder of what is now Communities In Schools.

With the withdrawal of federal funds, private dollars had to be raised for what had formerly been the Postal Street Academies. This is when I began to understand another aspect of what "magic eyes" can mean because I watched Neil's indefatigable efforts to partner, persuade, and create community with all strata of society on behalf of the children of Atlanta. This man saw possibilities *everywhere:* small foundation grants, a little state-government funding, loans from generous (and trusting) board members, borrowing from one bank to pay off another. . . . We never knew how we'd meet payroll from one pay period to the next, but somehow Neil kept the ball rolling and by the mid-'70s we had four Street Academies operating in Atlanta. They were very much on the New York City model: storefront schools for dropouts. We also opened an academy inside Saint Luke's Episcopal Church.

From the beginning of our Atlanta adventure, we had a critical ally. Robert H. B. Baldwin was a top executive at Morgan Stanley in New York, someone I'd first met in our Street Academy days and who believed in us from the start. When he learned that Neil and I were relocating to Atlanta, he called a friend of his there, Justus Martin, the president of a major regional stock brokerage firm, the Robinson-Humphrey Company. He asked Martin and R-H board chairman Sandy Yearley to meet with us and learn more about what we were trying to do.

I well remember the looks these ultrarespectable stockbrokers gave us when we entered their boardroom, so I can say without hesitation that it was Bob Baldwin's influence and reputation that convinced them to provide some crucial start-up funding for the Atlanta Academies. This was neither the first nor the last time that he would make the difference between success and failure for us. Five years later, he became the first chairman of our national board of directors. From his position as president and eventually chairman of Morgan Stanley, he gave us the credibility we needed in the business and political communities. He also held me personally to a very high standard of professionalism. As an early funder said, "Bill, I've grown to like you a lot and believe in your mission, but I can sleep at night because Bob Baldwin is your board chair."

In 1974, we took a major step: Neil and I convinced the Atlanta public education system to assign teachers to our Academies. Dr. Alonzo Crim was the superintendent of schools. Relatively new to the job in Atlanta after having led several other major school systems, Dr. Crim was aware that his students needed help, and he was open to new ideas. He'd met Dave Lewis when Dave was running the Postal Street Academy and was powerfully impressed. So when Neil and I came in and explained that we were teaming up with Dave, it gave Dr. Crim the confidence to back us. I believe he could see that we were for real, that we meant what we said about our commitment to kids, even if our methods were untried locally.

Neil approached Dr. Crim with the idea of repositioning teachers into our Academies. "We could call them 'Satellite Learning Centers,'" Neil said. The superintendent agreed to roll the dice. We weren't quite *in* the schools yet, but we were getting very close. And finally, Neil, Dave, and I saw the necessity of crossing that boundary and actually setting up a project inside the public schools, to reach kids before they became dropouts. With the unwavering support of Dr. Crim, we started working in an elementary school and a high school.

Neil helped me understand how important it was to build positive relationships with teachers at the same time that we connected with students. He used to sketch a little picture: It showed the school surrounded by a moat with the drawbridge raised. Outside the moat were weird-looking blobs that seemed like they could swallow the school in one gulp.

"This is how teachers and principals get to feeling sometimes," he said. "They believe they're surrounded by amoeba do-gooders, all circling around the school and trying to absorb them. Is it any wonder the drawbridge stays up? We need to show them every day that we're partners and allies, not threats."

The "magic eyes" of a guy like Neil Shorthouse are indispensable to rallying the community around its children. Knowing Neil as well as I do, I can't say that I've *never* seen him discouraged or uncertain. But like the nurse whose job was also a calling, he makes it his business to see life, joy, and possibilities everywhere he looks. "It provides meaning for me," he says. "It's my purpose on Earth." He has remained, next to my wife, my best friend and partner.

Something's Going to Happen . . .

The good news is, there are people like Neil in *your* community. We've located hundreds of them around the country as we search for Champions for Children to fight the dropout epidemic.

I remember one early funder saying to me, skeptically: "This job isn't exactly for your Junior League types, is it?"

Well, you'd be surprised.

In 1985, when I first met her, Cynthia Marshall was president of the Charlotte, North Carolina, Junior League, which had rallied 600 women volunteers to improve the civic life of their city. Cynthia called the CIS office in Washington to ask me to come speak to her group. Somehow I'd gotten through life without ever having heard of the Junior League. When my assistant, Haleh Samii, passed on the request, my reaction was: "Great—I love baseball!"

Haleh straightened me out, and I headed down to Charlotte. Even before I gave my talk, I could tell that Cynthia and I saw things in similar ways, although her beautiful Southern manners were quite a bit different from my urban style.

Cynthia had helped develop Charlotte's Family Center, a resource for abused and neglected children. The idea of creating caring teams of agency personnel to help kids in trouble wasn't new to her. I guess we were fortunate that our paths crossed at the moment they did, because she latched onto the idea of Communities In Schools and vowed to start an affiliate in Charlotte.

I don't think I've ever met a more tenacious and energetic advocate for children. Her "magic eyes" are supersharp. "Cynthia is one of those rare people who never sees a 'problem,'" says CIS of North Carolina's president, Linda Harrill. "She sees *everything* as an opportunity. She grasps ideas quickly and sees how to implement and expand them. I can say, 'Cynthia, have you ever thought of doing a Mall Academy?' and she'll get that twinkle in her eye and say, 'Oh . . . yes, we can do that,' and you can just tell she's already putting the pieces together in her mind."

One of my favorite statements of Cynthia's is this one: "In any community, if a cross section of key leaders gets together and sees an issue that needs attention, especially one with economic implications, something's going to happen." I agree wholeheartedly, but I would add that the "something" depends on the vision and abilities of people like Cynthia, Charlotte's Champion for Children.

Cynthia Marshall has told me that she holds out three crucial principles for her CIS team:

1. Be wide open to any idea or person who happens to come your way. She says, "You can be talking to a person in a grocery store and find that they know someone who has a call to be connected."

2. Listen with your heart as well as your head.

3. Use the network you have, the people you've known for many years, not just whatever group of agencies or organizations the board of directors may help locate. Find a way for them to understand that *everyone* is part of the big picture, that everyone has a role to play.

It's easy to see how these principles have influenced some of the important successes that Cynthia has achieved over the years. Consider this situation, which took place shortly after she got CIS off the ground and had begun her practice of remaining constantly alert to new ideas and new ways to serve students and families:

Kim, a fourth grader at a Charlotte elementary school with a CIS presence, came from an Asian American family who'd been in the U.S. for just a short time. Kim's CIS coordinator noticed that he was absent a lot. When she asked him what was wrong, he told her that his head hurt. He also didn't seem to be getting enough to eat.

The coordinator took him to the school nurse, who looked in his mouth in the course of her examination. It wasn't pretty: Twelve teeth were either decaying or abscessed. I'm guessing that Cynthia's principle about "using your own network" was already being instilled among her colleagues, because the CIS staffer thought first of a dentist who belonged to her own church. She knew that this practitioner was used to treating middle- and upper-income people, but she also knew he had a good heart and cared about the community. And in fact, when the dentist heard about Kim, he was appalled and volunteered to treat the boy for free.

Getting the right dental attention took care of the headaches; and of course once Kim could chew without wincing, his appetite improved, too. The site coordinator was even able to extend the benefits to Kim's family, making a home visit to counsel them on the importance of nutrition and checkups for the other children.

But for Cynthia, the seed of an idea had been planted. *How many more kids,* she wondered, *have the same problem?* The county health department was already one of her partners, providing physical screenings for CIS students but not dental hygiene. So Cynthia forged a new agreement with them to perform dental screenings for every CIS child.

With that program in place, her team was able to gauge the scope of the problem—and it was huge. Many, many students were suffering from poor dental health, and it wasn't hard to extrapolate from Kim's case and assume that a number of the kids' daily academic performance was being affected.

The dentist from the CIS staffer's congregation put the word out to his colleagues: Did they realize how bad a problem this was in their community? Shortly thereafter, the number of dentists providing free care for CIS students began to increase.

This was also an issue that Cynthia was able to use to engage the entire community. "People can buy toothpaste and toothbrushes and give them to every CIS kid," she says. "They may feel: 'I can't prevent dropouts but I'll help kids this way.' And the amazing thing is, it *does* prevent dropouts."

One person and one partnership leads to another and another. Cynthia learned that the local community college had a program that taught high school graduates how to become dental assistants. They also operated a free clinic so they could learn their trade—and they needed patients to work on. In short order, dozens of CIS kids were being taken there regularly to get their teeth cleaned. One student got into a conversation with his hygienist, became a dental assistant after graduating from high school, and went to work in the office of one of the volunteer dentists. Today his aspiration is to become a dentist himself. It's amazing how these things come full circle . . . but as Cynthia says, "As we adults learn to be more open to possibilities, that attitude is transferred to the young people."

Almost 20 years after its start, the dental-volunteer program now involves 25 private dentists who see students in their offices. They handle the tougher jobs—fillings and worse—while the community college continues to provide cleanings. These same dentists, many of whom have been steady volunteers for 10 or 15 years, helped expand Give Kids a Smile Day in Charlotte. This is a national effort to provide one day of free dental care every year for children. Charlotte CIS's partners have been able to attract important funding in the wake of the affiliate's successes with dental health and now plan to sponsor dental clinics several times a year. One dentist will close his practice for the day and "open up his chairs," and other dentists come in to help, seeing as many kids as possible. A group of dental hygienists offers a similar volunteer service.

Cynthia is matter-of-fact about the whole thing. "People care," she says. "You just have to give them a way to catch your vision. Our volunteer dentists *want* to give back in a way that makes a difference. Now they know how."

Aim for College . . . and Stay in School

Jack Tate, Cynthia's founding board president, is a former bank president and one of Charlotte's most powerful and respected businessmen. He's also a "consummate child advocate," in Cynthia's words. One day in 1994, Jack walked into Cynthia's office and said, "Okay, I'm done. I've raised $500,000 for a college scholarship fund. So . . . can you build a program?"

This wasn't quite as out of the blue as it might sound. A few months earlier, he'd begun to develop an idea partly inspired by a man named George Lewis, a Charlotte entrepreneur and founder of Cogentrix Energy. Jack had two connections with the other businessman: They shared a common enthusiasm for CIS, and Jack's son John was George's banker. When George mentioned to John Tate that he was interested in doing something to help Charlotte's children, John said, "Well, my dad is really involved in this Communities In Schools program, and they want to start a small alternative high school for hard-to-reach kids on the top floor of a Methodist church. They're looking for someone to 'adopt' the school."

George Lewis paid the lease to the church so the Wesley Uptown Academy could begin its work. He got his employees at Cogentrix involved, too, as tutors and mentors. And as if this weren't enough, he declared, "Your mission is to keep kids in school. That's fantastic, but I think we can do even better. Young people need college these days. I'm going to give a four-year scholarship to every senior who graduates from the academy."

When CIS board president Jack Tate heard this, the inspiration struck. He said to Cynthia: "We need a college scholarship program here for the other CIS kids who aren't at the Uptown Academy. I'll raise the money." Cynthia agreed that it was a wonderful idea, thanked him, and went on with her busy life.

Nine weeks later, he returned, saying: "I'm done . . ." and CIS of Charlotte-Mecklenburg was half a million dollars to the good. Now Cynthia *really* needed to come up with a scholarship program.

What happened next is a perfect illustration of how to use magic eyes to see creative possibilities. A scholarship is a great thing, she reasoned, but if you're not prepared for college, it's not going to do much good. You have to engage students early on and imbue them with a college-bound mentality—and of course, the academic and social skills needed to succeed in higher education.

Cynthia also realized something else: The very process of grooming kids for college could act as a powerful deterrent to dropping out of high school. "You can tell a student that they'll make X thousand dollars more with a diploma than as a dropout, and even more as a college graduate, but it may not mean anything. Words without experiences often don't sink in. You have to *show* them the jobs and *show* them the connection between the education and the jobs. Demonstrate how math and computer skills make a difference in your prospects. Show how punctuality and reliability and courtesy are part of success in life."

A lot of us take these truths for granted because they're part of the culture we grew up in. But children bring a diversity of experiences to school. It's a frequently mistaken middle-class assumption that all kids already know about the values of the dominant culture.

Cynthia and her colleagues matched the money Jack Tate had raised with a grant from the Z. Smith Reynolds Foundation and hired the first director of the ThinkCOLLEGE program. Kemal Atkins had been an admissions officer at Appalachian State University and was ideally suited to plan an initiative that would identify the best practices used nationwide to prepare kids to go to college.

ThinkCOLLEGE has been operational since 1996 and now includes a wealth of college-bound components for hundreds of young people every year. Career advisors provide one-on-one counseling, study-skills instruction, career exploration, job shadowing, and internships. The high school students go on campus tours, and a five-week

THE VERY PROCESS OF GROOMING KIDS FOR COLLEGE CAN ACT AS A POWERFUL DETERRENT TO DROPPING OUT OF HIGH SCHOOL.

"Summer Bridge" program held at Central Piedmont Community College shows CIS high school graduates firsthand what college life is like, helping them shake the fear that they "aren't college material." The career advisors help with admission information and financial aid and admission applications.

The seed of the whole program—scholarships for worthy students—hasn't been lost either. Teens are invited to apply for scholarships from numerous sources, including the original ThinkCOLLEGE fund begun by Jack Tate. Recipients are chosen based on motivation, financial need, and academic achievement. Most recently, 62 seniors were awarded scholarships valued at $84,000, in addition to federal Pell grants. An additional $171,400 in renewal scholarships was given to 129 high school graduates already enrolled in college.

We also have clear indications of ThinkCOLLEGE's effectiveness as a dropout-prevention strategy. Comparative data provided by Charlotte-Mecklenburg schools for the 2005–06 school year show that among kids from low-income families at eight high schools, only 6 out of 349 CIS/ThinkCOLLEGE students dropped out, compared with 496 dropouts out of 7,379 who weren't enrolled in the program.[2]

The dropout epidemic *can* be stopped . . . if a Champion for Children with heart, vision, and a strategy is there to rally the community around its schools.

Seeing Differently

Cynthia Marshall retired in 2006 after 21 years at the helm of CIS of Charlotte-Mecklenburg. She left an organization that serves more than 2,000 young people every year in 25 elementary, middle, and high schools. It's one of the most lauded human-services programs in the nation.

Cynthia has received just about every honor you can think of, including Charlotte's Woman of the Year, the Charlotte Business Journal's Women in Business Achievement Award, and the Order of the Long-Leaf Pine, the highest civilian honor given by the governor of North Carolina to reward outstanding leadership.

Looking back on her years with CIS, she told me: "At the start I had so much to learn. I grasped the whole agency-coordination idea, but I didn't really understand how much volunteers could mean to young people. But when our board member from IBM recruited 120 IBM employees in one year, then I understood. The kids can't believe an adult is coming to spend time with them and not getting paid for it! It's a miracle to them, and it changes how they feel about themselves and about adults. And after a while, I learned something just as important: The change is reciprocal. The tutors who gave their hour a week were being transformed in just as great a way as the kids receiving the gift."

Cynthia believes that this two-way transformation will be a lasting legacy to Charlotte's youth. "We've discovered that many of our CIS graduates have either gone into a helping profession or found a way to give back. One former student was a teenage mom in high school. Now she's an executive assistant at Bank of America and mentors other teen mothers. Bill, I've often heard you say, 'You can't give away what you don't have'—and these kids got it. They're living it out, and as a result the positive cycle goes on and on."

Barb Pellin, immediate past president of the Charlotte CIS board of directors, told me: "As I've talked to CIS leaders at the state and national level, it's clear that Charlotte has been blessed with an executive director that every CIS organization in the country would like to duplicate."

That's true: Cynthia Marshall is a model Champion for Children, an inspiring leader for our entire network. But she would be the first to tell you that her principles and approach are easy enough to duplicate if you consistently see opportunities and possibilities in the maze of challenges confronting schools, kids, and families.

> We have an "adult problem," not a "youth problem," and it's up to us to *see* differently, *think* differently, and then *act* differently. The result can be a true turning point for thousands of young people in our communities.

■ ■ ■ ■ ■

CHAPTER SIX

The
Third
Side
of the
Triangle

Thinking about Failure

"No child left behind" . . . if ever there was a great goal for America's students, this is surely it.

The No Child Left Behind Act (NCLB) was first signed into law by President Bush in January 2002. It is the cornerstone of the school-reform movement that the U.S. Department of Education has implemented.

As I write this, Congress and the education community are gearing up for the reauthorization of NCLB, which will surely entail substantial modifications to its initial provisions. In its current form, NCLB offers some important strategies to achieve what its creators call "the four principles" of reform:

1. Accountability for results

2. More choices for parents

3. Greater local control and flexibility

4. An emphasis on doing what works based on scientific research

The first principle, "Accountability for results," has probably gotten the most attention. Essentially, it calls for state-level standards for students in grades three through eight and annual statewide progress objectives ensuring that all groups of students reach proficiency within 12 years. School districts and schools that fail to make adequate yearly progress (AYP) toward statewide proficiency goals will, over time, be subject to improvement, corrective action, and restructuring measures aimed at getting them back on course.

The second principle, "More choices for parents," is understood to mean more opportunities to transfer children from low-performing schools to better schools. If the current institution has failed to meet standards for three of the four preceding years, additional options are available, including funds for low-income students to receive supplemental educational services from public- or private-sector providers. "No child [should] lose the opportunity for a quality education because he or she is trapped in a failing school," the Department of Education declares.

The third principle, which focuses on local control and flexibility, in essence permits states and local school districts to use federal education funds in more diverse ways. Since only about 7 percent of public school funding comes from the federal government, the impact of this strategy remains uncertain at this point.

The fourth principle is aimed primarily at literacy, focusing on the goal that all children should be able to read by the end of the third grade. Nearly a billion dollars a year has been invested in the Reading First program, which targets kindergarten through third-grade students in low-income schools. Preschoolers are reached through Early Reading First, using "instructional strategies and professional development drawn from scientifically based reading research to help [them] to attain the fundamental knowledge and skills they will need for optimal reading development in kindergarten and beyond."[1]

I applaud these principles *as principles,* though serious doubts and concerns have been raised about how they're playing out. But there are deeper and graver problems with No Child Left Behind that go beyond questions of implementation. *The NCLB legislation offers no coherent treatment of the fundamental importance of community involvement as a means of achieving the legislation's goals.* When NCLB speaks of "supplemental education services," what's called for is primarily tutoring and academic coaching. But this is just one of a whole set of resources that are necessary for successful schools and students.

A Challenge to the System

No Child Left Behind paints a picture of our education system that resembles a triangle with only two sides. The first side of the triangle is about *governance*. Reform in this area involves training principals and teachers, improving school administration, and introducing efficiency and standards-based accountability. The idea is to professionalize the system, often by adapting management practices from the private sector, with the aim of making the school more effective. Improvements to the physical plant— which is often in disgraceful shape—are part of this area, too. And should the school still fail to meet standards, "governance" takes on a whole different meaning, since mayors can and will take over such institutions and become the new bosses.

The second side of the triangle is about *pedagogy*. Reform efforts focus on teaching strategies, curriculum innovations, and the options we provide students to help them learn. We work to inculcate different teaching styles and fresh approaches (such as distance learning and service-learning), along with proven programmatic elements to more effectively teach phonics, math, and writing. Educators consider the most basic questions about "the project of education": what it's set up to do and achieve in terms of preparation for citizenship and economic empowerment in the growing global marketplace. Broadly speaking, this side of the triangle is about the *content* and *purpose* of education, while the first side is about the *form*.

What's missing is the third side of the triangle: the coordinated involvement of community members who can meet the non-academic needs of students and help schools truly become places where no child is left behind. Neither of the first two sides of the triangle address the issues of the most vulnerable kids. The best teacher, the top administrator, the most outstanding curriculum, the highest standards—none of these will put food in a child's stomach or a roof over his head. And these "extracurricular" issues are so pervasive in our country that when ignored, they undermine the huge and necessary investment we're making in the other two sides of the triangle.

Think of a business that's run very well, with great employees and a terrific product—except that their intended customers have no money, so the whole thing is pointless. Even if NCLB-inspired reforms worked perfectly to strengthen governance and pedagogy, you'd still be missing something huge: Are the students themselves coming to school ready and able to succeed?

Integrated, school-based services aren't just an addendum or a support to reform of the other two sides. Rather, they must be welded into the triangle as a firm, equal third side. *Community resources and support are a necessary—but not sufficient—condition for true school reform and for the success of millions of children,* especially those whose social well-being is threatened.

THE BEST TEACHER, THE TOP ADMINISTRATOR, THE MOST OUTSTANDING CURRICULUM, THE HIGHEST STANDARDS— NONE OF THESE WILL PUT FOOD IN A CHILD'S STOMACH OR A ROOF OVER HIS HEAD.

To believe otherwise is to allow middle-class presuppositions about "what kids need" to frame the debate. It may well be that your children and most of the other kids in your community come to school after a good night's sleep, a nutritious breakfast, and a short walk through a safe, pretty neighborhood. NCLB and similar reform perspectives assume that *all* kids come to school this way: ready to learn and succeed. They think the kids are fine—it's those darn *schools* that are failing them. And if there *is* some inequality among children at the starting line, it can be ameliorated through academic-support services and maybe a mentor.

In thousands of schools across the U.S., that picture is tragically inaccurate and far from reality, and it's about time the reform movement faced up to it.

Historically, CIS has been something of a thorn in the side of the education-reform movement because we point to these issues that schools aren't equipped to handle, and we refuse to accept that the problems aren't directly related to a child's failure. We necessarily challenge an institution—public education—that isn't set up to respond. A homeless child needs a stable place to live, but getting her one isn't a "school-reform strategy."

It's all too understandable that the education establishment may respond defensively to our critique of traditional, "two-sided" reform efforts. That's why it's so important that we approach educators in a spirit of empathy and respect. It's not their fault that they aren't housing experts—or family therapists, nutritionists, or employment counselors. That's not their job. Moreover, most of them know perfectly well that there's something vital missing from the equation. We need to help provide an environment in which they, too, can speak out about the inadequacies of reform efforts that ignore the third side of the triangle. Without this baseline, many kids literally drop out.

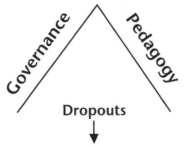

All the school reform in the world won't provide the Five Basics. That's up to the community.

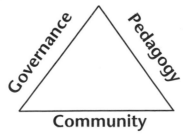

Blaming educators and schools for "failing" is no more helpful than the previous generation's tendency to blame the kids. If you really want to put it in those terms, it's the *community* that's failing both schools and children. We need to accept our share of the solution instead of expecting teachers to be superheroes. And we certainly can't keep telling our teachers that they aren't any good. Either they'll start to believe it—just as kids do if you criticize them enough—or else they'll get mad and devote precious time to organizing ways to *force* us to give them respect (and money). And if that doesn't work, many will simply quit the profession.

I'm not trying to let teachers and principals off the hook. They have an incredibly important role to play; they have to be accountable, and if they're not getting results, the next step is to find out why. Some just need to find another job—that's true in every business. But the majority of educators *are* good; they're just overstressed and underresourced. I've seen teachers who were considered mediocre become much better once they had an environment created for them that respected them and provided the resources they needed to do their job.

Herb Alpert, legendary musician, cofounder of A&M records, and one of my and CIS's oldest friends, once came with me to visit a high school in a very tough New York City community. The principal was a former star basketball player; he stood about 6'10" and was pretty tough himself. Everything in that school was neat, orderly, and well managed—not even a piece of paper on the floor. Herb took all this in and then asked the man: "So why do you need CIS?"

"I'm good at my job," the principal replied. "I can keep it calm and professional in here and make sure we have good teachers, high standards, and a strong curriculum. But I have no control over what happens outside the school grounds. The CIS team is my arms and legs to all the housing projects around here. They make sure kids get safely to school with the resources they need."

That, in a few words, says so much about how all three sides of the triangle can come together in a coordinated way. Great principals need help, too, and conversely, once the students arrive safely at school, they expect and deserve a high-quality education.

The problem is that most school districts—*especially* those where the dropout epidemic is most dire—don't have any obvious person or group that superintendents can turn to and say, "Please handle the third side of the triangle. Please be our Champion for Children. Please help these young people come to school ready to learn." The goal of a Communities In Schools local affiliate is to be that organization. And our overall "reform strategy" is to articulate this approach, provide effective examples of it, and help create national momentum leading to the day when *every* school district, with or without CIS's presence, will have a triangle with three strong sides.

In this as in everything else, the power of community, of working together, is all-important. Neil Shorthouse has a list of what he calls "The Magnificent Seven"—seven community sectors that, in partnership, can make the biggest difference in creating change.

The Magnificent Seven

1. Educators (including college-level teachers and education departments)

2. The private sector (including business, labor, the media, and funders)

3. Faith community leaders

4. Government and civic community leaders

5. Professionals (including health services, housing, the justice system, counselors, United Way–supported agencies and other nonprofits)

6. Parents, guardians, and extended family members

7. Students

Creating an environment in which these seven community groups can be part of the process, bringing the third side of the triangle together with governance and pedagogy, requires the encouragement and collaboration of professional educators. And yes, there can be resistance from school authorities; we'll go into that in more detail later in this chapter. But many community leaders may not realize just how open their school system is to their involvement. **Educators can't do it alone, and they will welcome your help.**

Let me pause right here to emphasize the word *help*. We're talking about committed, experienced professionals—the thousands of superintendents, principals, teachers, and administrators who've dedicated their lives to the education of our young people. They do *not* need you, me, or anyone else to stroll into their schools and start telling them what to do. That's a terrible abuse of whatever influence we might wield as a community. (They also don't need politicians passing legislation that commits them to "reforms" without the means to implement the changes.) The superintendent of your local school district would never think of walking into Microsoft and telling the managers how to do their work. Why then would a CEO—no matter how gifted at running his own business—think he could tell a school system how to do its job?

We're speaking once again of *partnership,* of the kind of collaboration in which each member of the orchestra offers what they do best. When community leaders—especially those in the business world—approach school officials with this attitude, they'll receive a warm welcome.

"People Who Do What He's Done . . ."

Once upon a time there was a boy named Paul who grew up in a small, poor town called Davis Creek, West Virginia. He was a slow learner in elementary school and didn't learn to read until he was in the third grade. That label "slow learner" stuck with him for years. In junior high, they started calling him an "underachiever" because they discovered he was pretty smart, even though he wasn't doing well in class. Then in high school, his grades shot up and suddenly he was "gifted."

But in his heart and soul, he knew that he was still little Paul, the slow learner. He didn't think like other people. The school wanted him to conceive of the world sequentially, in order from A to B. He tended to see ideas holistically, metaphorically. He made connections that seemed perfectly clear to him, but when he voiced them, most adults didn't get it. "You're being too random!" they told him. "Stop going off on tangents and then trying to pull everything together into some 'big picture.'"

So despite his good grades and the fancy new label of "gifted," Paul knew he wasn't going to college. *No one* from his high school went to college.

One teacher disagreed.

Mrs. Sang taught Latin and French, and she wouldn't leave Paul alone. You're going to college, she insisted. You *are.* "I'm not college material," he'd mutter, but she showed him and his parents how to fill out the applications and declared that he *would* be accepted.

He was. Paul went off to Ohio State University, and well into his freshman year he continued to get letters from Mrs. Sang, letters full of exhortations to believe in himself, to remember that he was still being formed, that he was young and capable of anything.

A number of years passed, and the adult Paul decided to make a trip back to his old high school. Mrs. Sang was still there and delighted to see him. She'd followed his career with interest and pride. She promptly pulled him into her fifth-period class and sat him up in front of the students.

"Did you go to college?" she asked him.

"Yes, I did," Paul replied. "I went to Ohio State."

"Do you have a master's degree?"

"Yes, from the University of North Carolina."

"Do you have a doctorate?"

"I do."

"From where?"

"Harvard University."

"What sort of jobs have you worked?"

"Well, I started out as a teacher. Then I became a principal, then an assistant superintendent. At the moment I'm superintendent of schools in Princeton, New Jersey."

Mrs. Sang allowed a moment of silence, then asked Paul, "Where did you go to high school?"

"Right here."

And the classroom erupted in disbelieving catcalls and shouts. "You did not!" the students yelled. "No way! Who are you *really?*"

Mrs. Sang told them to be quiet, then asked, "Now why don't you believe this man? He just got done telling you he's from Davis Creek, just like you."

One boy raised his hand and said, "People who do what he's done don't go to this school."

Dr. Paul D. Houston has never forgotten that day. *People who do what he's done don't go to this school.* It reinforced his passion to work for the day when our public school system will *never* provoke a student to speak such sad, negative words.

Raising a Village

In 1994, Paul Houston became the executive director of the American Association of School Administrators, and for more than a dozen years he has been a brilliant and tireless advocate for breaking down the barriers between schools and communities.

It's startling how much we have in common. Both of us were called "slow," and neither of us would have been a good bet for adult success. We're both "right-brain" people, thinking metaphorically and holistically. A caring adult made the crucial difference in each of our young lives, helping us believe in ourselves and reject the negative labeling.

Paul Houston has some very good news for community leaders who want to be involved in stopping the dropout epidemic: "The schools have to change, they have to involve communities, parents, the greater world. It's the only way they're going to be able to keep kids in school. I tell superintendents: 'You have to stop thinking of yourselves as superintendents of *schools* and start thinking of yourselves as superintendents of *education,* of *learning.*' There's a big difference."

Some administrators are unsure and perhaps anxious about what this means for their own school districts, but Paul declares, "We're past the point of people saying, 'I don't think it's the right idea.' Now the whole conversation is about the right *ways* for this idea to be realized. How can communities step up and support the work school superintendents are doing? The schools are looking to community leaders and saying, 'Help—we can't do this alone.'"

So as Paul likes to ask, if it takes a village to raise a child, what does it take to raise a village? Public schools play two essential roles here. First, if you're looking for a rallying cry, a cause to believe in, you can't do better than the schools. Regardless of what political or social divisions may exist in a community, *everyone* wants kids to do well in this area. It's a place to plant your flag and call others to join the battle. Second, these facilities are physically central to the community as well. A village has to *happen* somewhere— what better place than the schoolhouse? It's right there, it's a place where families are already used to going, it's a public trust, and all too often it's underutilized once classes are over for the day.

> *"The schools have to change; they have to involve communities, parents, the greater world. It's the only way they're going to be able to keep kids in school."*

— **Dr. Paul D. Houston**, executive director, American Association of School Administrators

Community involvement (the third side of the triangle) is, as I've said, a necessary but not sufficient condition for successful schools. Paul Houston is well aware that the other two sides of the triangle—the ones for which educators and policy makers are accountable—are badly in need of true reform. He doesn't see community involvement as the be-all and end-all, the miraculous solution to every school's problems. We need to reexamine how school experiences—teaching, testing, assessments—are presented to our young people.

"We make kids failures and then say, 'Why do you want to quit school? You don't like failing? What's wrong with you?' We educators bear a big chunk of the burden for that situation," Paul says.

He sees a particularly crucial role for the business community to play in creating a "tipping point" for genuine school reform.

"Are businesspeople going to read your book?" he asked me the other day.

I sure hope so, I replied.

"Okay," Paul said, "please say this to them: The head of the American Association of School Administrators needs you to be part of the solution to our schools' problems. We need you to speak out and take action on behalf of community involvement with our kids' education. As a superintendent, I could say, 'Schools need this kind of help,' and people think, *There he goes, just bellyaching and whining again.* But if a business leader says the same thing, people are going to pay attention: 'Wow, we'd better do something about this. The president of the electric company said the community has to partner with the schools—it must be true.'"

So business leaders have credibility that they can apply in a positive fashion. They can use their influence in the political process to get politicians to focus on the right set of issues. The basic argument should be that we can't sustain democracy without a strong public school system because citizens need to be literate, informed, and able to participate knowledgeably in civic life. That's why *public* education came into existence in this country, and its mission has, if anything, grown even more critical. Business leaders need to say to politicians, loudly and clearly: "Every one of us has a stake in this. We've got to keep our kids in school."

I hear Paul talking about three things: **awareness, advocacy,** and **action.** Local business leaders and other power brokers must first become **aware** of the true problems confronting their school system; then they must firmly claim a role as **advocates** for the right kind of change. Last, they can take appropriate **action** to support a coordinated community response to the needs of children—and their teachers. These are themes we'll continue to explore in the final section of this book.

I also hear Paul making a clear case for why schools need the third side of the triangle. Without community support, educators and administrators simply can't provide the safety net that will prevent students from leaving school, branded as "failures," long before any reforms in the other two sides of the triangle have a chance to work. If only all kids started from the same place, equipped with the same resources and supports that you provide for *your* children, then school reform alone might be the answer to our troubled public education system. But that's not the case—it's not even close. The majority of kids who drop out are suffering from deficits that no curriculum can make up, and these are *all* our children.

Truly, we put our educators in a terrible bind. "No child left behind" is both a moral obligation and an economic necessity. But the deteriorating conditions that millions of families face make it virtually impossible for the schools to fulfill this mission. They just don't have the resources or the expertise to address all the deficiencies. Without the third side of the triangle, we have an unstable, inadequate structure, and kids literally drop out of it. Once again, the need for the community's involvement as an equal partner is clear.

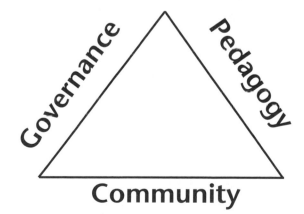

Bringing Power, Authority, and Idea Together

I want to turn to some of the practical implications of what we've been discussing. One problem with a good image or metaphor (such as "the third side of the triangle") is that its simplicity and clarity can fool you into thinking that *everything* connected with the concept is likewise simple and clear. But the real-world challenges are extremely complex.

I know that Paul Houston is right when he says that superintendents will welcome your help as an advocate for community involvement. He points out that the debate is no longer about *whether* this partnership should exist. When administrators have questions and doubts, they focus on *how* this should be done, not *if* it should happen.

But just because a school superintendent may be familiar with the general idea of using a school as a delivery point for needed social services for children and families, that doesn't mean he'll be an easy sell on the *specifics*. With the best intentions—and these leaders are overwhelmingly good, smart, dedicated people who are completely committed to the children in their school system—those in authority tend to be skeptical of ideas that arise from *outside* their own area of expertise, especially if those concepts seem to call their expertise into question. And the natural response when you're feeling skeptical is to focus on the negative, to quickly point out all the problems and drawbacks.

What's the result? When a grassroots community leader manages to get five minutes with a school superintendent to "sell" CIS or its equivalent, he or she may have to spend four of those minutes being told why the ideas wouldn't work in this school system—or worse yet, "We're already doing that" when they aren't.

Superintendents and school boards represent *Authority:* They make the decisions about what will happen in the education system. And a group like CIS is offering an *Idea,* a strategy, a new way of approaching an old problem. The fact is, a one-on-one meeting between Idea and Authority can be a tricky proposition.

Fortunately, there's another way to do this, one that brings to the table the missing voice. This is the voice of *Power*—and it might be *your* voice, if you're a respected business leader, local government official, foundation director, or leader of a faith community. This is one of the most time-tested principles of community organizing: *Power, Authority, and Idea need to sit at the same table.* It's the same principle that Paul Houston invokes when he talks about the critical role of business leaders in advocating for a new approach to the dropout epidemic.

People in positions of power in your area—and again, you may be one of them—have a stake in the community. If there's a serious problem, they want it solved.

The dropout epidemic is about as serious as a problem can get. Enlightened self-interest alone would dictate that community leaders need to *take* it seriously and play a major role in stemming the tide of young dropouts. Unemployment equals crime and unsafe neighborhoods, affecting every family who lives there. And the business sector in particular simply can't afford this constant, worsening drain on the economy and the labor force.

> POWER, AUTHORITY, AND IDEA NEED TO SIT AT THE SAME TABLE.

I'm happy to say that for many, many powerful individuals, self-interest isn't the only motivator. Beyond that, these people simply care. They see the human cost of the dropout epidemic, and they feel a moral responsibility to help their community—especially if part of that morality is an ethic of giving back, of making a contribution to society as a way of expressing gratitude for the gifts and benefits they've enjoyed in their own lives.

When Power Speaks . . .

Some people get nervous when they hear the word *power,* as if it's a nasty secret that no good-hearted person should know about. The truth is that *every* community has its centers of power, and everyone knows who those people are. Often they're the ones with money (but not always). Using power simply means using your internal and external resources to get the job done. Those with this strength have respect and influence—when Power speaks, Authority *will* listen.

This idea isn't new or unique to CIS. Almost every successful agent for community change has followed a similar path, and CIS local affiliates are no exception. At some point, there was a "power lunch," convened by Power, that brought Authority and Idea to the same table.

There's a hitch that can sometimes occur when Idea talks to Power about convening a "power lunch." Generous, civic-minded individuals (and corporations and foundations) are often accustomed to exercising their might with their checkbooks. I'm the last person to refuse a contribution in the name of kids, but as valuable as funding is, it's *not* always the best use of power.

Neither is personal involvement in the schools, necessarily. We need volunteers, as many as possible—at this writing, 49,000 people volunteer with CIS affiliates—but putting you on the front lines to work directly with kids and families may not be the best use of your talents.

A good case in point is my friend Brad Currey. He and I went to the same adult Sunday school at St. Luke's Episcopal Church in Atlanta back when we were trying to launch the first prototype Communities In Schools sites. Brad was the second in command at Atlanta's largest bank, and he had a big heart and a strong desire to give back to his community. One Sunday morning we were pondering how the scriptural message of loving your neighbor could be put into action for Atlanta's youth.

"Well, I know you've started these 'Academies,'" Brad said to me. "Do you want me to be a tutor?"

Much as I appreciated the offer, I already had something different in mind. "Uh, not really, Brad," I replied.

I think his feelings might have been a little hurt, but he hung in there. "Then how can I help?"

"Simple. Give me one hour of your time. Call the superintendent of schools and ask him to lunch at your club—tell him you'd like to discuss a great idea for helping kids succeed. Then bring me along. I'll be the Idea."

So we brought Power, Authority, and Idea together for lunch. And by the time we'd had our coffee, Superintendent Crim had agreed to another meeting with me and my colleagues to explore the CIS idea.

Yes, I could have encouraged Brad to just become a tutor. And who knows—he might have been great at it. But by encouraging him instead to use his power on behalf of *thousands* of kids, not just a few, we took a big step forward. He had a unique gift to give, and fortunately he was willing to share it.

A New Deal in Vegas

A revealing case study of how to bring Power, Authority, and Idea together to introduce the third side of the triangle into a school system took place just in the last few years. The setting was Las Vegas.

You probably associate the city with glitzy casinos and 24-hour action. But Clark County, home to the gaming mecca, also happens to be the fastest-growing school system in the United States. And when you leave the Strip, you'll find thousands of children living in the most dire circumstances imaginable. An estimated 3,500 school-age children are homeless, and more than 40 percent qualify for free or reduced-price lunches, a measure that's reliably correlated with economic disadvantage. These children need the community to stand up for them, and fortunately we are seeing that happen today.

Elaine Wynn and her husband, Steve, started their hotel-casino company in 1973 with one little hotel in downtown Las Vegas called the Golden Nugget. Over the years, they've expanded their business and created some of the city's most well-known spots, including the Mirage, Treasure Island, Bellagio, and the Wynn. Elaine is definitely a force to be reckoned with, a true community Power. She's charming, intelligent, and extremely motivated to succeed.

However, I've had the privilege of knowing Elaine in a very different context. Like most mothers, she wanted to make sure her kids grew up healthy, happy, and well educated. But what makes Elaine special is that she decided early on that *all* children should have these same benefits. And she has walked her talk ever since, working hard to ensure that Las Vegas provides educational and cultural opportunities for all who live there.

Over the years, she has offered her time and her heart to organizations like the University of Nevada–Las Vegas Foundation, the Golden Nugget Scholarship Foundation, the Nevada Institute for Contemporary Art, and the Nevada Gaming Foundation for Educational Excellence. She serves as a member of the Nevada Council to Establish Academic Standards and chairs the Greater Las Vegas After-School All-Stars.

We've also had the great good fortune to have Elaine on the CIS national board of directors since 1999. She got up to speed with our mission and strategies about as fast as anyone I've ever known. She wanted to speak up for Idea right from the start, in addition to using her power in the usual ways a board member might. So her contributions to our work around the country have been enormous, but Las Vegas and its children have always been close to her heart.

She called me one day in 2003 with two pieces of news: There was a new school superintendent in Clark County whom she believed might be receptive to the CIS idea. And the Omidyar family, owners of the very well-funded Omidyar Foundation (as it was then called; now it's the Omidyar Network), had just relocated to Las Vegas. Didn't this sound like a potential "power lunch"?

It did. But I reminded Elaine about our previous experience in Las Vegas, nearly ten years earlier. It's not a story I like to dwell on, but it's instructive in this context. It's a great example of what happens when Power, Idea, and Authority do *not* find a way to talk.

How to Reject a Good Idea

In the mid-1990s, CIS was keen to offer its services in Las Vegas. Naturally Elaine was spearheading our efforts there. Well, one of the drawbacks of being a Power is that sometimes you get into a power *struggle*. That was what happened almost immediately. It wasn't Elaine's fault, and at this late date the details really don't matter. But the result was that Authority—represented by the school board—was unwilling to give the CIS idea a fair hearing.

Of course, a reason was needed for rejecting the idea. When you're looking for apparent negatives, you can always find one. Certain people pointed out that among dozens of other services, CIS affiliates offered health clinics in some schools. And didn't these do family-planning counseling? Did they make birth control available? What about abortion referrals? In short, the CIS idea was turned into an official "pro-choice" platform, which went over very badly in this largely traditional community. (You might be surprised to know that the Las Vegas powers that be hold quite conservative values.)

Now, none of this was accurate. As I've described in previous chapters, the whole essence of the organization is that it's locally accountable to the community. *Nothing* can happen through CIS that isn't approved by the board of directors and the school system. We have no "laundry list" of required services that a local affiliate must provide to the schools; it's entirely up to the stakeholders. So this notion that CIS as a whole—as an Idea—was somehow pro–teenage sex or pro-abortion was absurd. We're just pro-kids, pro-parents, and pro-communities.

So it was up to us as holders of the Idea to convince Authority in Las Vegas of the truth of this. Power, represented by Elaine, had gotten us a seat at the table. The players were staring at us, waiting to hear what we had to say.

And we failed. We couldn't find the right words, the right arguments, to convince them that CIS had no political ax to grind. Authority was unable to accept Idea, was ultimately threatened by Idea, and rejected it. Maybe there *were* no right words; the political infighting and power struggle may have been insurmountable. But ten years later when this same issue came up again, we were a decade wiser, and knew that we would take a different tack . . . and this time Authority listened.

Showing the Results

I said that I "reminded" Elaine of our failure in Las Vegas when she called me with the news about the new superintendent and the Omidyars, but that's not really true. She didn't need any prompting. I could tell from her voice that the memory was still vivid—and distinctly unpleasant. Yet she was convinced that things were different now, that we could reengage with the Clark County school system without repeating the mistakes of the past.

I agreed. I also pointed out (not that she needed reminding of this either) that we now had a terrific asset in our favor. His name is Daniel J. Cardinali, and he has since become (and I hope will remain, for many, many years) president of the national Communities In Schools organization. At the time, he was our executive vice president for field operations. I told Elaine that Dan wanted to personally represent us in Las Vegas, side by side with her.

A brief word about Dan Cardinali: This young man (at 41, he sure seems young to me) is one of the brightest moments in the CIS story. He came to CIS in 2000 and I immediately thought, *If we can keep this guy from quitting over how scattered and unfocused we can sometimes be, he'll end up running the place.* Thank goodness Dan hung in there, and my prediction came true.

Trained as a community organizer in Guadalajara, Mexico, he started his career in service as part of a team organizing a squatter community of 120,000 individuals to secure land rights, running water, and public education. He came back to Washington, D.C., to receive a one-year research fellowship at the Woodstock Theological Center at Georgetown University. While working for Partners for the Americas, he coordinated its leadership training program, the International Fellowship in Community Development.

These are the kind of résumé facts anyone could learn about Dan. But what I also knew about him at the time of Elaine's call was that he was one of the hardest-working, most gifted community organizers I'd ever met. All of us at the CIS national office were coming to rely on him more and more. I knew that if anyone could bring CIS to Las Vegas, he could.

So Dan flew off on what would be the first of many trips for this project. Reviewing the situation with Elaine, he learned that the new school superintendent, Carlos Garcia, had come to Clark County from Fresno, where he'd heard good things about CIS through some mutual friends. Elaine was right: Carlos was predisposed to give us a hearing, and she was also correct that the Omidyars were willing to listen. But she warned Dan: This foundation is *tough*. They expect all their potential grantees to treat the process like a business deal. They want a plan and outcomes— don't think you can go in there and sell the Idea without a clear, solid strategy to back it up.

So Dan devised an incredibly detailed three-year business plan. It laid out exactly what CIS's mission in Las Vegas would be and how we'd go about achieving it. He matched the goals of the Clark County school system with the kinds of outcomes a successful CIS affiliate can achieve. Then he showed how both of these supported the Omidyar Foundation's mission. If approved, CIS would begin at just one school, Reynaldo Martinez Elementary, whose desperately underserved students were struggling against the most basic, heartbreaking deficiencies. They lacked food, clothing, shelter . . . and hope.

So Power, Authority, and Idea were ready to sit down together. Dan and Elaine spoke with Carlos Garcia and the Omidyar Foundation's representative in a series of three meetings. A couple of things soon became clear. One was that the new superintendent was keenly aware of Clark County's status as the fastest-growing school district in the country. Carlos had his hands full just trying to find qualified teachers and administrators to handle the burgeoning enrollment. But he also felt a moral responsibility to see that *every* child got the knowledge that he or she deserved. "No child left behind" was already his motto. Second, Carlos wanted to be what Paul Houston calls a "superintendent of education," not just a superintendent of schools. In other words, he was open to the idea that the schools can't do it alone. He wanted a way for the community and the educators to work together—the only question was how.

Dan also discovered that Elaine's role as a champion of the Idea was invaluable. She had the respect of all the movers and shakers in Las Vegas, and here she was, able to put the CIS argument in the clearest and most compelling terms. Moreover, her role as the Power member of the trio was ideal: She and her husband, Steve, could easily have written a check to help get CIS off the ground and left it at that. But instead she insisted upon using her influence as a convener, as the one who could get all the others to talk to each other, and to take seriously the ideas being proposed. Hopefully, the Omidyars would exercise the power of the purse and other foundations would follow.

These meetings were hard. Dan would call in and say, "Yes, they're still grilling us. Gotta run. . . ." Authority and Power wanted to know exactly what CIS was doing around the country, and Dan had the data that pointed to concrete results. *He was backing up Idea with evidence.* For Carlos, the plan was starting to look attractive: This independent, nonpartisan group could leverage significant resources on behalf of his students. Dan and Elaine weren't asking him to come up with "development dollars" or, in fact, any start-up funding at all. The flow would go the other way, *into* the school system. As for the Omidyar Foundation, they could see that the CIS Idea wasn't just theory. We had an idea about how to get things done, too.

There was still the school board to win over. The head of the board came from a highly respected—and highly conservative—family. Her name was Sheila Molton, and she was a wonderful leader by all accounts. She was there at Dan and Elaine's next "power lunch."

Her very first question was: "What's your formal relationship with Planned Parenthood?"

Dan responded truthfully that we had none. Local CIS affiliates around the country often developed relationships with Planned Parenthood, but that was up to them and those they served. "We function *by invitation only,*" Dan explained. "We can't exist without the superintendent's permission, and we do nothing that hasn't been approved by the community." The head of the school board seemed pleased with that answer, but Dan decided to follow it up with an invitation: Why not make a personal visit to a CIS community as similar as possible to Las Vegas?

As I look back on our failure to start CIS in Clark County ten years earlier, I can't help but wonder if an offer like that might have turned the tide. Sometimes you have to give voices and bodies to Idea—you have to show Authority the flesh-and-blood results, the daily operation of a successful initiative.

Sheila Molton took Dan up on his offer. A month later, during a meeting of the Council of Great City Schools in Chicago, the two of them were in the office of Chicago CIS Executive Director Jane Mentzinger. Jane laid out the precise strategies that allowed her CIS affiliate to operate in 138 Chicago schools, connecting more than 150 local service providers with children and families in need.

> CIS IS COMMITTED TO GETTING THE BEST POSSIBLE RESOURCES IN PLACE FOR YOUNG PEOPLE, BUT WE ALWAYS RESPECT THE POLITICAL AND ETHICAL SENSITIVITIES OF THE SCHOOLS WHO INVITE US IN.

She also made a telling point about local ownership versus some kind of official "CIS line." As it happened, Chicago CIS partnered with Planned Parenthood in a number of school sites. *But* the Chicago school system has an "abstinence only" policy in regard to what can be taught to young people about sexual activity. Both Chicago CIS and Planned Parenthood rigorously respected this policy, and the latter's role was limited to teen-health issues that did *not* involve reproduction. CIS is committed to getting the best possible resources in place for young people, but we always respect the political and ethical sensitivities of the schools who invite us in.

To put it another way: CIS has an Idea about local ownership— we think it's critical to success with schools. What Sheila saw was the Idea in the flesh. Thanks to Elaine Wynn's superb "convener" skills, an important Authority was getting a close-up look at how a good Idea really works. Sheila was willing to give it a try.

Back in Las Vegas, Superintendent Garcia gave a thumbs-up, too, and we had funding in place from the Omidyars. We held a big community meeting at which, among many other issues, we expressed our desire to hire a local liaison. Almost immediately we found a fantastic candidate in Louise Helton, who went on to become CIS of Southern Nevada's first executive director.

This is a very abbreviated version of the entire process, of course. I don't mean to imply that it was all smooth sailing once Power, Authority, and Idea were in the same boat—it never is. But I do hold this up as a fine example to illustrate the crucial importance of such a trio.

CIS of Southern Nevada officially launched in June 2004, and three years later more than 850 students at Martinez Elementary are receiving free meals *seven* days a week, along with health care provided at a new building on the school campus, and much more. It's a beginning, and a good one. It's also a perfect illustration of why educators can't do everything alone. Is it the job of the Clark County school system to feed its students over the weekend or to provide health care for them? Of course not. And yet the lack of these basic human needs was destroying the ability of students to succeed in school—and in life. So the community had to step up and bring its helping resources into partnership with the schools.

All the "school reform" in the world wouldn't have accomplished this. But as we know, a triangle needs three sides. Integrated, school-based services are the missing third side, and when they're in place, we can foresee the day when, truly, *no* child is left behind.

■ ■ ■ ■ ■

PART III

From Charity
to Change

CHAPTER SEVEN

A New Way of Thinking about Schools

How Far Can Charity Go?

The United States is very good at charity. We're a generous people. After the Gulf Coast hurricanes of 2005, there was an outpouring of support from institutions, foundations, congregations, entertainment and sports figures, and ordinary American citizens. Millions rallied round the survivors of the disaster. And thankfully, this is typical of how our country responds to unexpected tragedy.

But charity only goes so far. The problem is that every call on our help and generosity eventually moves out of the headlines and off our TV screens. We go back into our ordinary world—some of us to our gated communities and "safe neighborhoods"—and life goes on. It's similar to the aftermath of a funeral: Someone close to us has died, and neighbors and relatives all come and give us cakes and casseroles and surround us with love . . . but six months later, we're alone.

How could it be any other way, really? No one wants to be a

perpetual "charity case," and even the most generous givers have priorities in their own lives.

As I write, the dropout epidemic is front-page news. Major national magazines, prime-time television shows—they're all reporting the grim facts about what's happening to one-third of our kids every year. I'm sure that millions of Americans are learning about this for the first time and perhaps asking: "What can I do?"

My greatest fear is that this will become *yesterday's* news. There may well be an outpouring of giving amid statements of support for public schools, families, and students—but life goes on. . . .

The fact is that **curing the dropout epidemic will demand** *change,* **not just charity.** We have to alter our fundamental way of doing business where schools are concerned, although it's extremely important to understand that such a shift doesn't *replace* charitable support. A generous personal response that reflects our deep desire to give and help is always needed. But systemic reform is essential, too. It does no good to keep putting resources into a failing system; instead, the plan has to change. But once the switch is successful, that doesn't mean that we suddenly stop funding it. Instead, we keep giving as before, the difference being that now the resources are used effectively.

This word *charity* is really a synonym for *giving,* for providing resources. In the business world, no one calls it charity, of course, but every time a CEO approves a budget item for a particular project, he or she is making a decision to *give,* to *invest,* to allocate resources in the expectation of accomplishing an objective. Similarly, a local government agency that approves a grant to fund, say, a reading initiative in the public school system, is approving a particular type of gift.

But if the *system* needs to change, all of the giving and investing won't make enough of a difference. When people talk about the uselessness of "throwing money at a problem," this is what they mean. Always remember, though, that once the necessary transformation has been effected, the resources must continue. Now we're no longer "throwing money," we're *using* it to fund a truly effective plan.

In a sense, the Five Basics are charity. A positive one-on-one relationship with a caring adult, a safe place, a healthy start, a marketable skill, and a chance to give back—these are all things we can and should *give* every child. But the coordination of these resources around the schools is *change*. In fact, it's the necessary difference that will allow the Five Basics to be effective in meeting the needs of kids and families.

Once a community embraces the idea of modifying how resources are delivered to schools and families, there's no limit to the creative possibilities. In Houston, for instance, juvenile courts are now "sentencing" young offenders to enter the Communities In Schools program. This isn't charity, nor is it punishment. Rather, it's a change in the way the pieces of the system are configured. The school is at the center, and young people in trouble are being directed to a place where they can receive coordinated, accountable, personalized assistance.

People in your area who give to or work for charities often have an appetite for systemic change and feel frustrated because they don't see the opportunity to be part of it. They're tired of Band-Aids applied to specific problems that crop up again and again, with no vision to stem the flow of young people bleeding out onto the streets. They're fed up with commissions and meetings that investigate some tragic circumstance and make recommendations about how it could have been better addressed—without asking why it happened in the first place.

A First Step Toward Change: United All the Way

Businesspeople can have an enormous impact on turning charity into change on behalf of kids. Many such leaders either support the community through corporate-giving programs or sit on the boards of charitable foundations. The vitally important thing you can do if you're one of these decision makers is to *fund cooperation and coordination* among your grantees and in the community at large.

This is the efficient way to operate, not only for its desirable results, but also in terms of the investment you make. Your money will go a lot further when organizations are able to use the leveraging power of the grant to secure in-kind support from others. CIS affiliates regularly achieve leveraging effects as high as $13 for every dollar of foundation support. A truly cooperative community effort creates a convergence of resources and energy that's far greater than the sum of its parts.

When I speak to groups of business leaders, I'm often asked, "What sorts of changes are you asking us to implement?" In response, I request that they think about the United Way, which has done a truly exceptional job of changing how people make contributions to social causes. What if the process was united *all* the way? That is, what if the money was not only collected together, but also allocated so as to encourage integration and collaboration among the many community charities? We need to *reward cooperation* and stop the bad habit of giving funds to 20 different groups without creating conditions and incentives for them to work together. The new expectation should be: *Okay, we're funding you—now how are you going to help each other do your jobs more effectively?*

WE NEED TO *REWARD COOPERATION.*

Let's say that your corporate or nonprofit foundation decides to fund Teach For America, which places recent top college graduates as teachers in troubled schools. You also want to support New Leaders for New Schools, which recruits, trains, and supports talented principals. And perhaps there's a local health clinic that badly needs a way to expand its outreach to poor children.

Each of these organizations is worthy of your support. They'll know of each other and respect each other's missions, but realistically they aren't going to find time to *work together* unless you make that a condition of their funding. And at this point, you may decide that you need to add a Champion for Children into the mix as well—an organization similar to CIS that knows how to broker and coordinate all the players together into a holistic team for youth.

But one way or another, it's critical that social service and volunteer agencies understand that they'll be supported and rewarded *to the extent that they not only talk and work together, but truly integrate their resources.* The aim is to create a safety net for children and families based on shared goals, information, and supplies. In effect, the various local organizations are being asked to think of themselves as part of the same "company." There's no competition, no hoarding of assets or data. What CEO would willingly permit that from the various departments of his or her business, all supposedly engaged on a single project? We need to foster the same attitude in the community.

This is genuine institutional change at several levels. Not only are you changing the way your organization gives its funds, but you're shifting how the grantees view their mission. Even better, when Teach For America, New Leaders for New Schools, the local health clinic, and CIS are all working efficiently as one, they're affecting the most important institution of all—the public schools. Educators no longer have to go it alone, overextended and ill equipped for the demands being placed on them. They can now confidently rely on a coordinated community team to meet students' nonacademic needs. It's a fundamental shift in the relationship between the school as an institution and the community it serves.

This is easy to recommend but often difficult to implement. No one likes to change, and many a book has been written about why this is so. When I was working on the streets, I used to believe there was a conspiracy on the part of the powers that be, a deliberate plan to maintain the status quo and keep poor people poor. That was before I moved to Washington, D.C., and saw that many federal government bureaucrats had enough trouble understanding and navigating through this red tape themselves without also trying to launch a scheme to oppress anyone. I now believe that our failure to support systemic change results largely from two factors: the natural inertia of people and institutions when called upon to do things differently and a deeply felt uncertainty, bordering on despair, about *how* to change.

This despair leads to a retreat into small areas of personal responsibility, just as we saw in the example of Tara Larson and the many social services available to help her. If people can't feel good about changing, they at least want to feel good about doing their own jobs. This has the paradoxical effect of making the work tougher because we create little silos of expertise that often fail to communicate—let alone integrate—their efforts and end up pointing fingers of blame. Everyone's trying to "outgood" everyone else.

Philanthropic and corporate foundations unwittingly contribute to this mind-set when they select a single organization—no matter how worthy—to address a problem that by its nature demands cooperation from many sources. Instantly, potential partners become competitors, first in their grant applications and then in the inevitable turf battles that follow. "Looking good" when you file your end-of-grant report becomes more important than truly *doing* good. And, sadly, this often means demonstrating that your organization is better than A, B, or C. If only A, B, and C were working *with* you! The combined results would be truly impressive.

It's important to note that cooperation and coordination are nonpartisan values that transcend political ideologies. Given my roots in the social changes of the 1960s, my organization and I frequently used to be accused of being "left wing." In the mid-1990s when the Republicans achieved their majority in Congress, I was asked by a leading politician to attend one of a series of meetings he was holding among some of the new members of the House and Senate. He invited people whose ideas interested him, offered them a chance to present some of their key concepts, and then opened the floor for a question-and-answer session.

After I explained some of what CIS does, one of the first questions came from a first-term congressman. Actually, it wasn't a question so much as a complaint: "You sound like a Kennedy liberal," he told me. I protested that nothing I'd said was remotely connected with either liberalism or Senator Kennedy. "Well, how *do* you feel about the conservatives taking over Congress?" he retorted.

"I'm disappointed," I said.

"See? That's what I mean. You're a liberal."

"Not at all," I replied. "I'm disappointed because I was

hoping that all this talk about 'the new conservatives' would bring a truly conservative spirit to Congress. What I've heard here today doesn't sound conservative *enough* to me. The best way I know of to conserve resources is to spend them wisely on programs that produce the kind of synergy and leveraging effects I was just describing to you. But that's not what's happened, as far as I can tell. You believed that the previous Congress was spending too much money and spending it inefficiently. So now you want to spend *less* money, in an equally inefficient way. It's not about how much money you spend, Congressman. It's about spending it to support personal, accountable, and coordinated responses to our students' needs."

A Second Step Toward Change: Taking the Time

Another important aspect of turning charity into change takes us back to the basics: the necessity for personal relationships. If institutions are to cooperate and work together on behalf of children and families, they really have to spend time in each other's company. Much as we depend on and value the new technologies of the 21st-century workplace, we all know that an electronic exchange is never the same as a face-to-face meeting. E-mails are short and (hopefully) sweet; they're efficient; they get the job done. But I'm not sure how well they build community.

Communication serves two purposes, one informational and the other relational. We rely on our face-to-face interactions with others to build a sense of trust and even love, not just to provide facts. Only proximity can create the all-important relational aspects of community.

Remember, we adults have a call to build this environment for our young people. It's something that far too many kids never get to experience. So all our talk of cooperation and working together has got to result in action that *models* community. Children learn from what they see—and so do adults. If you want staff and volunteers from a half-dozen different agencies to work together at a school site, demonstrating community for kids, then you'd better be willing to demonstrate it for the staff yourself. Physical propinquity—actually getting leaders into the same room together to talk and learn from each other—is an essential step in changing institutions.

A Third Step Toward Change: Patience Is a Virtue

Change takes time. In particular, the positive *results* of change take time, and the bigger the problem, the longer it can take. We aren't going to see the last dropout this year, or next year, or the year after that—not even if every district in America changed overnight and used the schools as delivery points for personal, coordinated, and accountable services. We all understand the importance of persistence and patience when trying to turn around a huge social issue—or a huge corporate one, for that matter. CEOs need to be patient, too, as long as the signs are clear that they're on the right track toward making their company profitable.

SYSTEMIC CHANGE SHOULDN'T BE EVALUATED AS IF IT WERE A SCIENTIFIC EXPERIMENT OR A SMALL DEMONSTRATION PROJECT.

This is all to say that systemic change shouldn't be *evaluated* as if it were a scientific experiment or a small demonstration project. In other words, we've got to stop basing our funding cycles on three-year grants (as many foundations do) or on four-year administrations (whether federal, state, or local). It's like planting a delicate new tree and then digging it up a year later to examine the roots. It hasn't completely developed yet? Oh well, throw it away and try something else. Our educational system didn't get where it is overnight. Reversing its negative aspects will also take time, and the last thing we need is a series of shortsighted benchmarks based on timetables that aren't relevant to the problems.

So we need to urge our partners and funders to stick with us for the long haul. This isn't the same thing as sitting back while no progress is made in the hopes that "something" will improve. Every local CIS affiliate has specific benchmarks for success, and funders rightly expect these goals to be met. Rather, it's an attitude of commitment and perseverance.

We mustn't promise any quick fixes or magic bullets. What we can predict is change in—finally—the right direction. And if a funder is truly determined to get a quick result for its investment, we can suggest a donation to any of a number of veteran CIS affiliates where the infrastructure for change is already in place and the school system is partnering with the community to create a new way of delivering services for its students. In such a community, an infusion of new funds can lead to CIS coordinators at new schools and hundreds more young people who are connected with needed resources.

The Communities In Schools movement ultimately aims to put itself out of business. Our vision of change will be realized on the day when our concepts are so institutionalized, so truly a part of how every community responds to the needs of its children, that no special "neutral third party" is required. No one has to advocate for cafeterias in schools. They're just *there* because everyone knows that kids have to eat lunch. Do we need a special Gymnasiums In Schools organization? Of course not. Gyms are taken for granted and planned for in every school system. It's my hope that someday all of the Five Basics will be similarly available, delivered by caring adults who view the students as human beings, not statistics.

New Orleans: Every Child a "CIS Student"

When the levees broke in New Orleans in August 2005, the devastation triggered an outpouring of charity. Especially in light of the disgraceful response to the initial disaster from all levels of government, the private sector and individual givers were willing to dig deep and commit themselves to getting the Big Easy back on its feet.

Once again, the charity was there when it was needed. But

something else began to stir in the city, as the region's education leaders recognized that their broken community had been handed an opportunity in the midst of tragedy.

The New Orleans schools, which served between 50,000 and 60,000 students, were on the brink of failure before Hurricane Katrina arrived. The state was preparing to take over and restructure the system. A small CIS affiliate was operating in one school, but its efforts were overwhelmed by a chaotic and bureaucratic structure and a 46 percent dropout rate for the city's students.

Then the hurricanes hit. Thousands of young people and families were displaced, many to be absorbed by nearby school systems, as I described in Chapter 4. But students gradually began to return to a city and a school system that were starting from the ground up. Every one of these kids, along with their families, would need special attention and a variety of social services just to recommence their ordinary lives.

Suddenly, *every child was a "CIS student."*

By this I mean that there was no longer a perceived division between haves and have-nots, between young people who might need additional help to succeed in school and those who presumably already had the necessary resources. It was a citywide educational emergency, and if anything good could be said to have come out of the floods, it was this: We now had a situation in which the coordination of social services around kids and families was a *must*, not just a nice idea. All eyes were on the problem. It was truly a golden moment for systemic change.

The state of Louisiana stepped in to run the New Orleans school districts—a move that likely would have occurred anyway, given the difficulties the system was experiencing before the hurricanes. The state offered an open door to a variety of models, charter schools and parochial schools included. Basically, anyone who was ready and willing to operate classrooms and could measure up to state standards was welcomed. Finding undamaged buildings was a major challenge. In the midst of this unprecedented attempt to meet students' needs as rapidly as possible, CIS of New Orleans stepped forward to act as a service-delivery coordinator that could operate in any or all of these environments.

In the weeks immediately following the hurricanes, the CIS national office outside Washington, D.C., had organized a hurricane relief fund that raised $437,000 from corporate, foundation, and individual givers. Most of these funds were transferred to 21 local CIS affiliates in six states to provide direct services to 19,000 displaced students and their families.

During this same period, CIS of New Orleans, whose staff and board members initially had to evacuate the city, began to return as services were restored and plans implemented to begin opening schools. Education officials asked CIS to coordinate services beginning in December 2005 with six newly opening schools serving 3,555 students. Success in these locations led to requests for additional support as more opened, and by the fall of 2006, CIS of New Orleans was ready to add as many as four more schools.

As of the first semester of the 2006–07 school year, the needs of the young people of New Orleans are still immense. About 27,000 students have returned, with another 100 to 200 reenrolling every week. CIS brings free mental-health and general medical care to students and their families one day per week, using Tulane University School of Medicine's mobile unit. Family Services of Greater New Orleans offers help for students referred for post-traumatic stress and anger management. A variety of tutoring and cultural enrichment programs are starting to cope with the deficits and challenges of the interrupted educational lives of these children.

CIS of New Orleans put more than 500 local and out-of-town volunteers to work, producing 7,200 hours of community service over eight months, in projects such as repainting classrooms and landscaping campuses, one-on-one tutoring and mentoring, and painting murals and planting gardens. In-kind donations of office and school supplies are also matched with the needs of different institutions as they prepare to reopen.

A year following the floods, New Orleans was still a city in crisis, but when I attended a series of meetings and events commemorating the first anniversary of the disaster, I saw many signs of hope, indicating that systemic change for the region's children is now a reality. CIS President Dan Cardinali was with me and recalls speaking with a doctor who serves on the board of directors of a local private school.

"This man had a reputation for charitable giving, for truly caring about the issues confronting New Orleans children and families," Dan said. "He told me that for the past several years, he'd been increasingly frustrated by the sense that his efforts and those of his colleagues, no matter how generous, were simply not making enough of a difference. He said it was the system that had to change, that New Orleans had to get serious about figuring out how to stop kids from failing in school. I urged him to get involved with our CIS initiative, and after we'd talked a little about it, he said it was the first real sign of hope he could remember in a long while. He wanted a way to change the system, and he told me he wasn't the only one—that plenty of local leaders would rally behind this idea."

Another New Orleans leader told me the same thing in a simple and memorable phrase: "We have a fresh canvas to paint on. We want to get it right this time."

I hope and believe that a *new* New Orleans can rise out of the ashes. It's still too early to tell, and I don't want to exaggerate the ability of a single small entity like Communities In Schools to create the many partnerships necessary to meet the needs of all of the city's children and families. It isn't just about schools. A personal, accountable, and coordinated response at *every* level of society is critical for this great city. The principles we've been discussing as a strategy for stopping the dropout epidemic can and do apply to other social institutions. *Everyone* needs community—especially when their former way of life has been shattered beyond repair.

The future of the New Orleans schools will depend on careful planning and management of resources. But it seems to me that the *idea* of that vital third side of the triangle is now in place. I haven't talked to a single local or state leader who didn't acknowledge—indeed, *assume*—that ongoing coordination of community resources into the schools was necessary in order to re-create an educational system that the city can be proud of.

Do we need a catastrophe to focus our attention in this way? Can cities and towns across America really stand still until the next opportunity arises to build a school system from scratch in the wake of tragedy? For the sake of our children, the answer has got to be *no*. Instead, I encourage you to think—and advocate in your community—as if the catastrophe had already happened. *Because it has.* The dropout epidemic is doing more damage, ruining more lives, and costing more money than any natural disaster. With one-third of our young people quitting school without a diploma, the levees aren't holding—we're in the midst of a national emergency.

There's great potential and enormous promise for true systemic change in your community and others across the U.S., but you'll need to begin by acknowledging and helping others see the rising waters that are turning our children into evacuees from the America we've known and loved.

■ ■ ■ ■ ■

CHAPTER EIGHT

Going to Scale— the Evidence Is In

Fourteen teenagers, most of them former dropouts and disciplinary problems, sat in a math class taught by Harold Finkelstein, a Ph.D. from Emory University.

The subject was the addition of positive and negative numbers— an invitation to instant boredom in the enervating heat. But the young teacher, swinging his gaze from the blackboard to the desks, rallied his students with rapid-fire questions. There was the same intense involvement found in the last 30 seconds of a tight basketball game, everyone on the edges of their seats. And there were cheers, groans, and laughter as they caught the excitement of the properties of additive inverses.

"You wouldn't believe that most of these kids were classified as functional illiterates by their schools, would you?" said a member of the staff.[1]

That was how *Washington Post* columnist David S. Broder described the action at one of our Atlanta Street Academies in the 1970s. The excitement—and success—was real. We knew we'd created something important.

By 1974, our EXODUS program was operating in two Atlanta public schools, as well as four Street Academies and the Academy at Saint Luke's Church. We had some key local business leaders on our side; George Johnson and Anne Cox Chambers in particular were tirelessly opening doors for us, holding "friend-raisers" and luncheons, and showing up personally at the schools to see first-hand what we were doing. (Anne, who was head of Cox Communications, made it a real "family thing," introducing her son Jim to us, and both mother and son have continued their support to the present day.)

Largely thanks to Neil Shorthouse and Dave Lewis, the Postal Street Academy cofounder who joined us in starting the program, we felt we had a prototype that could be expanded to new communities and cities—anywhere in America, really, where kids were dropping out. That had always been our dream. We wanted to take this thing to scale, to affect the entire system, not just the young people on the street. Our vision was to help schools work better so that kids didn't drop out in the first place.

For me, there was an element of conflict, too: On the one hand, I loved streetwork and found it very difficult to adjust to the Establishment's ways. But on the other hand, I knew that if I stayed on the streets forever, our exciting, precious new prototype would probably never grow beyond those streets.

So Neil, Dave, and I set our sights on replication. We had no idea what an important—and challenging—principle was at stake. With near-perfect hindsight, I can see now that *replicability is the precondition of any truly transformative action.* If your program can't be adopted by others in new places and new circumstances, it's at best a limited, localized success. And even replicability doesn't guarantee that the program will "go to scale"—that is, provide a means for change that's large enough and powerful enough to meet and overcome a major social problem head-on. **Scalability, sustainability, and *evidence-based strategies* are essential to creating permanent change in the way our education system combats the dropout epidemic.**

Bringing the community "inside the system" . . . creating a model for coordinating services with the school as a "community center" . . . weaving a safety net of "wraparound services" for kids . . . providing "asset-based resources" to keep students in school

. . . these concepts sound familiar now, even obvious, because a lot of people use that language and a great deal of research has demonstrated their validity, but in 1974 it was all new.

When Neil, Dave, and I made the decision to try to take our Atlanta program to other cities, we were regarded by Power and Authority as energetic idealists at best and upstart hippie radicals at worst. We quickly learned the reality of what *Catch-22* means. We went to potential donors and said, "Please fund us to expand our prototype to new communities and prove our theory that the principles can apply in many different circumstances and settings."

And the funders replied, "We've never heard of this approach before. We'll give you money once you've replicated it and shown that it can be done."

We'd tell them: "But we don't *have* any money to replicate—that's the whole problem!"

One foundation head made a memorable remark: "Bill, we're worried that this thing is built on charisma and unusually dedicated people." My short fuse nearly burned all the way down. Charisma, huh? Gee, maybe I should get the Centers for Disease Control to look into this. Is it some kind of virus? What's wrong with passion, caring, and fresh ideas?

"In the '60s," I said to the guy, "I saw that we had a whole country full of 'unusually dedicated people,' and now you're telling me that they're all in one school? They're everywhere, and sometimes all they need is the vision to show them how to act differently and not just try harder. This is *not* about us—any community leader can use these principles."

In today's language, we were *social entrepreneurs,* a phrase invented by the innovative humanitarian Bill Drayton to describe people who "are not content just to give a fish, or teach how to fish. They will not rest until they have revolutionized the fishing industry."[2] This may sound like a fine thing to be, but it turned off a lot of folks precisely because we were so passionate. We still had to find a way to convince potential supporters that our dedication to keeping kids in school was based on principles that, when shared, would evoke similar passions in communities across the country.

I had little patience for requests for research or evidence. Just come see a school, I urged those who asked. You want evidence? Look: These kids are making it, they're getting their diplomas or GEDs, they're not in jail, on drugs, or dead. *There's* your "evidence-based evaluation."

I'm amazed by how much we didn't know—about the expectations of big foundations confronted with a small, experimental program and about the building of community with these potential friends. But we were still driven more by passion than professionalism. For years we'd distrusted the system and bitterly resented attempts to evaluate us.

Equally amazing, though, is what happened next. A combination of God-given opportunity and perseverance on our part took us from the projects to the White House, and it all started when a peanut farmer got himself elected governor of Georgia. . . .

Catching the Dream

President Jimmy Carter was addressing a national Communities In Schools conference in 1998, reflecting back on a hot Atlanta day in 1974. "These two scraggly looking guys came into my office at the governor's mansion," he told the audience, "and I had to turn to my state policeman and say, 'Are these the people who are supposed to help the school system? They look like *they* need help.'"

Okay, I suppose Neil and I were a pretty scraggly pair. We were also desperate and could hardly believe we'd been given this chance to speak with the governor of Georgia to share the dream of replicating our EXODUS program beyond Atlanta.

The meeting came about thanks to Dr. Wayne Smith, a minister who had become interested in our attempts to create a Christian commune and had broken bread with us a number of times. Dr. Smith was also Carter's liaison with several communities in South America as part of a plan to create "sister city" relationships with municipalities in Georgia. After listening to me describe our frustrations with funders, Dr. Smith took pity on me and said he'd get us a meeting with the governor, on two conditions: We'd only stay for 20 minutes, and we wouldn't embarrass him. We were still from the streets, looked it, and acted it. He was worried about how we'd relate to a powerful man who also happened to be his friend.

So Neil and I showed up at the governor's office (not knowing until years later, of course, how dubious Carter was about our initial appearance), and he got right down to it. In the nicest possible way, he looked at us and just asked, "What do you want?"

We answered, "We need resources to replicate what we're doing with kids here in Atlanta." The governor said nothing, but made a gesture that invited us to go on. So we gave him a brief explanation of our commitment to young people and our strategies and goals—what today would be called the "elevator speech."

We could hardly believe our ears when he nodded and said, "All right. Let me see what I can do." By God's grace, we'd managed to intrigue Carter in two ways that were extremely important to him. He could hear the passion we had for poor kids, and he had the same feelings. Moreover, as we later learned, our program appealed to his intellectual side because he could see we'd thought about the principles and had a replicable way to address the dropout problem. That meeting was the beginning of a relationship that has continued to this day, and has included the privilege of knowing most of the Carter family.

Not long after that initial visit, I was presenting at a conference, and one of the other speakers was the late Ruth Stapleton. We hit it off, and she said, "The next time I'm in Atlanta, I'd like to have dinner and hear more about your work." So when she and her husband came to town, they took my wife, Jean, and me out for Chinese food and intense conversation. When the meal was finished, Ruth said, "Let's go back to my brother's place and hang out with them."

Her brother, of course, was Jimmy Carter, and his "place" was the governor's mansion. When we arrived, he was sitting on the couch reading. He remembered me and was friendly but clearly had work to do, so he excused himself to go to his study. But Rosalynn Carter was there, too, and she stayed up half the night talking to us. She really seemed to understand the concept of what we were trying to do.

With Rosalynn's support a major factor, we were soon the grateful recipients of $5,000 from Carter's emergency fund and a letter of endorsement from him that opened the door for us to raise the then-unbelievable sum of $100,000 from Atlanta leaders such as Bert Lance, George Johnson, and Anne Cox Chambers.

Then, in December 1974, I got a call from Phil Alston, a leading Atlanta attorney who had become a member of our fledgling board. He said, "The governor is going to announce for President."

"President of what?" I asked.

Phil explained, and I was excited but, to say the least, skeptical. He asked if I could get some of our folks to come to the press conference at which Carter would make the announcement because the governor believed it was important that some grassroots supporters be there. Neil and I and our families were living communally at the time; I showed up at the press conference wearing sneakers and jeans and looking very grassroots indeed. When it was over, Rosalynn invited me back to the mansion for dinner along with a number of other friends and supporters.

I rode over in a car with Frank Borman, the astronaut, who undoubtedly thought I was the gardener or somebody. It was one of those nights I'll never forget: I was chatting away at the dinner table with Ruth Stapleton, Rosalynn, and Miss Lillian (the governor's ebullient mother). His sons, Chip and Jack, were there, too, and you could tell what a strong, close family they were. Then the 11 o'clock news came on, and we all watched Jimmy Carter say he would be the next President of the United States.

That same night, he told me that he wanted something in writing about our dreams of a national program. I agreed, thinking that if by some amazing chance he got elected President, then *maybe* we'd actually have a shot at achieving those dreams.

Anything but a Plan

And a year later . . . Governor Jimmy Carter was the President-elect. Neil and I just shook our heads in wonder. It's the kind of thing that confirms my belief that our journey was a response to

God's invitation to do good work. We can't take credit for it.

Years after these events, I was interviewed by someone who had a chip on her shoulder for some reason. She kept asking, "Come on, really, how did you invent this thing and get it to be so successful?" What she meant was, how did someone like *you* do it? I told her, "Well, I'm brilliant. In 1974 I figured out that our first-term governor in Georgia was going to be elected President two years later, so Neil and I wrote a strategic plan based on that."

The point is that it wasn't brains or political experience that got us together with a future President. We were simply staying open to possibilities, following our hearts and our faith, and Jimmy Carter, a man of faith himself, could hear our message and it was part of his dream, too. You can call it synchronicity, luck, or humility—anything but a plan.

After Carter won, I got a phone call asking me to come down to his home in Plains, where he was interviewing people for cabinet positions. That was definitely not why he wanted me there! It turned out that he just wanted to ask, at Rosalynn's urging, how he could help. This is when he told us how intrigued he'd been by the ideas and principles we were trying to replicate. They appealed to his intellectual side, his "scientist's mind" (for science and engineering comprised his original training). Everyone knows how big Jimmy Carter's heart is, but he's also one of the smartest people I've ever met. He reads constantly and remembers everything. Mutual friends would meet him and come away telling me, "He knows more about my area of expertise than I do."

Still, there were mixed feelings about suddenly being in Jimmy Carter's world. Part of me had never expected to leave the streets and my one-on-one mission with kids—and that was fine with me, because I loved the work. But Neil and I knew that we had to make our commitment bigger than that. Well, there I was with the next President of the United States. It was hard to believe he wanted to help us, but it was true.

I came to Washington for the inauguration and wound up staying the night at Blair House. Later, I went to the prayer breakfast, and in the middle of it I received a message to call Rosalynn. She told me that she'd decided to make "Project Propinquity" (as we were then calling our national program) her personal cause. That was why *Post* writer David Broder did a long story about us later that year. "Bill Milliken has shaved his beard," the piece began, "but he slides in and out of the Executive Office Building in Washington dressed as casually as he did when his hangout was an abandoned church building in the shadow of Atlanta Stadium." Thank God, the story went on to focus on our work and not on me. It ended: "The combination of faith, fund-raising, and the First Lady is putting Project Propinquity on the move." That was absolutely true.

Jimmy and Rosalynn let me use space in the Old Executive Office Building (OEOB) whenever I was in town. I had a title, too— Advisor on Youth Issues—but no paycheck and no place to stay in D.C. The first time I came up as an "advisor," Rosalynn said in that warm way of hers, "Oh, why don't you just stay with us?" So that night I called my mother in Pittsburgh and said, "Guess where I'm calling from? The Lincoln Bedroom!" I couldn't resist; even at the age of 37, I was still trying to prove that my parents' low expectations of me were wrong.

At the OEOB, I was working on the document the President had requested with help from two friends and colleagues: Landrum Bolling, former president of the Lilly Endowment, and Dean Overman, who'd been part of the Street Academy movement and was now the managing partner of the Washington office of a major law firm. I sent Rosalynn memos on our progress every week just to make sure she didn't forget about us. I needn't have worried. She was a wonderful and dedicated friend, opening so many doors for us in the new administration. Rosalynn told Broder: "I have asked the department heads to see Bill because I think what he's doing is so important. We spend money, money, money on these problems, and so many of the services don't even reach the people who need them."

In May 1977, Rosalynn, Senator Richard Lugar of Indiana, and Bert Lance, our Atlanta supporter (who had become director of the Office of Management and Budget), sponsored and spoke at a breakfast intended to introduce Project Propinquity to the private sector. We had more than 200 businesspeople there, and out of that morning grew some extremely important relationships. Around the same time, Harv Oostdyk and I began to sketch out what a national organization might actually look like. We had the invaluable help of Burt Chamberlin, head trainer for the Postal Street Academies and one of the key players in our fledgling movement.

Together we spent what seemed like endless days on retreats and in planning sessions, trying to figure out how to launch an organization that would stay true to our principles and still be able to affect the dropout problem nationwide. We didn't want to be seen as "just another charity," but as a movement for change. In Atlanta, corporate leaders would say dubiously, "Well, I help a lot of charities . . ." We'd answer, "This isn't a charity; it's an *investment* —in kids and in the future."

At this stage, we needed to create an independent board of directors that would still carry weight with educators. Dr. Crim was on our board in Atlanta—would other superintendents also join us at the national level? How could we build a structure that would last, that could survive changes in administrations and economic climate? And what roles would each of us take? How would we *pay* everyone?

In the end, the consensus was that Neil would continue to refine the Atlanta prototype and I'd head the national office. Burt agreed to be executive vice president. Harv stuck with us until the office was launched, then moved to Dallas to pursue his dream of using these principles to address the way entire neighborhoods coordinate services.

Bob Baldwin at Morgan Stanley came through for us once again, taking on the chairmanship of the national board of directors. Despite also serving as the chairman of Morgan Stanley, Bob always found the time to give back. Without him, there would have been no Communities In Schools. But his involvement wasn't a blank check: He made it clear that while he respected our passion and vision, we had a long way to go in learning how to run a business—caring wasn't enough.

Bob insisted that we become *professionals,* and although it took us some time to accomplish this, I'll always be grateful to him for setting the standard. He also *passed on* these principles: Shortly after he agreed to lead our board, he introduced me to a colleague of his at Morgan Stanley named James M. Allwin. "This young man is interested in your work," Bob told me. Today, Jim Allwin is Bob's successor as chairman—a strong leader, a great friend, and one of the few people I've ever met who can stand tall in Bob's shoes.

But in 1977, all this was far ahead of us. We finished our "white paper," turned it over to Rosalynn and the President, and held our breath. When the answer came, it was better than we could have hoped for: $2.7 million in federal funds to expand our prototype in Atlanta, Indianapolis, and New York City.

Smallness on a Large Scale

One of the first decisions we made was to change our name from Project Propinquity to Cities In Schools. It seemed to capture the essence of what we were advocating: bringing the resources of the city into the schoolhouse to help kids graduate. The "cities" part was a given. We were city boys and felt comfortable in that environment, and we believed that the majority of the youth problem was urban. We watched country people in Georgia coming to the cities, full of hope for the future. Instead, the next generation of kids was "fresh meat," falling into drugs, crime, and unemployment. They were naïve, and they were preyed upon.

As we launched our national movement, the question was: *How will we manage something so big, a multicity effort?* The answer was: We won't. We decided that we'd replicate smallness on a large scale. Every unit would have its own sense of community rather than being run from Washington. Each city would incorporate as a separate, locally owned nonprofit. Our role would be to supply the model, the experience, and—as best we could—the initial funding. But we knew that sooner or later these new programs would have to survive on their own. Their boards needed to be able to raise their own budgets.

It's become a hallmark of the CIS movement and a key to

scalability and sustainability. If local leaders aren't able to take ownership of the problem and the solution, then the effort will ultimately fail.

CIS used decentralization as a key to "going to scale," with each community taking ownership of the problem and the solution.

With the benefit now of 30 years of national replication, I can say that the Communities In Schools model is demonstrably adaptable to just about any location that wants it—urban, suburban, or rural. The key is to retain the *form*—integrated student-support services delivered at the school site—while leaving the *content* flexible, depending on each community's particular strengths and challenges. Like hot wax, we take the shape of whatever place we become part of. It's not as if we're saying: "In order to change the way you deliver services to kids, you have to have Big Brothers Big Sisters, AmeriCorps, and the local university involved." The particular players in each orchestra are up to you—or rather, up to the community—and any effort to create a CIS-like initiative has to start with a really good assessment of local needs and wants. We must scratch where people are itching. We need the input of parents, faith communities, the students themselves, and the helping agencies, not just the school or local-government authorities.

Replicability involves a tension between adaptability to unique community conditions and fidelity to successful, proven models.

Similarly, funding sources can vary enormously. We think that the Champion for Children should be a neutral third party who's paid by a nonprofit board, but beyond this, the relative percentages of funding from public, private, and foundation sources run the gamut in our nearly 200 affiliates. Local CIS executive directors show amazing creativity in finding funders who really do work as partners, because again, we're looking for a change in the way we do business around kids, not just a collection of givers, no matter how generous.

Far too many projects aimed at improving schools are unique— in the worst sense of the word. They may be successful, but they depend on a special set of circumstances that others can't replicate or adapt. Sometimes these situations involve a particularly generous amount of financial support. Sometimes it's a "model program" with many experts focusing their attention on one school. And indeed, the result may be genuine institutional change at that location. But how do you do the same thing elsewhere? How does the change become systemic?

Replicability should be the goal *within* districts, too. If you succeed in bringing a personal, coordinated, and accountable team of adults into one high school, consider how to adapt that same configuration to the elementary and middle schools whose students will go on to attend that high school—and to other high schools as well. Ideally, an unbroken continuum of services should go beyond K through 12 and be available from preschool through graduation—and then continue through the postsecondary years. This "P–16" (preschool to college graduation) movement is reminding us that college students often need the same kinds of integrated services to assist them with their educational goals.

A Justice Issue

We were hoping for—even expecting—eight years of President Jimmy Carter, but it was not to be. After his defeat in 1980, we were left with six half-developed prototypes, limping along. The plan was always to let these sites go once they were strong enough to survive on their own—rather like young people. But without federal funding, it was extremely difficult to keep them alive.

We were considered "Carter's program," even though I tried

to show how CIS was completely independent of political ideology. By now my wife and I, with our children, Sean and Lani, had moved to Washington, and the national CIS office was officially located there. We were committed to finding a base for our work in the nation's capital.

Our big break came when I was introduced to Barbara Bush, wife of the then–vice president. I poured my heart out to her about needing assistance, and she said, "I'd like to help but my particular cause is adult literacy."

"So is ours," I replied.

"But I thought you were a youth program."

"We are—we're trying to keep young people from *becoming* adult illiterates."

I was afraid she'd be offended, but to her credit she just nodded and said, "You're right. Okay, I'll help you."

She connected us with Ed Meese, President Reagan's attorney general, at my request. This was for two reasons: First, we could argue for the impact CIS had on juvenile justice in the communities we served. It was simply another illustration of how dropouts affect *everyone*—the fewer kids on the streets, the less crime. (In fact, we used a very similar argument ten years later when the Clinton administration supported us through HUD: How are you going get any successful urban development if half your city kids are dropping out?) Second, I wanted someone on our side whom *nobody* would expect to support us. That way we couldn't be accused of being Jimmy or Rosalynn Carter's pet program anymore. I'd done my homework on the attorney general, and I knew that in addition to his well-deserved reputation as a hard-core conservative, he cared a lot about kids and was committed to helping them.

He became our champion and succeeded in reinstating our federal funding through the Department of Justice. He knew Bob Baldwin, our board chair, and Bob had him come up and speak at Morgan Stanley. It helped our standing with the business world a lot, and people were really starting to see that this wasn't a Democratic or Republican issue—it was about all of us.

> Being nonpartisan is a precondition for scalability—the future of our children is not a partisan issue.

Under Meese's leadership, we crafted the "Partnership Plan," an arrangement in which four cabinet-level departments—Justice, Health and Human Services, Labor, and Education—all put money into a pot that was used to support CIS. This was an almost unprecedented interagency approach at the time. The cooperation of these four groups made a strong statement about our basic philosophy. All along we'd been saying that the dropout issue was *not* just about education; it affected every segment of society. Its roots were often outside the academic world, and it would require the participation and coordination of resources far beyond the school building.

The Partnership Plan was a vote of confidence in this approach. The federal government was saying, loud and clear: "If your mission is juvenile justice, you have a stake in helping kids graduate. If your mission is health and human services, then keep these young people healthy. If your mission is jobs and a vibrant economy, you've got to stop the dropout epidemic. And we need to work *together* and coordinate our efforts."

Slowly, painfully, the CIS movement grew through the 1980s. Our Partnership Plan funding helped us attract matching private-sector and foundation grants. Barbara Bush's stalwart support continued to help us publicize our work. Had we learned all we needed to know about replication and sustainability? Our prototypes were now in 25 cities and all independent of us, which was exactly what we wanted. Yet this very success created the next challenge in our understanding of how to take CIS to scale: how to turn it into a solution that was truly national in scope and commanded the respect of a wide diversity of partners.

The problem, put simply, was this: Why did local CIS affiliates and prospective CIS communities need *us?* What did the national office bring to the table? I used to fend off that question by saying: "Why do you need a United States? Why not just be the Country of Illinois, the Republic of Florida?" But I knew that was too easy. CIS National really wasn't much like the federal government, which could do things that no state could—such as print money, amend the Constitution, and declare war. So what precisely *were* the things that we as a national organization could uniquely contribute?

The issue came to a head shortly after George H. W. Bush was elected President in 1988. To our astonishment, he'd mentioned Cities In Schools in one of the Presidential debates as an example of what he meant by a "Point of Light." He'd visited one of our school sites at Bob Baldwin's request and remembered us, and out it came when the question about volunteerism was put to him and Democratic candidate Michael Dukakis. Then, less than a month after the election, he videotaped an endorsement for us to use that sounded like something we'd written ourselves. After drawing attention to the gravity of the dropout crisis, he said, "I urge all of you—business leaders, educators, parents, human service providers—to give your support to Cities In Schools, and to find out how you can become involved."

One of our founding board members was Dan Burke, the head of Capital Cities/ABC. Dan was close to the Bushes, and he, too, could see that we were poised to make a big leap—*if* we could take the necessary steps. Early in 1989 he invited me to his office for a talk.

"CIS is starting to take root in more and more states," he pointed out. "New communities are asking for our help. President and Mrs. Bush respect our work. And yet you and Neil still act like nobody wants you, like you're outsiders banging on the door. That's no longer the situation. What's more, you're killing yourselves trying to get this message personally to every community in the country. Do you two ever see your families anymore? How much travel time are you logging every month? Bill, you need to get all this down on paper as a training program so that others can use it. And if you don't, I'm going to leave the board and suggest you get a real job."

Flexibility—with Standards

Dan Burke's caring directness was the right voice at the right time. I realized that he was pushing us to a new understanding of what "replicability" means. With a curriculum and a place to conduct training sessions, we could empower hundreds of others with the CIS concepts. We could say, in effect, "We're not going to control how you implement the ideas. We'll share this set of values and principles, framed around implementation parameters that are very wide, so you can adapt and benefit from them."

Capital Cities/ABC and the Department of Justice provided initial funding for our training curriculum, and Lehigh University in Bethlehem, Pennsylvania, got the contract to develop it. Jim Hill, our vice president of administration at that time, worked tirelessly and creatively on shaping the words and ensuring that a generation of firsthand knowledge was captured in print. Lehigh produced one of the first "hypermedia" curricula in that proto-computer era. It used laser discs, interactive video, a variety of groundbreaking teaching tools.

> Replicability involves training others and letting others take ownership of the results.

The actual training was done at the Iacocca Institute for Competitiveness at Lehigh. Lee Iacocca was on the university board and had just launched this institute to focus on what he saw, correctly, as the imminent danger to America's competitiveness resulting from our failure to educate our young people.

Dan Burke set up a meeting for me with Iacocca, telling me: "Just don't try to 'explain' hypermedia to him, all right?" I had no desire or ability to do that. I just told Iacocca that in my opinion, our efforts to train new CIS practitioners would strengthen his own mission. How can you foster competitiveness if you're losing 30 percent of the kids? After visiting one of our school sites in Atlanta, he agreed to let us affiliate our work with his new institute. And when he learned more about our successes through the 1980s, he gave us a ringing endorsement: "All of us in the business world like a program that gets results. CIS gets results. . . . I am solidly behind it."

The CIS Training Institute rapidly became essential to our expansion. To the question, *What does CIS National offer?* we could now answer, *A flexible, practical training program that equips you with strategies you can take home to your own community and use to begin fighting the dropout epidemic.*

There was another side to this "value-add" as well. In creating our training materials, we inevitably found ourselves emphasizing certain standards, both of program quality and of management, that we believed were necessary for success with kids and schools. It was the flip side of flexibility: Our model was highly adaptable, but it wasn't "whatever you wanted." There were bottom-line practices that we knew had to be embraced.

So here was something else we could offer as a national organization: the criteria that would allow a fledgling local initiative to call itself "CIS." This led directly to our Quality & Standards program, which we developed throughout the '90s and which resulted in "chartered" CIS affiliates (not to be confused with charter schools). These organizations had been peer-reviewed by others in the CIS network and by our own trainers and could be demonstrably shown to adhere to the highest standards of non-profit management.

> Scalability and sustainability require core standards for the national network to follow.

The emphasis on standards also helped us make what was probably a long overdue decision in 1996: to change our name from Cities In Schools to Communities In Schools. We were striving for more uniformity among our local affiliates and that extended to their names. They were getting very creative with what they called themselves, but we could hardly blame a small community in east Texas for not wanting to be "Cities In Schools"!

Increasingly, affiliates in Texas and North Carolina were choosing the name "Communities In Schools" instead. Not only was this more accurate demographically, but we realized that the name captured a whole other level of meaning. Yes, we bring the city—or the community—into the school, but our fundamental mission is to *create* community where before there was none. This is at the heart of our whole approach to integrated, caring delivery of resources. So when it came time to settle on a single name for the national organization and all the state and local affiliates, "Communities In Schools" was the overwhelming choice.

Throughout this period, it was fascinating to watch the interplay between flexibility and core standards. To our surprise, we learned that they weren't truly opposites. Codifying our bottom-line principles actually encouraged innovation because new affiliates had a stronger base to stand on. And once they'd come up with innovations that worked for them, they could communicate them to other affiliates because we all shared the common language of core beliefs and standards. It was like jazz players improvising on well-known tunes: Everyone could hear what you were basing your creativity on.

The goal, always, was replication on a national scale. We didn't care much about the philosophical question *Why does CIS National exist?* for its own sake. We just wanted to be the best, most effective organization we could, the better to spread the CIS movement to as many schools, families, and kids as possible. And this in turn would create a "tipping point," a change in the way communities thought about their schools, whether or not CIS was present. We never imagined our organization in every school district in the country. Our vision—then and now—was to engender a critical mass of successful affiliates that would inspire and instruct others and eventually transform how our nation delivers resources to students and families.

Business expert Jim Collins's book *Good to Great* talks about "inflection points," those moments in a corporation's journey when some key decision is made that spells the difference between middling success and a fantastic upswing in productivity. There's no doubt that the decision to replicate through training was one of those inflection points for CIS, and I think it led directly to a second such moment for us.

As we began to train hundreds, rather than dozens, of people every year, we saw that some of our most cherished, time-tested implementation strategies were going to be questioned and reworked by these talented trainees. And so we didn't try to contain innovation, even at that basic level. We took a deep breath, swallowed hard, and *encouraged* the questioning and creativity. Our ideas had to be malleable enough to work in urban centers such as New York City, Chicago, and Los Angeles, as well as in rural North Carolina, in Appalachia, and in the suburbs of Washington, D.C. That just wasn't going to happen if we beat people up about not doing it "the way Neil and I did it in Atlanta in the good old days."

A direct result of encouraging such an entrepreneurial approach among our local affiliates was a willingness to fall flat and an acceptance of the missteps of others. Failure can lead to greater and deeper learning than success. Bill Gates has often said that he built Microsoft by fostering a culture in which it was *expected* that everyone would risk, fail, and risk again.

> Replicability demands risk and a tolerance for failure, whereas scalability calls for innovation and refinement.

Being okay with failure wasn't something new for me personally. I couldn't count the number of mistakes and losses that marked my journey since 1960. But there was a key difference at this point. In the beginning, our defeats often resulted from a lack of understanding of key principles—the very ones we had to learn, codify, and eventually share with others, such as the Five Basics or the idea of personalism, accountability, and coordination. We were like musicians who didn't know our scales.

But by the '90s, we had those scales down cold and could teach them to others. We'd still permit and even encourage failure, but within a context of excellent musicianship, so the improvisations were more intelligent and even the errors provided information. You can see that this is directly tied to that yin-yang relationship of flexibility and core standards.

Managing from Washington

One of our most informative failures helped us clarify even more precisely just what a national-level organization like CIS can and can't do for its local network. Throughout the '90s, we'd routinely accept funding from corporations that had a specific agenda relating to kids, families, or schools. In effect, we'd act as a contractor for them, and if we didn't know quite how to do what they wanted, we assumed that we'd figure it out as we went along. But it turned out that the uniformity of results that these businesses expected wasn't something we could always deliver.

A classic example of this misguided approach was our three-year partnership with a major retailer. Its CEO sat on our board, and his support was generous and consistent. When he suggested that we talk to his corporation's charitable foundation, we were happy to do it. They had ten markets they wanted us to work in, and we agreed to regrant their dollars to our local affiliates in those areas. The plan was to encourage the retailer's employees to volunteer at CIS school sites. While the foundation let us set the indicators of "success" for the kids involved, they wanted these benchmarks to be uniform. They intended to grant the same amount of money to each of the ten affiliates and expected the same results in all locations.

There were so many reasons why this couldn't have worked. Most important, none of the ten affiliates had even *asked* for the partnership with the retailer, which went against the core principle we'd taught them of responding to community needs from the bottom up, not by bringing in programs from outside. In addition, we had no business trying to manage the work of the local affiliates, but that was exactly the position we found ourselves in since we were responsible for the results of the grant money.

So we learned that we would never again direct a local series of initiatives out of the national office. With 25 affiliates, we might have a shot at doing that effectively, but not with 200. If this same retailer (which, by the way, was extremely understanding and forgiving about our failures) asked us for a partnership today, we'd say, "We have a strategic plan that emphasizes a few clear goals. These are achievable because they're based on the things we do well. If you can suggest a partnership that fits, there are a lot of options for working together. But if not, it's better for all concerned that we part ways."

We're still willing to regrant money to local or state CIS affiliates because many corporations are simply not set up to manage 15 or 20 small grants themselves; they want to deal with one larger organization. But we won't do it just to subsidize the grantor's particular programmatic ideas. They have to be interested in supporting our core business, as well as the particular goals of the grantee in question. By agreeing to administer their resources in subgrants to local affiliates, we're making a pledge that those gifts will be used effectively and will show measurable results. We're offering our guarantee that an investment through the national office will be used in a high-quality way by a high-quality network.

The State Strategy

Another key inflection point that occurred in the 1990s made a huge difference in our ability to replicate and sustain the CIS movement. We decided to emphasize independent, state-level CIS affiliates as the most efficient way to grow and institutionalize our work, rather than using a regional structure staffed by employees of CIS National. Our original idea had been to manage replication from five regional offices. But we discovered that whatever benefit this structure might confer in terms of national leadership was more than offset by the "top-down" headaches involved and, ultimately, by the simple fact that Georgians should replicate in Georgia and Floridians in Florida.

Our first state office, which was in Texas, had been successful from its start in the mid-1980s, thanks to our original state director, Jill Binder, and the support of Democratic Governor Mark White and first lady Linda Gale White. This was a case where public-sector support led to a degree of institutionalization that in turn spurred rapid growth of CIS within Texas. CIS wasn't quite part of the state education department, but most of its funding came from the state legislature and there was no question that CIS of Texas was able to operate effectively and independently from the national office.

Around the same time, Neil convinced John Clendenin, chairman of BellSouth, to approve funding for statewide CIS operations in Georgia, North Carolina, South Carolina, and Florida. John was also chair of the U.S. Chamber of Commerce and a conservative southern Republican, and he saw the value of replicating and sustaining CIS at the state level. Thanks to the superb leadership of the four state directors—Neil Shorthouse in Georgia, Linda Harrill in North Carolina, Martha Gale in South Carolina, and Lois Gracey in Florida—the investment quickly paid off.

The success of the "state strategy," as we came to call it, rested on several factors. First, it placed ownership and control of the dropout issue where it belonged: not with us in Washington, but with the state decision makers directly affected by the performance of their young people. Second, it encouraged information sharing and networking among communities that operated in the same educational environment, especially in terms of funding and academic standards. And third, state CIS directors found that they could become important players in the education policies being developed by state legislatures and boards of education.

> State-level organizations are the most effective way for networks like CIS to go to scale, and they sustain the most successful local affiliates.

All these factors led to a strong surge both in numbers of new CIS communities within the states with CIS offices and in the success rates of the local affiliates. It wasn't until 2004, however, that we received the final validation of the state strategy.

Our national board of directors had come to realize that the organization needed a refocusing of its basic strategies if the CIS movement was truly to go to scale. They approached the prestigious Bridgespan Group, which agreed to study CIS and help us craft a new strategic plan. One of their strongest recommendations was that we support the state strategy almost exclusively. They urged us to stop local replication in states without state-level CIS offices, no matter how interested the community might be in receiving our help.

Bridgespan was responding to our continuing desire to go to scale, to make a measurable national impact on the dropout epidemic. Essentially, they said, "You want to reach a half million more kids every year? You can launch three more state affiliates that operate as well as North Carolina, Georgia, and Texas . . . or you can start 87 new local affiliates." Put that way, it was no decision at all. However, Bridgespan agreed that certain cities were simply too important—and too devastated by the dropout epidemic—to overlook, whether or not they were located in a "CIS state." So at this writing, we're actively supporting and growing the affiliates in New York City; Chicago; Los Angeles; Las Vegas; and Washington, D.C., even though we don't have state offices to oversee them. We also provide special support for CIS of New Orleans in the wake of the 2005 hurricanes' devastating impact. No one could have anticipated what happened there, and a strategic plan has to be flexible enough to respond to such a tragedy.

Profitable Nonprofits

Nonprofits in America provide a way for citizens to mobilize to address social problems that the government can't or won't work on effectively. This blunt truth may in part explain why it's so difficult to sustain a national nonprofit network.

Since the 1970s, when there were around 300,000 nonprofits in the U.S., about 170 nonprofit networks have broken through to the $50-million-or-more network-wide budget level—a pretty good benchmark of national sustainability. Today the total number of nonprofits has soared to about 1.8 million. CIS remains one of the very small group that has hit the $50 million mark (actually, about $223 million as of the 2005–06 academic year).

Looking back on our story, I think it's clear that we had a great vision and many good ideas going in. And without false modesty, I can say that Dave Lewis, Neil Shorthouse, and I—along with Harv Oostdyk, Burt Chamberlin, Jim Hill, and so many other early leaders of the CIS movement—worked our tails off to keep the dream alive for children who had no hope and no future. But by themselves, good ideas and dedication to kids wouldn't have done it. We had to become a *replicable, effective, sustainable* process that communities across the country could adapt as their own.

To summarize what we learned:

- CIS used decentralization as a key to "going to scale," with each community taking ownership of the problem and the solution.

- Replicability involves a tension between adaptability to unique community conditions and fidelity to successful, proven models.

- Being nonpartisan is a precondition for scalability— the future of our children is not a partisan issue.

- Replicability involves training others and letting others take ownership of the results.

- Scalability and sustainability require core standards for the national network to follow.

- Replicability demands risk and a tolerance for failure, whereas scalability calls for innovation and refinement.

- State-level organizations are the most effective way for networks like CIS to go to scale, and they sustain the most successful local affiliates.

I think these lessons apply well to the nonprofit world in general. There's no question that they made the difference for us. They were the result of the collective intelligence of many, many CIS practitioners. This isn't the same thing as consensus, which tends to water down principles and strategies. Rather, it allows a high level of risk and disagreement.

Ultimately, we just have to stay open to the right combination of elements coalescing at the right time. Dan Cardinali, for instance, has been a catalytic agent for CIS ever since his arrival, and we're incredibly fortunate to have an individual of his caliber at the helm. So the combination of circumstances and personal traits—collective intelligence, right leadership, a tolerance for risk, the ability to learn from success and failure, and trust in God and each other—creates an almost magical alchemy. If one element is missing, nothing works.

But Does It Work?

I want to end this chapter by discussing one of the most vexing yet essential aspects of fighting the dropout epidemic. Scalability and sustainability are two of the vital ingredients necessary for creating a permanent change in the way our education system combats the epidemic. The third is a reliance on *evidence-based strategies*.

As I've said, my colleagues and I came from a street culture that had little patience with the rigors of formal evaluations. We could see with our own eyes that young lives were being turned around, and that was all the proof we needed. Many of the original Street Academies were funded by corporations that regarded their dollars as "investment money." They basically said, "We don't understand how you do it, but we love what you do, so just go to it!"

I'm sure that my personal experiences with "standards" back

in high school also contributed to our dislike of being evaluated. I was one of those kids who was set up to fail by the school system—not out of any malice on the part of teachers, but because I learned differently and never did well on tests. So I had a strong negative reaction to the idea that objective, measurable standards could ever really capture the worth of something I cared about. Whether I realized it clearly or not, my own self-worth was tied up in the issue.

That attitude is unacceptable today, and rightly so, for an organization that claims to be going to scale on combating the dropout epidemic. Corporations, foundations, and government leaders at all levels want to know that their funding dollars are being well spent and that nonprofits like CIS are truly making a measurable difference. When it comes to dropout rates, I can't imagine a more difficult area in which to demonstrate success.

To begin with, everyone counts dropouts differently. Up until quite recently, most people accepted a severely underreported dropout rate, often couched in terms of an "event rate"—that is, the percentage of high schoolers (defined as 10th through 12th graders) who leave school every year. That's one of several measures used by the U.S. Department of Education, along with many states. By that measure, the dropout rate is around 4.7 percent overall, and between 6 and 10 percent for poor and minority students.[3]

But when John Bridgeland and his colleagues completed *The Silent Epidemic* for the Gates Foundation, they used a different way of counting: the "cohort rate." This measures the number of ninth graders who don't graduate with their class four years later. By the study's estimate, this number is around 30 percent.

I believe that the cohort rate provides a much clearer picture of the gravity of the dropout crisis, since it begins with a ninth-grade class. If you limit your percentage to 10th through 12th graders, you ignore the fact that millions of students *already* dropped out. In fact, ninth graders form a significant portion of the total number of dropouts.

Now, the sad truth is that we've seen little political will to achieve clarity on this issue. States vary in how they count, superintendents within states vary in what they measure, and a lot of the variance is self-protective. No one wants the political black eye of a "dropout problem" in his or her community, so there's not much interest in highlighting what's going on. In short, political institutions obfuscate the issue in complex ways.

Communities In Schools is independent of the school system, so we have the freedom to say loudly that there *is* a problem. And thanks to *The Silent Epidemic* and many other excellent media reports ranging from *Time* magazine to the Oprah Winfrey show, Americans are gradually achieving a consensus that the problem is grave. In my opinion, the dropout crisis has been this bad for many years—it's just that the self-protective cover-up is finally unraveling.

However, the very structures that have obfuscated the problem also inhibit our ability to clearly show our effectiveness. We have to rely on different and highly politicized systems in each state and school district to count and validate student success. But the systems weren't designed to show effectiveness; they were set up *not* to show *in*effectiveness, and the positive gets covered up along with the negative. They not only cloud the bad news, they conceal the potential solutions. Student ID numbers, for example, would allow CIS to follow its highly mobile kids from school to school and thus rate its own effectiveness much more clearly. Without a uniform way to track them, we can't confirm whether they're still in school; even more important, we can't ensure continued support and services to these children.

So—to our frustration—we don't have a cohort rate we can use to compare with the estimated 30 percent national cohort rate. We use our own calculation, which most closely approximates the event rate. Even against that most conservative of estimates, our 3.5 percent dropout rate—half the 6 to10 percent national event rate for poor and minority students—is remarkable. The kids we serve are almost exclusively those young people who, without intervention, would likely fall far below the national averages for student success. So keeping 96.5 percent of such a group in school is strong evidence indeed of the effectiveness of our strategies.

We believe that we could show an even greater impact if we could use the public system to produce a cohort rate that included the vulnerable ninth grade. We support the National Governors Association's call for a uniform way of calculating each state's graduation rate, and we're confident that it would add even more credence to our strategies.

For now, though, there's still plenty of evidence to rely upon. The Five Basics, for instance, are recognized today as an early, prescient example of an "asset-based model": If you provide kids with these assets, they will do better in school. A wealth of research is available to validate this approach (see Appendix 4).

Asset-based strategies were the focus of great attention in the 1990s, as were prevention-based models—which it turned out we had also been doing all along. Some kids are in such deep trouble that the immediate goal is to keep them from getting worse. Most CIS affiliates offer access to services and resources for the entire school—broadly, the Five Basics—while also providing targeted, case-managed services to a smaller, more at-risk group. This work tends to be preventive—interventions that can turn around a potential drug addict or criminal, for instance.

Our local affiliates submit end-of-year reports on student outcomes in areas such as attendance, behavior issues, promotion, and academic achievement. These are self-reported data, but we hold the affiliates to the highest standards of such accounting. At this writing, we have data from the 2005–06 academic year, and the numbers are remarkable:

- 80 percent of students tracked for poor attendance improved their attendance.

- 88 percent tracked for behavior problems had fewer behavior incidents.

- 80 percent tracked for suspensions had fewer suspensions.

- 82 percent tracked for academics showed improvement in academic achievement.

- 83 percent were promoted to the next grade.

- 81 percent of eligible seniors graduated.

- 96.5 percent remained in school.[4]

We also have a lot of data about the cost-effectiveness of this approach. Here's the statistic that says it all: The average cost per student to connect him or her with the needed resources and services is $182 a year. That's what I call a bargain.

I want to emphasize once again that the majority of these young people bring enormous problems and needs to school with them. They've already been stigmatized and abandoned by many in our society. Not to put too fine a point on it, these kids are *supposed* to drop out. The percentages above are nothing short of astonishing for this group, but we're committed to doing even better.

In the midst of this rather dry discussion of rates and percentages, let's pause to remember what's at stake. These children aren't statistics. Consider, deeply, the words I used in the previous paragraph: *stigmatized and abandoned . . . kids who are supposed to drop out . . . enormous problems and needs.* We're talking about a tremendous human toll, a legacy of deprivation and hopelessness being visited on the most innocent members of our society. If you can't feel heartbroken and outraged about this, you're probably reading the wrong book.

So when we seek evidence about practices that help these children succeed in school and in life, it's not just a matter of pleasing funders or adhering to sociologists' standards of what counts as "evidence-based strategies." We have a *moral* obligation to collect the very best proof—a point I didn't always understand but now believe passionately. We can't give ourselves any slack. If something works, it's our duty to demonstrate it objectively and share the news as widely as possible. And if something *doesn't* work, or doesn't do the job well enough, we have to stop doing it. Our children are too precious for anything less.

Changing the Climate

Looking past the percentages for a moment, we can also say that CIS, through its interventions, is aiming to change a school's entire climate—admittedly a difficult thing to measure but a reality nonetheless. We believe that when a team of caring adults is creating community in a school, the institution becomes a safer place, both physically and emotionally. When the most pressing needs of the hardest-hit students are being addressed, everyone breathes easier. Teachers can devote more time to teaching, discipline is no longer a daily crisis for administrators, and families reconnect with the school, seeing it as a place where other adults believe in their children too. These "climate changes" will be reflected in the hard numbers—but also in a growing sense of optimism and empowerment.

There's still one piece of the evidence puzzle missing, and as I write this we're in the process of adding it. We can show the *correlation* of CIS-provided services with improved student outcomes and overall better school climate. What we're now studying is whether CIS *caused* this.

Thirty years ago, I would have laughed at such a distinction, or maybe lost my temper. Of *course* CIS made the difference—what else could it have been? Today, I'm a little older and wiser, and I see the importance of this point. To really nail down our effectiveness, we have to show that CIS was the deciding factor, the catalyst for change, not just a wheel turned by some other, more important wheel in the school system.

To this end, the Atlantic Philanthropies has funded us to do an independent, research-based, three-year evaluation of our network aimed at demonstrating exactly what role CIS plays in student achievement. The study will pay particular attention to the impact of integrated school-based services as a strategy. Strangely enough, there isn't yet much literature available on this key point. Our project will look at the effect of multiple services targeted to specific student needs.

So when we claim that our strategies and principles are evidence based, we know that decision makers can rely on that statement.

But what about programmatic tactics? Are there, for instance, better and worse ways of providing the Five Basics? Shouldn't we be able to offer communities some guidance on content, too, not just process?

In partnership with the National Dropout Prevention Center at Clemson University, we've identified risk factors in elementary, middle, and high school that may lead to dropping out. We've then gone on to examine programs that are successful in mitigating those factors. Then we analyzed what the best programs have in common and extracted the "critical elements." Now we can say to a local community, "If you want to create or 'broker in' a mentoring program or a family engagement program, make sure to incorporate these six elements and you'll have a much greater chance of success."

Throughout much of our history, we stood firm on the Basics. They formed our only criteria for partnership (remember that national retailer?) and our message to communities across the nation: Provide the Five Basics and you're doing good, as long as they're part of a personal, accountable, and coordinated effort on behalf of kids and families.

But as Wichita CIS's Judy Frick asked in a more positive context: "What doesn't fit the Basics?" They're like world peace: Of course everyone agrees they're good, but they're also extremely broad. We had to make a decision that merely "fitting the Five Basics" could no longer be a criterion for endorsement by us. We now won't settle for just *any* caring adult, *any* tutoring or skill-building program. If it really works for kids, there has to be evidence for it.

■ ■ ■

Today, Communities In Schools reaches 1.2 million young people annually in 27 states and the District of Columbia, along with a quarter million of their family members.

That's not nearly enough.

As an organization, we can't possibly expect to stop the dropout epidemic alone. I've written so much about the scalability, sustainability, and evidence-based approach of CIS for one reason—*to convince you to take these principles and make them your own in your community.* I want you to agree that this approach not only makes sense, it also *works* and is capable of creating a lasting impact on the education system. You don't have to call it Communities In Schools as long as you're committed to the principles.

In the final chapter, we'll consider what the thorough adoption of these ideas would really mean and how you can help us get even closer to that day when we see the last dropout.

■ ■ ■ ■ ■

CHAPTER NINE

From Awareness to Advocacy to Action— *Stop the Epidemic!*

The state of Georgia has benefited from Neil Shorthouse's leadership for more than 30 years, and it shows. The state CIS program, which Neil has headed since 1989, is one of the strongest in the nation, with 54 local affiliates reaching more than 100,000 children and their families every year.

Georgia is also a prime example of how integrated school-based services for students are being institutionalized in a way that's going to *stop the dropout epidemic* in that state. I realize this is a bold claim, but here's why I believe it.

A Graduation Coach in Every School

Georgia Governor Sonny Perdue has made his position on the dropout epidemic clear: He calls it a *moral* issue, and he's determined to turn around the 29 percent noncompletion rate of Georgia's students. (This, by the way, is the official number; many in the state, including Neil, believe the rate to be higher.)

Over the years, Communities In Schools of Georgia has received regular funding from the governor's office and the state department of education. In 2005, the state legislature's House Appropriations Committee called for an audit of CIS's effectiveness to determine if the state dollars were being well spent. The audit revealed three key findings:

1. CIS attracts $24 in funding and services for every dollar of state funding. In other words, a school system using the CIS methods is benefiting from an extraordinary leveraging effect.

2. By the most conservative measures, the students who graduate as a result of CIS's intervention generate twice as much revenue for the state, in terms of income tax dollars, than the cost of supporting CIS of Georgia.

3. The graduation rate of students in school districts with a CIS presence was consistently higher than the state average.

Based on these results, Governor Perdue and State School Superintendent Kathy Cox turned to CIS as their partner in a new statewide initiative to combat the dropout epidemic. They contracted with CIS to develop the Georgia High School Graduation Coach Program. It's a critical step in the journey to *change* the way our communities organize services around the schools.

As Neil explains it, the governor's Graduation Coach Program is a 21st-century adaptation of one of the oldest CIS principles: personal, one-on-one relationships with struggling students. A "graduation coach" has been placed in every high school in the state of Georgia. This person's first responsibility is to literally *know the name* of every student who may be at risk of leaving school. "If you don't even know a person's name, how can you have a relationship?" asks Neil. Then the coach will develop a support system for each teen based upon the unique reasons that led the young person to enter the "dropout pipeline."

Perhaps Henry Jones failed the high school graduation test and is ready to give up—he thinks he's dumb. Perhaps Mary Williams is missing so many credits as a result of being a mother at 17 that she can't even picture graduation. Maybe Oscar White is absent more than present because his family needs him to help earn money. . . . By now you know that the reasons kids quit school are many and varied. There's no single solution. It's the graduation coach's job to discover the *particular* answers that will work for Henry, Mary, and Oscar.

The next step, of course, involves the community. No coach, however many hours he or she puts in, can turn around the futures of the dozens, perhaps hundreds, of struggling students at a particular high school. "The community has to own responsibility for these kids and multiply the effectiveness of the graduation coach," Neil explains. "Faith communities, business communities, social service agencies, United Ways, police departments, housing authorities—anybody who can take the time to invest in a kid's future or whose mission is to do precisely that will be asked to partner with the graduation coach on behalf of students' identified needs."

> THE COACH'S FIRST RESPONSIBILITY IS TO LITERALLY *KNOW THE NAME* OF EVERY STUDENT WHO MAY BE AT RISK OF LEAVING SCHOOL.

The governor's office and the state department of education are providing some, but not all, of the necessary financial resources. Georgia's private sector needs to support the Graduation Coach Program, too. Georgia Power has contributed funds, and Neil believes that the ultimate success of the initiative will be greatly strengthened if the community literally buys in to the program. This of course reflects our years of experience in CIS, where we've learned that public/private partnerships are by far the most effective and reliable vehicle to weave a stable safety net for kids.

As an example of how this is coming about, Kerry Campbell of Georgia Power, board chair of CIS of Georgia, is now developing a "Community Coach" program to supplement the governor's initiative. The vision is to match a community coach with each graduation coach to help identify and coordinate the necessary local support for students and families.

So the Graduation Coach Program employs strategies that Communities In Schools has used for the past 30 years. Indeed, in the Georgia school districts that already have a CIS affiliate, the graduation coach works with that organization. A successful CIS affiliate already offers what amounts to a portfolio of resources, programs, and strategies to choose from, all aimed at keeping kids in school. CIS helps mold the system around the child rather than forcing the child to fit into the system. We meet kids where they are. The goal is always the same—every student must graduate prepared for life.

But there's one crucial difference: The Graduation Coach Program *institutionalizes* the changes that CIS has long advocated. I can't emphasize strongly enough how important this is. If change, not just charity, is what's needed to stop the dropout epidemic, here's an example of how to do it. A graduation coach makes this portfolio approach part of the school's day-to-day practices, regardless of whether it's an official CIS site or not. He or she is like a gatekeeper or entryway into the portfolio.

Imagine . . . not too many years from now, this individual will simply be part of any successful high school's team. Nobody will point in amazement and say, "Wow! That school really cares about its students—look, they have a *graduation coach.*" When parents come to Back-to-School Night, they'll meet teachers, administrators, guidance counselors, the school nurse, the student teachers— and the graduation coach. No surprise, no big deal. *Of course* this school has such a person—doesn't every school?

It's an inspiring picture. But we can't forget that the success of any graduation coach depends on whether the community portfolio of resources is diverse and responsive enough to meet the unique challenges that each student presents—whether, to use our earlier image, the third side of the triangle is robust enough. Here, too, Georgia is taking the lead in providing a strong array of options for the future graduation coaches to choose from. One of these options in particular also involves the talents of the Georgia CIS team, including one of CIS's oldest friends, Reginald Beaty.

Performance Learning Centers®:
Street Academies for the New Century

Reginald Beaty is waging a new campaign these days.

You remember Reggie: In Chapter 1, we followed his story from the rough streets of Atlanta to his graduation from one of the first of the city's Street Academies. This much-decorated Army officer retired from military service in 2000 after being honored as the nation's best ROTC instructor and receiving Oklahoma's "Man of the Year" award.

What next? Fortunately for the children of Georgia, Reggie Beaty decided to rejoin his old colleagues and mentors at the state Communities In Schools office. Almost immediately, he was handed one of the toughest challenges of his life.

Neil Shorthouse's "magic eyes" had meant so much to all of us as we struggled to launch what would become the CIS movement in Atlanta. Those remarkable eyes were now focused on a new vision—or perhaps I should say a new way of implementing one of the oldest and best-tested approaches to keeping kids in school: the original Street Academy.

Neil's idea was to prepare a plan for creating academies for the 21st century. They'd be called Performance Learning Centers® (PLCs), and they'd function much as the original Street Academies did. Our former CIS state director in Pennsylvania, Mort Stanfield, had done the original prototype; and he passed it on to Neil to develop based on Neil's long experience with alternative education sites.

Housed in freestanding facilities, the PLCs would target high school students at serious risk of dropping out. Services, both academic and social, would be matched with student needs. The big difference between these institutions and the Academies of the 1970s, however, was that PLCs would from the outset be fully supported initiatives of the public school system.

Reggie Beaty was given the task of figuring out how to get this done. "The concept goes back to our roots, obviously," he says. "It's the holistic approach, making a marriage that addresses the academic and social barriers that cause kids to be unsuccessful."

It took Reggie and his colleagues more than a year to research and develop the PLC plan. He traveled around the state, visiting the school districts with CIS affiliates to find the best candidates for homes for two pilot PLC sites. Finally, 23 superintendents were invited to a meeting to "bid" on the sites. Lowndes County was chosen for one site. The second involved a conversion of one of the oldest Street Academy sites in Atlanta, the West End Academy.

"We concentrated on creating an environment where I'd want to send my own kids," Reggie remembers. "We made it modern and business-oriented."

The curriculum is just as rigorous as a regular high school program. "The kids we selected for the first PLCs were unsuccessful in a traditional academic setting for a variety of reasons. We were determined that they would and could meet the same standards as any other student—same credits, same tests."

The academic goal is mastery of the curriculum at a pace geared to each student's abilities. Nonacademic goals are also individualized: Teen mothers receive the services they need, youth on probation are helped through the intricacies of the juvenile justice system, students who lack family support are matched with mentors who can help set educational and career goals. Each PLC, in addition to using teachers "outstationed" from the public school system, has a service coordinator whose role of brokering in community resources is similar to the coordinator at traditional schools with a CIS presence. The result is an extremely tight safety net woven around these young people.

In the fall of 2002, 75 students in grades 9 through 12 were enrolled in each of the first two PLCs. Graduation from high school was a must, of course, but Reggie's purpose went further: His strategy called for an "individual development plan" for each student that would help create personal, academic, and career goals.

He says, "Making all A's was *not* the point. That was a means to an end. We needed them to own the importance of building a future for themselves. Excelling in classes was the gate; then they needed to focus on goals beyond high school."

Raising expectations and doing everything needed to help meet them are two different things, as Reggie and his CIS colleagues discovered. The two pilot sites did extremely well at helping their students graduate, but the former Army officer wasn't satisfied with either the quality of their education or their ability to go on to meaningful careers. So as other communities began asking to be part of the initiative, improvements in the range of academic options were built in, along with summer training courses for PLC teachers.

"We became more deliberate, more methodical, about preparing students for college work. We put it out there as the norm, the expectation. Most of our students didn't grow up in a 'college-bound atmosphere,' you might say," Reggie explains.

Some students, he discovered, just weren't suited for the new schools: "It wasn't realistic to expect a 17-year-old who reads at the fourth grade level to do well in our kind of environment. That was a bridge too far. He or she clearly needed remedial help before applying to enroll at the PLC. Love, eagerness, motivation—they weren't the only requirements for admission." Students who weren't ready for the program were referred to local CIS affiliates for one-on-one help with their academic and social challenges.

In its second year, the PLC initiative added six more sites in other Georgia communities. The network grew to 15, then to 22, then to 27 . . . and in 2006 added its first out-of-state PLC in Charlotte, North Carolina. At this writing, more than 1,200 students have earned Georgia diplomas through the program—young people who, given their track record of poor success in traditional schools, were almost certainly fated to drop out.

This is a great achievement in itself—Neil calls Reggie Beaty "an organizational wizard"—but it's also a striking example of how systemic change can happen in a relatively short time. The Performance Learning Centers are now the only statewide drop-out-prevention initiative to be made part of Georgia's official education strategy. The state board of education and legislature have approved funding and other support and have asked Neil and Reggie to continue to expand the network into school systems that until now haven't had a CIS presence. This work is being greatly aided by a major grant from the Bill & Melinda Gates Foundation, which also calls for replicating the PLCs in four additional states:

Pennsylvania, Washington, Virginia, and North Carolina.

Coordinated delivery of services to keep kids in school and graduate prepared for life is now becoming *institutionalized* in Georgia, and the means to reach some of the most challenged students—the Performance Learning Centers—is also part of the overall governmental strategy. The ideas I've been discussing throughout this book are slowly becoming the *rule,* not the exception, in how one state responds to the dropout epidemic. As Reggie says, "When the Gates Foundation gives you a seven-figure grant, people look at you and say, 'This must be working. This must be worth our time to investigate.'"

Moving Outward

Georgia isn't the only state where this is occurring. Texas, site of our first state program, has been pioneering this direction for years. The CIS network there is funded through the state legislature, and its work is aligned with the Texas Department of Education's strategy. As we saw in Chapter 4, state and local government turned to CIS to help children and families displaced by the 2005 Gulf Coast hurricanes. The point isn't that CIS as such has become institutionalized in Texas, but rather the larger significance of what this *means:* A state is committing funds to a non-profit network because that network can rally the community to help keep kids in school and on track for graduation.

Communities In Schools is certainly not the only vehicle for bringing about this change. Under the leadership of Chancellor Joel I. Klein, New York City's Department of Education launched its Office of Multiple Pathways to Graduation in September 2005. Klein, a Clinton administration veteran, has set the office's goal to significantly increase the graduation rates and college readiness of overage and under-credited high school students. It supports the development of new and enhanced schools and programs designed specifically for older students who may be truant or thinking about dropping out or are looking for another educational option. I must say, it's nice to see that the spirit of the New

York Street Academies is alive and well—but better still, it's thriving as part of the *official school strategy to combat dropouts.*

Chancellor Klein has also spearheaded the Office of Youth Development. Teams from this agency work to find specific, customized solutions for the challenges to graduation that New York City kids face. Areas of support include guidance and counseling, crisis intervention, school-based health services, help for students living in temporary housing, substance abuse and violence prevention and intervention, college planning, and youth-leadership opportunities.

The city's success in combating the dropout epidemic through this approach was highlighted by *Time* magazine in its May 3, 2007, issue. Staff writer Claudia Wallis focused on "some 13,000 students who dropped out or were on the verge of doing so but have been recovered in the public school system. The city's secret? Finding out who was dropping out and why and offering a variety of paths—complete with intensive social support and personalized instruction—back to school." Wallis describes how at-risk youth are connected with "a community-based organization that focuses on the social, emotional and family issues that tend to weigh down these students." After all, as Chancellor Klein explains, "We [educators] don't have the expertise for these complex challenges." A principal of a Brooklyn high school declares that, now that the community resources are in place, "Teachers can focus on the best way to educate students. That's huge!"[1] It is indeed. It's also—almost word-for-word—a restatement of the principles we've been examining throughout this book.

The Office of Youth Development has certain principles that underlie its work. Here's how it describes its mission:

> [T]o provide all students with a system of supports that prepares them for a successful adolescence and adulthood. . . . When students attend schools in which they are understood and cared for, school staff are able to respond effectively to the full range of administrative, environmental, pedagogical and social issues that may arise. Teachers, administrators, counselors and support staff in effective schools understand how the community, age

and grade levels, economic status, and culture affect the student populations they serve. They have the appropriate training to respond to student needs, have a working knowledge of applicable policies and procedures, and have access to service providers to meet the needs of students and enhance the teaching and learning process.[2]

Notice those key phrases: *a system of supports . . . schools in which they are understood and cared for . . . the full range of issues that may arise . . . access to service providers to meet the needs of students and enhance the teaching and learning process . . .* This is substantially the same vision that a Republican governor wants to implement in Georgia, and once again it's an example of the principles I've tried to illustrate in this book. New York City's schools are joining the growing chorus of voices speaking out for the *absolute necessity of the third side of triangle: community involvement to meet the non-academic needs of students at risk of leaving school.*

Stop the Epidemic!

The day when all school systems routinely connect community services for students who need them as an ordinary part of their commitment to educate *all* children will be the day we glimpse the last dropout.

It can be done—it *is* being done. And now is the time to start getting it done in *your* community. **Our children need three things from you: your *awareness*, your *advocacy*, and your *action*.**

The most important thing to be *aware* of is exactly how serious the dropout epidemic is. We're losing somewhere between one-quarter and one-third of our young people every year. The fiscal and human consequences are huge. The epidemic is costing our society billions of dollars in lost economic productivity. It's catastrophic for the workforce, and it's dooming millions of young adults to lives with little hope for a future.

What's the dropout rate in your local school system? In your state? Answering these questions can be tricky since, as we discussed in the previous chapter, there's wide variance both in method and in integrity when it comes to counting these kids. The U.S. Department of Education's official publication that contains state-by-state figures, "Dropout Rates in the United States: 2004," is available online at **http://nces.ed.gov**. Another excellent source of statistics is the Stand Up Website, **www.standup.org**, which offers a wealth of state-by-state information on students' educational progress. An inquiry to your local school board or superintendent of schools should also produce a helpful response—and if it doesn't, that, too, will be informative. It's particularly important to ask questions about poor and minority student success. The dropout epidemic is a *justice* issue, in large part because the least advantaged young people in our society are bearing the brunt of our systems' failures.

What steps are schools taking to respond? As you become aware of the facts that reflect the extent of the dropout epidemic in your community and state, find out what resources and strategies are already in place to stem the flow of students leaving the classroom. It's a most unusual school system that isn't doing *something*. Our challenge is to help educators and administrators apply the principles of integrated, school-based service delivery in a way that will maximize their already-existing efforts.

Charter schools, for example, are operated independently of the traditional public school system and tailor their programs to community needs. According to the U.S. Department of Education's US Charter School Website, nearly 3,000 new schools have been launched since state legislatures began passing charter legislation in the 1990s. "Policymakers, parents, and educators are looking at chartering as a way to increase educational choice and innovation within the public school system," says the Department of Education.[3] It's an excellent opportunity to include integrated, school-based service delivery into the mix of choices.

When it comes to *advocacy* and *action,* the choices are many, all of them rich with possibilities. These possibilities depend on personal circumstances, and of course I don't know yours. Writing a book is an odd experience, especially for someone like me who thrives on one-to-one relationships. If only I knew exactly who you were, reading these words! In that case, I'd be better able to offer very specific recommendations about how to move forward on behalf of the kids in your school system, based on your level of energy, time, commitment, and standing in the community.

Since that's not possible, I'll try to suggest some general paths to follow. If I've done my job well in writing this book, most readers will close the covers with a new understanding and, I hope, new energy and willingness to advocate, to speak out, to join a movement dedicated to ending the dropout epidemic. These readers, in short, are willing to be part of the solution.

IT'S A MOST UNUSUAL SCHOOL SYSTEM THAT ISN'T DOING *SOMETHING.* OUR CHALLENGE IS TO HELP EDUCATORS AND ADMIN-ISTRATORS TO APPLY THE PRINCIPLES OF INTEGRATED, SCHOOL-BASED SERVICE DELIVERY IN A WAY THAT WILL MAXIMIZE THEIR ALREADY-EXISTING EFFORTS.

In addition, there are probably a few of you—a much smaller number—who are in a position to *take this on* as a major life activity, a cause to which you can devote considerable energy and commitment. The Communities In Schools movement is nourished by people like you, and I certainly want to connect with you. But first, let me offer some suggestions to the other, larger group of readers.

Advocacy and Action Online

The Communities In Schools network Website, **www.communitiesinschools.org**, is intended to be a portal for everyone looking to stay in touch, to keep learning, and to find opportunities, both locally and nationally, where they can speak out on behalf of youth in jeopardy of leaving school. I also want to urge you to utilize two other virtual communities: **MeetUp.org** is an Internet tool that can create a huge community in very short order, one that's also able to mobilize for real-world action. In addition, the Stand Up Website (**www.standup.org**) offers a regular e-newsletter and some excellent forums with content shaped for specific geographical regions, highlighting the advances and challenges of the integrated, school-based services movement.

The goal of all this online activity is to create a critical mass of public connection on behalf of the personal, accountable, and coordinated delivery of resources to students—in fact, to create an online version of the kind of adult community that we so badly need if we're going to weave that safety net for kids. Through MeetUp and Stand Up, you can alert each other to important local opportunities—town meetings, school board meetings, bond issues, and the like—while urging the adoption of a "third side of the triangle" perspective on school reform across the U.S.

Advocacy and Action in CIS Communities

What about the specific role of Communities In Schools? Certainly we welcome your support, wherever we are and wherever you are, but most school districts don't have a CIS affiliate. At this writing, the nationwide CIS network consists of 195 local affiliates in 27 states and the District of Columbia, providing services at more than 3,400 public schools. (See Appendix 2 for a complete list of CIS communities.) If you're one of that smaller group of readers who really wants to put significant time and energy into combating the dropout epidemic, and you find that CIS is already in your community or state—welcome aboard! We'll surely find plenty of work for you. Among other things, you can:

- Visit a school with a CIS presence to observe directly the work we do with and for students

- Serve on a school or community committee, sharing your expertise to make a difference

- Build and support relationships between schools and community programs and businesses through your CIS local affiliate

- Identify appropriate funding sources or contribute to needed school and community programs through the CIS affiliate

I can't emphasize strongly enough that along with specific advocacy, we need to change our attitudes and responses to solving our education system's greatest problem. If you're a businessperson, rethink how your company is using its influence in the community. If you're involved in social services, take a look at how your people are positioned. If you're a faith-based leader, use the brainpower and influence of your congregation, not just their charitable impulses.

The most important action you can take is often within your own sphere of activity. The responsibility for stopping the dropout epidemic rests with each one of us. Communities In Schools President Dan Cardinali puts it this way: "Americans will never have a strong, successful education system unless they take more of a role in their schools than just paying property taxes."

Other Responses to the Dropout Epidemic— and How You Can Help

I love imagining the day when we've doubled or tripled the number of school systems with a CIS presence. That may be a long time coming, though; and even then, many states won't have CIS. Realistically, Communities In Schools will *never* be in every school system. Indeed, that's a point I've tried to make throughout this book: If these principles depended on CIS for their success, something would be wrong.

Fortunately, a number of other organizations are doing excellent work in helping stop the dropout epidemic. In Appendix 3, you'll find brief descriptions of some of our national partners, many of whom may have a presence in your community or state and may be able to suggest a role for you to play in addressing the dropout epidemic.

The National Dropout Prevention Center's Website, **www. dropoutprevention.org**, is also a good source of information. The NDPC offers 15 strategies that are firmly evidence based and supported by the most current research:

1. **Systemic renewal,** understood as a continuing process of evaluating goals related to school policies and practices

2. **School-community collaboration**

3. **Safe learning environments**

4. **Family engagement**

5. **Early childhood development**

6. **Early literacy development**

7. **Mentoring/tutoring**

8. **Service-learning,** a process that connects community service experiences with academic learning

9. **Alternative schooling**

10. **After-school opportunities**

11. **Professional development** for teachers who work with youth in jeopardy of dropping out

12. **Active learning,** a concept that emphasizes teaching and learning strategies that engage students in new and creative ways

13. **Educational technology** that can deliver instruction adapted to individual students' learning styles

14. **Individualized instruction**

15. **Career and technology education**

Each strategy is linked to supplementary resources as well as model programs that are implementing the idea. It's a first-rate guide to what's working and a good way to identify practices that may fit your community.

In addition, I want to call your attention to five specific recent responses to the dropout epidemic that are taking place in communities across America. Learning how you can combine forces with the work of these organizations may be a perfect way to satisfy your appetite for change.

The National Education Association has crafted a 12-point plan to reduce the dropout rate. In announcing this in October 2006, NEA President Reg Weaver said, "We've identified the crisis, and it will take everyone sharing responsibility to correct it. This is no longer about students slipping through the cracks of our educational system. Those cracks are now craters." I couldn't have said it better myself.

Here are the NEA's 12 steps:

1. **Mandate high school graduation or equivalency as compulsory for everyone below the age of 21.**

2. **Establish high school graduation centers for students 19 to 21 years old** to provide specialized instruction and counseling to all students in this older age group who would be more effectively addressed in classes apart from younger students.

3. **Make sure students receive individual attention** in safe schools; in smaller learning communities within large schools; in small classes (18 or fewer students); and in programs during the summer, on weekends, and before and after school that provide tutoring and build on what students learn during the school day.

4. **Expand students' graduation options** through creative partnerships with community colleges in career and technical fields and with alternative schools so that students have another way to earn a high school diploma. For students who are incarcerated, tie their release to high school graduation at the end of their sentences.

5. **Increase career education and workforce readiness programs in schools** so that students see the connection between school and careers after graduation. To ensure that students have the skills they need for these careers, integrate 21st-century skills into the curriculum and provide all students with access to 21st-century technology.

6. **Act early so students do *not* drop out** with high-quality, universal preschool and full-day kindergarten; strong elementary programs that ensure students are doing grade-level work when they enter middle school; and middle school programs that address causes of dropping out that appear in these grades and ensure that students have access to algebra, science, and other courses that serve as the foundation for success in high school and beyond.

7. **Involve families in students' learning at school and at home** in new and creative ways so that all families—single-parent families, families in poverty, and families in minority communities—can support their children's academic achievement, help their children engage in healthy behaviors, and stay actively involved in their children's education from preschool through high school graduation.

8. **Monitor students' academic progress in school** through a variety of measures during the school year that provide a full picture of students' learning and help teachers make sure students do not fall behind academically.

9.   **Monitor, accurately report, and work to reduce drop-out rates** by gathering accurate data for key student groups (such as racial, ethnic, and economic), establishing benchmarks in each state for eliminating dropouts, and adopting the standardized reporting method developed by the National Governors Association.

10. **Involve the entire community in dropout prevention** through family-friendly policies that provide release time for employees to attend parent-teacher conferences; work schedules for high school students that enable them to attend classes on time and be ready to learn; "adopt a school" programs that encourage volunteerism and community-led projects in school; and community-based, real-world learning experiences for students.

11. **Make sure educators have the training and resources they need to prevent students from dropping out,** including professional development focused on the needs of diverse students and students who are at risk of dropping out; up-to-date textbooks and materials, computers, and information technology; and safe, modern schools.

12. **Make high school graduation a federal priority** by calling on Congress and the President to invest $10 billion over the next ten years to support dropout-prevention programs and states who make high school graduation compulsory.

Most of these steps (which appear on the NEA's Website, **www.nea.org**) are very much in keeping with the principles I've discussed in this book. I urge you to visit the Website to see what local or state action may be appropriate to take with them.

Also in October 2006, The Pew Partnership for Civic Change launched the Learning to Finish campaign, whose stated goal is to address the dropout problem "in communities ready to meet this challenge as a community-wide concern." Shreveport, Louisiana, and Jacksonville, Florida, are the pilot communities for the Pew Partnership's campaign, with plans calling for rolling out the initiative in 25 more cities by the end of 2008. So it's well worth taking a look at their Website, **www.pew-partnership.org**, to see if your community is one of the beneficiaries of this promising campaign.

Learning to Finish will focus particularly on academic and social interventions for eighth graders, based on a community needs assessment of the challenges these students may face. The campaign aims to "bring together both academic and community resources to assure students complete their eighth-grade year ready to tackle the challenging transition to high school."

The Pew Partnership points out what Communities In Schools affiliates have documented for many years: The ninth grade is a pivotal transition year for students at risk. "Those who trip at this threshold," the Partnership asserts, "often begin a downward spiral that results in leaving school permanently." The campaign's discussion guide, available free of charge on the Website, is also a fine resource for concerned parents and local leaders.

Anticipating the *Silent Epidemic* report and the media attention that made 2006 such a watershed year for the dropout issue, Jobs for the Future (JFF) issued an excellent report in June 2004 called "The Dropout Crisis: Promising Approaches in Prevention and Recovery." In addition to providing a solid overview of the subject that highlights the importance of making schools smaller and more personalized, JFF's statement focuses on a systemic approach to building an integrated system of responses to kids' failures to complete school. "Providing the diversified, flexible programming that some young people need," says the report, "will require districts to look across the various education, workforce, and public care systems (e.g., foster care, mental health, social services, juvenile justice) that address aspects of the needs of young people who disconnect from school."

Jobs for the Future also offers practical guidance for shaping state-level policy, and this may come in particularly handy if you've set your sights on advocating for a state CIS organization. You can download "The Dropout Crisis" at **www.jff.org**.

Feather O. Houstoun is president of the William Penn Foundation in Philadelphia. In January 2007, she published an article in *Education Week* titled "What Cities Can Do to Turn the Dropout Crisis Around." Houstoun offers eight pieces of advice that would be useful to anyone who's concerned about his or her local school system. Note that you don't necessarily have to take on these challenges yourself; instead, you and like-minded colleagues can advocate for them and insist that the dropout crisis warrants this strong, concerted action:

1. **Create a strong leadership body with cross-sector partners.**

2. **Identify and support a trusted convener.**

3. **Undertake high-quality data analysis and allow it to guide the work.**

4. **Set benchmarks that are challenging and attainable, measure progress each year, and hold civic leaders accountable.**

5. **Challenge the school district and city social-services system to set the tone for aggressive action.**

6. **Provide support to populations of young people most at risk of dropping out.**

7. **Challenge elected and appointed officials at all levels to make this issue a top priority.**

8. **Garner support from the private sector.**

The William Penn Foundation is walking its talk, too—it's providing major funding for Project U-Turn, a citywide campaign to address Philadelphia's dropout crisis. You can learn more about the program and whether some of its practical approaches could be adapted to your city by visiting **www.projectuturn.net**.

Finally, the Bill & Melinda Gates Foundation, which sponsored the *Silent Epidemic* report, followed up in 2006 by launching (along with The Broad Foundation) a nonpartisan national campaign to raise awareness about the dropout epidemic. Stand Up's manifesto is stirring: "We believe that everyone—not just parents and teachers—has a role in fixing our education system. Demand change in leadership and learning to make this happen. Talk to your elected officials. Change will happen only when we, as a nation, demand better."

In addition to the excellent state-by-state breakdown of education statistics that I mentioned earlier, the Stand Up Website, **www.standup.org**, offers information, resources, and tool kits to address a very wide array of challenges. There's also an active forum that connects people across the country who want to share in Stand Up's resources and advocacy.

■ ■ ■

While each of these five thoughtful responses to the dropout epidemic offers uniquely valuable approaches, it's also striking how much they have in common. And if there's one perspective that unites them, it's what we've been calling "the third side of triangle." Community involvement in meeting the non-academic needs of students is a pervasive theme throughout these responses. Once again, I think back to the 1970s when CIS was virtually alone in arguing for such a radical approach. It's enormously encouraging to see how our "voice in the wilderness" has slowly become a united, well-understood call to action.

The Last Dropout

There's an old saying: "You can't appreciate the good news unless you know what the *bad* news is." In the past year, as courageous reports like *The Silent Epidemic* breached the wall of denial and obfuscation around the dropout crisis, I often experienced a strangely mixed feeling. It seemed as if every week brought a grim new statistic about the young lives we were losing. I'd turn on the radio or stand in the supermarket checkout line and there would be yet another headline: *Dropout Nation, Nation of Failures, One-Third of Our Children* . . .

So much bad news . . . yet I realized that I was feeling more hopeful than I had in years. Perhaps now that the U.S. public was truly becoming aware of the gravity of the crisis, we could *take seriously* the need for immediate solutions. And I believe this is starting to happen. The bad news about the dropout epidemic has laid the groundwork for an unprecedented appetite for some *good* news about what we can do to stop it.

The nine principles I've described and the Communities In Schools success story represent that good news. We can work together to make these values a reality:

1. Programs don't change kids—*relationships* do.

2. The dropout crisis isn't just an education issue.

3. Young people need the five *real* basics, not just the three R's: a one-on-one relationship with a caring adult, a safe place to learn and grow, a healthy start and a healthy future, a marketable skill to use upon graduation, and a chance to give back to peers and community.

4. The community must weave a safety net around its children in a manner that's personal, accountable, and coordinated.

5. Every community needs a "Champion for Children": a neutral third party with "magic eyes" to see things—and people—differently, and to coordinate and broker the diverse community resources into the schools on behalf of young people and families.

6. Educators and policy makers can't do it alone . . . and they'll welcome your help.

7. Curing the dropout epidemic will demand *change,* not just charity.

8. *Scalability, sustainability,* and *evidence-based strategies* are essential to creating permanent change in the way our education system combats the dropout epidemic.

9. Our children need three things from you: your *awareness,* your *advocacy,* and your *action.*

If we succeed in practicing these principles, change *will* come. I would add only one caution: You can't pick and choose which principles you "like better" or the ones that you think will be easiest to implement. A *holistic, coordinated* approach is at the heart of what we're advocating, and that has to start with a big-picture commitment to institutional change. Only by adopting (and adapting) all nine of these principles to meet each community's challenges can we have any hope of seeing, someday, the last dropout.

I've called this book *The Last Dropout* because it *is* a phrase full of hope. It's Utopian, and it's "impossible," sure—but it's also the *only* morally acceptable vision for us Americans to endorse. And is it really impossible? I wonder. . . . My five-year-old grandson, Jack, might attend a high school where *no one* drops out. Not because it's such a wonderful place, but because . . . well, we just don't let that happen to our children anymore.

Conclusion: The Golden Triangle

I grew up in Pittsburgh, and by God's grace I met and married my wife, Jean, there. The two of us and our wonderful children, Sean and Lani, don't get back to the city as often we'd like now that our birth parents, extended family, and friends have moved on, and our lives remain so busy. My work at Communities In Schools always seems to involve 60-hour weeks, even after I made the transition in 2004 from president to vice-chairman. Jean has been an Episcopal priest since 1980 and has a doctorate in pastoral counseling, so she's extremely busy, too. As she likes to remind me, it's a good thing that she's a priest *and* a therapist, because her husband needs both!

I do love to visit Pittsburgh when I can, though. I still have great friends and CIS staff who are based there—and besides, I'm a huge Steelers fan. I never tire of driving from the airport into the city and, as I emerge from the Fort Pitt tunnel, seeing "the Golden Triangle." That's what a lot of folks call this great place, once known as America's steel capital. They call it that because it's where three rivers merge: the Monongahela, the Allegheny, and the Ohio. Pittsburgh produced a lot of golden times, with those three rivers bringing prosperity and fame.

There is a Golden Triangle that can bring prosperity to our children, too. If we can align the three sides of the triangle as I've proposed in this book, a Golden Triangle of reform will make our schools environments of learning and nurturing, keeping our young people on track for graduation and preparing them for life. It's going to take all of us—the entire community—to make it happen.

A few years ago, I had the privilege of speaking to the Chicago Communities In Schools annual meeting. This vibrant CIS affiliate has a presence in 138 schools, with more than 150 agencies bringing much-needed services and caring individuals into the schoolhouses. After my speech, Chicago's CIS executive director thanked me and then quickly said that she wasn't going to give a speech herself, but just wanted to take time to thank "the orchestra" of more than 200 people sitting before her. The crowd included representatives from the mayor's office as well as the superintendent's. There were health-care providers; corporations; parents and students; volunteers and leaders from the YMCA, Boys & Girls Clubs, the Urban League, Big Brothers Big Sisters, and many more.

I could feel my joyful tears starting as I watched them stand and applaud one another for bringing their gifts to the table on behalf of children. These men and women had come out of their various "silos" to weave a safety net of relationships and resources, freeing teachers up to teach and creating safe, caring environments in the schools they're privileged to serve.

After the meeting ended, I did what I love to do most, which is to visit a local CIS school site. The middle school I went to is a beacon of hope in the midst of a very poor neighborhood. Just walking in the door made me feel good as I took in the renovations, the new paint, the glistening clean walls. Students' art hung in the halls leading to their classrooms. This place has a great principal who'd taken over a failing enterprise and begun to turn it around. The teachers were energetic, and the administrators felt very much a part of the growing success of this wonderful school. They boasted of increased reading and math scores. The young people also seemed to love this environment of learning and care—they had smiles on their faces and a bounce to their walk, treating us visitors with respect and dignity. They weren't only studying the curriculum, they were also learning *community* and how to be part of it. The Golden Triangle was in place, and anyone could see the results.

A couple of people from the corporate community who'd also been at the Chicago CIS meeting were with me that day. At the end of our tour, we had a roundtable discussion with some of the students, a couple of parents, the principal, and some teachers. One of the businessmen asked a student named Clarence who was halfway through eighth grade what his experience had been like so far. Clarence responded that when he'd first arrived, he'd wanted to drop out after a couple of months. He said that he was behind in his grades and didn't feel comfortable at school.

Our business friend asked him what made the difference. Clarence replied, "I found out that there were a whole lot of people who believed in me and were willing to help me make it."

And what had Clarence gained from this experience? "I feel ready for high school, and *I got me a future.*"

There are millions of young people in our schools who are close to giving up. They're desperately searching for a future. By coming together as a community in and around our schools, we have the capacity and the resources to leave no child behind.

My prayer is that this will happen in your community. I pray that we all may have new minds to think differently, not simply try harder—that we may develop "magic eyes" to see the incredible assets already in place throughout our schools and communities. And may our hearts be filled with love that never quits until there truly is hope and a future for *all* our children.

■ ■ ■ ■ ■

APPENDIX 1

Prepared for Life . . . CIS Student Success Stories

So many students have been able to overcome enormous odds and reclaim their futures because they found themselves in caring communities where the principles described in this book were solidly in place. These kids—and their families, teachers, counselors, and other providers—are often willing to share their experiences so that others who are struggling with similar issues might find hope and a way forward on the path toward their own successes. Here are seven such stories. For more, visit **www.communitiesinschools.org**.

"ELECTing" Success

Rasheedah Phillips started her secondary education at Washington High School in Philadelphia, transferring to Lincoln High by her second year. "I was pregnant my freshman year of high school," she said, adding that she wasn't the first person in her family who became a parent early in life. "I come from a family of teen mothers. It has been a cycle in my family."

At Lincoln, she was referred to a special program offered by Communities In Schools.

Education Leading to Employment and Career Training (ELECT) is a statewide initiative of Pennsylvania's Departments of Public Welfare and Education, administered locally as a partnership between the School District of Philadelphia and CIS of Philadelphia. Through this program, Teen Parent Classrooms in 25 public high schools and two middle schools provide pregnant and parenting teens with the academic, health, and social-service supports needed to complete their education and make a successful transition from high school to entry-level employment, additional training, or postsecondary education.

Despite her situation, Rasheedah had a desire to achieve her dream of becoming an attorney. "Before getting pregnant, I had aspirations," she said. "But after I got pregnant, I didn't think I would achieve my goals. For a year or two, I found it difficult . . . but then something clicked and I started to do better. And here I am."

She credits CIS staff members with helping her move forward in life. "The counselors and social workers provided a safe place for me," she explained. "They would continually encourage me to go to school." Through the CIS program, she also received access to parenting-education classes, child care, and health-care services.

After Rasheedah had her daughter, she began to work hard to improve her grades. "The program has made me a model or example of what teen parents can do to be successful in high school," she said.

She graduated from Lincoln in 2002 and then went on to complete undergraduate studies at Temple University in three years. With her daughter now seven years old, she recently completed her first year of law school. "My first year was difficult," she said. "But no matter what I do, my degree is going to be an asset. I've also been doing a lot of public speaking through community programs, which helps me." She participated in a summer internship at a public law firm affiliated with Temple University Beasley

School of Law. "When I finish law school, I want to work with families and teen parents."

Rasheedah shared the following words of wisdom for teen mothers who know they're destined for greatness but unsure of their direction: "Regardless of your circumstances, your goals can be achieved, even if it takes you longer than you hope or expect. So many teens get discouraged because they think they are not good enough or cannot afford college. But I try to be an example of how you can use your situation to your advantage. There are a lot of resources out there for young parents. You have to work hard and look for them . . . no one is going to hand you anything. So many doors are open to you if you go out there to find them. Not everyone wants to go to college, because college is not meant for everyone. But whatever you want to do . . . just do it."

Hope for the Future

Denise Cook, a student at Communities In Schools of Atlanta's West End Performance Learning Center®, was one of six students who received awards in December 2006 for Student Achievement Month sponsored by CIS of Georgia. At the awards ceremony, she presented her contest entry, a poster-sized piece of artwork, and explained it to her audience saying, "This poster represents the past, present and future for me. Before CIS, my life was like death. Everything around me was dead. The CIS staff have been my heroes. Now, I have a future and I know that I'm going to make it."

Last May, Denise gave up any hope of a successful future when she dropped out of Grady High School. Just a few weeks before the school's graduation ceremony, she found herself short on academic credits, unable to pay her senior dues, and homeless. Denise's mother's had substance abuse problems that resulted in a long period of unemployment and the eventual loss of their apartment. What should have been a happy time for Denise became a time of loss and uncertainty.

While Denise's mother entered a shelter, Denise opted to live on the streets. "I was out by myself. Sometimes I stayed with friends, but I was never in the same place for long," said the Atlanta teen. After months on the streets, Denise decided to enter the shelter with her mother. "I got tired of not doing anything. I wanted to get help so I could go back to school. I knew that going to school was the only chance I had to get where I wanted to get in life," Denise said with quiet determination. With assistance from counselors in the shelter, Denise entered the West End PLC in August.

The West End PLC operates as a partnership between Atlanta Public Schools and Communities In Schools of Atlanta. This non-traditional school helps children who have dropped out or who are at risk for dropping out earn their high school diplomas.

Four months after entering the West End PLC, Denise is just one semester away from graduating. When asked about her plans for the future, the soft-spoken 19-year-old smiled, saying, "I'm going to Georgia Perimeter College for two years, then transferring to Florida A&M University. I want to study journalism because I love to write."

(Reprinted with permission of Communities In Schools of Atlanta)

Family's First Female Graduate

Yesenia Lupian is the third of seven children and the oldest daughter in her family. After she was expelled from her junior high school in Baytown, Texas, she was placed in a hospital program for 30 days due to severe depression and family problems and was treated for suicidal thoughts and repeated runaway attempts. She was then put in the educational-alternative school for the local district, where she enrolled in Communities In Schools of Baytown.

While in CIS, Yesenia took part in the Transition to Work program, a Ropes Adventure Course, and many after-school and enrichment activities. She was counseled, advised, and encouraged by her CIS case manager, who was there to listen, access services, and help her realize that she didn't have to be handicapped by past circumstances.

Today, Yesenia plans to attend college and become a certified nurse working with troubled teens. She currently has a job as an aide with CIS of Baytown's Gang Activity Prevention after-school program for elementary students. Since participating in CIS, she has received many high school academic and leadership honors and achievement awards. She'll graduate this year with honors, a year ahead of her class, and has received a $1,000 college scholarship. She's an amazing example of how the life of a troubled youth can be turned around into a positive, promising future, given the guidance and support of a caring community that refuses to let kids like her fall through the cracks.

Yesenia says, "The CIS of Baytown program has helped me to remain in school and graduate. My desire was to be the first female in my family to graduate from high school. Without CIS, I would have probably quit school and never tried to go to college. I would like the opportunity to work with teenagers with family problems like myself because it gives me the chance to give back—to help them like others helped me."

Suspended, Expelled . . . Then "Student of the Week"

Upon moving in the third grade from Chicago to La Porte County, Indiana, to live with his grandmother, Barron Moore struggled academically and socially as he adjusted to his new environment. He transferred in and out of three different elementary schools before arriving at Kesling Middle School in the fall of 2004 for what proved to be a very challenging sixth-grade year. After being suspended and then expelled from school due to poor grades and reports of fighting and disrespect toward his teachers, Barron needed to repeat the sixth grade.

Thanks to the strong partnership between Communities In Schools of La Porte County and the local Youth Service Bureau Big Brothers Big Sisters program—part of the oldest and largest mentoring organization in the United States—Barron gradually began to make a remarkable turnaround. Big Brothers Big Sisters of La Porte County was instrumental in bringing Barron together with his mentor, Dan Kaminski, vice president of General Insurance Services in La Porte County.

During Barron's expulsion from school, Kaminski continued to meet with him on a weekly basis. Allison L. Middlebrook, executive director of CIS of La Porte County, noted: "Barron would ride his bike to the Youth Service Bureau to meet with Dan. Even though there were times when Barron would not show up for their sessions, Dan patiently stood by Barron and helped him keep up with his studies."

When asked to describe his relationship with Dan, Barron responded, "Dan talks to me about sports and how to get out of problems. He's an awesome guy, and it's been great having Dan around."

The boy ultimately came to an important realization while expelled from school. "The revelation that there were so many things he couldn't do when he wasn't in school, such as play sports, really made a strong impression on Barron," remarked Middlebrook. "He recognized that if he didn't start making better decisions soon, he would risk repeating the sixth grade again."

Kesling Middle School principal Bill Wilmsen is thrilled by Barron's newfound triumphs in school, including being named student of the week. "It is so rewarding, seeing all of the successes that he has had this year," said Wilmsen. "Most important, I am proud of the choices that Barron has made for himself. His story personifies what can happen when agencies are working together toward the common good of the child."

The sixth-grade teachers echo their principal's sentiment. Kelly Troy, Barron's reading teacher, commented, "I have noticed a huge change in Barron this school year. He is not argumentative, takes pride in his work, and is respectful." Pam Miller, his language-arts teacher, summed it up: "Barron appears to care about his life and always has a smile on his face."

Thinking about College

Acton Archie moved from one government housing development to another as a child—12 times in 12 years, in fact. His father was murdered when Acton was a second grader; his mother was a drug addict. Each day was a struggle, walking past drugs and crime on the way to and from school and waking up with no power or water in the house. He remembers that many days he worried about whether he'd even have a home when he returned.

As a teenager, he made some bad choices as he struggled through the ninth grade, often absent and with no direction, personal interests, or career expectations. A caring grandmother and a strong faith in God kept him going—and Communities In Schools provided a helping hand as well. The CIS site coordinator at Acton's high school in Charlotte, North Carolina, made sure he had transportation to school, dental and health care, and connections to community-support personnel. She also became a mentor and a friend. He was exposed to college and career experiences and encouraged to form goals for himself. "I probably would have dropped out without that support," he says.

The CIS ThinkCOLLEGE program helps high school students find scholarship opportunities and qualify for higher education. Acton became a ThinkCOLLEGE participant and won two scholarships, renewing them each year he attended college. Acton graduated from North Carolina State University in May 2005 with a B.S. degree in business management, a concentration in information technology, and a minor in accounting. He's currently working at SAS Institute as a business analyst.

Small Is Beautiful

Although he's from a large family, Robert Guy appreciated the value of a small one when it came to his education. Robert and his seven younger siblings were homeschooled for a number of years, in part because the family moved so often. But there came a time for him to move into the public school system, and the first public school he attended was brand-new, with a low student-to-teacher ratio. He was active and successful there, but when the family moved again, this time to Athens, Georgia, Robert (then 16) was faced with attending a much larger, traditional high school.

This challenge, added to the economic and personal struggles of divorce that his family was going through at the time, led Robert to the Classic City Performance Learning Center® (PLC) in Athens, a Communities In Schools of Georgia alternative high school. "I've always known that my education comes first," Robert said. "After visiting the local high school and doing some research, my mom and I went to check out the PLC. We met with the principal, who talked to us and showed us around."

Robert was sold. He applied for admission to the school, which offers the advantage of being a small, self-contained learning environment with a low student-to-teacher ratio, high academic standards, personalized programs, and a flexible schedule. With his positive outlook, strong academic track record, and ambitious goal of graduating ahead of time, Robert was a natural choice for the Classic City PLC.

Once there, Robert fell in love with it. "It was like a family and became like home," he said of his two years there. "At the PLC, they get to know you as a person. They cared about what was going on in my life, and how it impacted my education and ability to focus on learning." Jaya Chauhan, Robert's learning facilitator and advisor at the PLC, said that building relationships with classmates and teachers was what attracted the teen to the school. "Robert's life wasn't always smooth, but he had an incredible inner strength and burning motivation to achieve his goal of graduating from high school. He was determined to succeed and be a positive role model; he was persistent, disciplined, organized, meticulous—and very caring," she said. "He was well liked by everyone."

His first year there, Robert had a lead role in creating the student council and, not surprisingly, served as president. He was also deeply involved in major fund-raising activities for the school's relief effort following the 2005 hurricane season.

"Robert also excelled in the creative arts," added Chauhan. "He was very interested in writing, producing, and acting. He produced a musical rap presentation in collaboration with two other students during the 2005 Thanksgiving holiday season, and it aired on a local radio station."

In a personal essay about his experience at the PLC, Robert wrote: "I have teachers who genuinely care about me and who would do anything to make sure I succeed. . . . I am at a place where people care about my dreams, goals and future. . . . Without this school, CIS, and Classic City PLC, I doubt I would have made it."

Last year Robert *did* make it, achieving his goal of graduating from high school and becoming the first in his family to do so. He continues his journey today as a freshman at Morehouse College in Atlanta, where he's studying political science. He's received scholarships to attend Morehouse—one of the most prestigious historically black colleges in the nation—and with a grade point average of 3.5, he'll continue to be eligible for academic scholarships. After completing his undergraduate studies at Morehouse, he plans to attend law school and become an entertainment attorney. He appears to be well on his way.

Jaya Chauhan said, "I feel certain that Robert is going to do really well in life. He has embarked on his journey and is going to just fly."

Around the World with Sweet Success

Lasheeda Perry is a 20-year-old culinary-arts student at Johnson and Wales University in Rhode Island. She grew up just outside of Philadelphia, one of eight children; and her family moved often and suffered many financial hardships. When she was just 15 years old, Lasheeda and her twin sister became the primary caregivers of their terminally ill mother. It was difficult to juggle schoolwork and family responsibilities, but Lasheeda persevered with a little help from Communities In Schools.

"CIS was always involved in activities at my school. When I was a student at Frankford High School, my teachers exposed me to so many new experiences," she recalls. "While I was at Frankford,

Mrs. Stephenson introduced me to the Careers Through Culinary Arts Program through CIS . . . and that changed my life. I knew that I had to work really hard to be in the program, but the payoff has been incredible. They helped me go to China! I also won a competition that awarded me a two-week trip to Australia, where I explored culinary delights. Many of my high school friends had never been outside of Philadelphia, but I was given an opportunity to see and experience whole different cultures. My mother pushed me to finish high school, although most of the people around me did not finish school."

Unfortunately, the teen's mother didn't live to see her daughter graduate. She died just weeks before commencement. But by that time, Lasheeda had already been awarded a $75,000 four-year scholarship through Communities In Schools of Philadelphia; and she was on her way to pursue a bachelor's degree in baking and pastry arts, with a minor in food-service management.

"When I was growing up, college wasn't an option," said Lasheeda. She never imagined that she'd be attending one of the country's most prestigious culinary schools on a full four-year scholarship. While at Johnson and Wales, she participated in a three-month internship at the Adare Manor Hotel and Golf Resort in Ireland. During the summer, Lasheeda works at Sweet Jazmine's pastry shop near Philadelphia. Owner Kimberly Davis Cuthbert has become one of many mentors to her.

"I love to learn, and I love baking and pastries. Thus far, it has taken me literally around the world."

■ ■ ■ ■ ■

APPENDIX 2

Communities In Schools— State and Local Locations

This list includes the network of state and local Communities In Schools affiliates that are operational as of this writing. For an updated list and contact information for each affiliate, visit **www. communitiesinschools.org**.

Alaska
CIS of Alaska State Office
    (Anchorage)
CIS of Anchorage
CIS of Bethel
CIS of Juneau
CIS of Mat-Su
CIS of Nome

Arizona
CIS of Arizona State Office
    (Phoenix)
CIS of Tempe

California
CIS of Greater Los Angeles
CIS of Sacramento
CIS of San Francisco 49er Academy

Delaware
CIS of Delaware State Office
    (Dover)

District of Columbia
CIS of the Nation's Capital

Florida
CIS of Florida State Office
   (Tallahassee)
CIS of Bradford County
CIS of Broward County
CIS of Gadsden County
CIS of Hillsborough County
CIS of Jacksonville
CIS of Leon County
CIS of Miami
CIS of Nassau County
CIS of Northwest Florida
CIS of Okeechobee County
CIS of Palm Beach County
CIS of Putnam County
CIS of St. Johns County

Georgia
CIS of Georgia State Office
   (Atlanta)
CIS of Albany/Dougherty County
CIS of Appling County
CIS of Athens/Clarke County
CIS of Atlanta
CIS of Augusta/Richmond County
CIS of Baldwin County
CIS of Berrien County
CIS of Bulloch County
CIS of Burke County
CIS of Candler County
CIS of Catoosa County
CIS of Cochran/Bleckley County
CIS of Colquitt County
CIS of Cook County
CIS of Coweta County
CIS of Crisp/Dooly Counties
CIS of Decatur County
CIS of Dodge County
CIS of Douglas County
CIS of Elbert County
CIS of Emanuel County
CIS of Fitzgerald/Ben Hill County
CIS of Glascock County

CIS of Hart County
CIS of Houston County
CIS of Jenkins County
CIS of Laurens County
CIS of Macon/Bibb County
CIS of Marietta City/Cobb County
CIS of McDuffie County
CIS of Miller County
CIS of Rome/Floyd County
CIS of Savannah/Chatham County
CIS of Screven County
CIS of Stephens County
CIS of Sumter County
CIS of Troup County
CIS of Turner County
CIS of Twiggs County
CIS of Valdosta/Lowndes
CIS of Wilkes County

Illinois
CIS of Aurora
Chicago-CIS

Indiana
CIS of Clark County
CIS of East Chicago
CIS of Elkhart/LaGrange County
CIS of La Porte
CIS of Starke County
CIS of Wayne County

Iowa
CIS of Cedar Valley

Kansas
CIS of Kansas State Office
   (Mulberry)
CIS of Grant County
CIS of Harvey County Partnership
CIS of Marion County
CIS of Wichita/Sedgwick County

Louisiana
CIS of New Orleans

Michigan
CIS of Michigan State Office
   (Holland)
CIS of Detroit
CIS of Kalamazoo
CIS of Lenawee
CIS of Mancelona
CIS of Ottawa
CIS of Tecumseh Area

Mississippi
CIS of Greenwood Leflore
CIS of Jackson

Nevada
CIS of Southern Nevada

New Jersey
CIS of New Jersey State Office
   (Newark)
CIS of Cumberland County
CIS of Newark
CIS of Passaic
CIS of Union County

New York
CIS of New York City

North Carolina
CIS of North Carolina State Office
   (Raleigh)
CIS of Asheville
CIS of Brunswick County
CIS of Cabarrus County
CIS of Caldwell County
CIS of Cape Fear
CIS of Charlotte-Mecklenburg
CIS of Clay County
CIS of Cleveland County
CIS of Cumberland County

CIS of Durham
CIS of Gaston County
CIS of Greater Greensboro
CIS of High Point
CIS of Lee County
CIS of Lexington
CIS of Lincoln County
CIS of Madison County
CIS of McDowell County
CIS of Mitchell County
CIS of Moore County
CIS of Northeast
CIS of Orange County
CIS of Perquimans County
CIS of Pitt County
CIS of Randolph County
CIS of Robeson County
CIS of Rockingham County
CIS of Rocky Mount Region
CIS of Rowan County
CIS of Swain County
CIS of Thomasville
CIS of Transylvania County
CIS of Wake County
CIS of Wayne County
CIS of Whiteville
CIS of Wilkes County

Ohio
CIS of Columbus

Oklahoma
CIS of Ardmore

Oregon
CIS of the North Coast

Pennsylvania
CIS of Pennsylvania State Office
   (Pittsburgh)
CIS of Greater Harrisburg
CIS of Laurel Highlands
CIS of Lehigh Valley

CIS of Philadelphia
CIS of Pittsburgh-Allegheny
    County
CIS of Southwest Pennsylvania

South Carolina
CIS of South Carolina State Office
    (Columbia)
CIS of Anderson County
CIS of Barnwell County
CIS of Berkeley County
CIS of Charleston
CIS of Cherokee County
CIS of Chester
CIS of Dillon County
CIS of Greenville
CIS of Greenwood County
CIS of Kershaw County
CIS of Lancaster County
CIS of Lee County
CIS of The Midlands
CIS of Oconee County
CIS of Saluda County

Tennessee
CIS of Johnson City

Texas
CIS of Texas State Office (Austin)
CIS Bay Area
CIS of Baytown
CIS Bell-Coryell Counties
CIS of the Big County
CIS of Brazoria County
CIS of Cameron County
CIS of Central Texas
CIS of Corpus Christi
CIS of Dallas Region
CIS of East Texas
CIS El Paso
CIS City of Galveston
CIS of the Golden Crescent
CIS of Greater Tarrant County
CIS of Hidalgo County
CIS of Houston
CIS of Laredo

CIS/McLennan County Youth
    Collaboration
CIS of North East Texas
CIS of North Texas
CIS of the Permian Basin
CIS of San Antonio
CIS of South Central Texas
CIS of South Central Texas
CIS Southeast Harris County
CIS Southeast Texas
CIS on the South Plains

Virginia
CIS of Virginia State Office
    (Richmond)
CIS of Chesterfield
CIS of Richmond

Washington
CIS of Washington State Office
    (Seattle)
CIS of Auburn
CIS of Federal Way
CIS of Kent
CIS of Lakewood
CIS of Orting
CIS of Peninsula
CIS of Puyallup
CIS of Renton
CIS of Seattle
CIS of Tacoma

West Virginia
CIS of Cabell County
CIS of Greenbrier County

APPENDIX 3

How to
Get
Involved

The following list includes dozens of outstanding national youth-serving and education-support organizations at work in thousands of communities across America. They represent some of the many worthy groups with whom Communities In Schools is proud to partner.

The Afterschool Alliance

The Afterschool Alliance is a nonprofit organization dedicated to raising awareness of the importance of after-school programs and advocating for quality, affordable programs for all children. It's supported by a group of public, private, and nonprofit organizations that share the Alliance's vision of ensuring that all children have access to quality after-school programs by 2010.

Website: **www.afterschoolalliance.org**

The Alternative High School Initiative

The Alternative High School Initiative is a network of youth development organizations committed to creating educational opportunities for young people for whom traditional school settings haven't been successful. AHSI was launched in 2003 as a response to the growing national trend of diminishing graduation rates; members work with local communities to generate and sustain safe, top-quality alternative high school options for vulnerable youth.
Website: **www.ahsi.info.org**

America's Promise—The Alliance for Youth

America's Promise—The Alliance for Youth grew out of the Presidents' Summit for America's Future in 1997 in Philadelphia, where Presidents Clinton, Bush, Carter, and Ford, with Nancy Reagan representing President Reagan, challenged America to make children and youth a national priority. Alliance partners—corporations, nonprofit service organizations, foundations, policy makers, advocacy organizations, and faith groups—work collaboratively to ensure that America's young people receive the Five Promises.
Website: **www.americaspromise.org**

Big Brothers Big Sisters

Big Brothers Big Sisters is the oldest and largest youth-mentoring organization in the United States, focused on developing positive relationships that have a direct and lasting impact on the lives of young people, ages 6 through 18, in communities across the country. National research has shown that positive relationships between youth and their Big Brothers and Big Sisters mentors have a direct and measurable impact on children's lives. Big Brothers Big Sisters currently operates in all 50 states and in 35 countries around the world.
Website: **www.bbbs.org**

Boys and Girls Clubs of America

The mission of Boys and Girls Clubs of America is to enable all young people, especially those who need us most, to reach their full potential as productive, caring, responsible citizens. With more than 3,900 clubs around the world, kids have access to a safe place to learn and grow; ongoing relationships with caring, adult professionals; life-enhancing programs and character development experiences; and hope and opportunity.
Website: **www.bgca.org**

Boy Scouts of America

The purpose of the Boy Scouts of America is to provide an educational program for boys and young adults to build character, to train in the responsibilities of participating citizenship, and to develop personal fitness. More than 300 local scouting councils provide quality youth programs, including Cub Scouting, Boy Scouting, and Venturing.
Website: **www.scouting.org**

Building Educated Leaders for Life (BELL)

BELL is a community-based, nonprofit educational organization founded in 1992 by a group of black students at Harvard Law School. Its mission is to enhance the academic performance and life opportunities of elementary school children living in low-income, urban communities. BELL's school-based programs are characterized by small-group tutoring and mentoring, curriculum-based instruction, rigorous evaluation of results, and strong training programs for staff.
Website: **www.bellnational.org**

Camp Fire USA

Founded in 1910, Camp Fire USA is one of the nation's leading not-for-profit youth-development organizations, currently serving nearly 750,000 children and youth annually. Programs include youth leadership, self-reliance, after-school groups, camping and environmental education, and child care. Camp Fire programs are delivered through 145 local and statewide councils and community partners across the nation.
Website: **www.campfireusa.org**

The Center for Social Organization of Schools (CSOS)

CSOS is an educational research and development arm at Johns Hopkins University. The Center includes sociologists, psychologists, social psychologists, and educators who conduct programmatic research to improve the education system and provide technical assistance to schools. Among its signature projects are studies on the graduation gap, so-called dropout factories and the promoting power of high schools across the country, and the National Network of Partnership Schools.
Website: **www.csos.jhu.edu**

Citizen Schools

Citizen Schools is a leading national education initiative that uniquely mobilizes thousands of adult volunteers to help improve student achievement by teaching skill-building apprenticeships after school. Programs blend real-world learning projects with rigorous academic- and leadership-development activities, preparing students in the middle grades for success in high school, college, the workforce, and civic life.
Website: **www.citizenschools.org**

City Year

City Year's mission is to build democracy through citizen service, civic leadership, and social entrepreneurship. Citizen service means citizens of all ages and backgrounds will unite to serve their community, nation, and world; civic leadership means every citizen will have the skills, values, and inspiration to be a leader for the common good; and social entrepreneurship means that one day human inventiveness and compassion will be unleashed systematically to solve the pressing social problems of the day.
Website: **www.cityyear.org**

Coalition for Community Schools

The Coalition for Community Schools is an alliance of national, state, and local organizations in education K through 16, youth development, community planning and development, family support, health and human services, government, and philanthropy, as well as national, state, and local community school networks. The Coalition advocates for community schools as the vehicles for strengthening schools, families, and communities so that together they can improve student learning.
Website: **www.communityschools.org**

College Summit

College Summit strengthens schools' capacity to prepare all students for success after high school. Trained student influencers build college-going culture, while teachers and counselors use a managed curriculum and technology tools to help all students create postsecondary plans and apply to college.
Website: **www.collegesummit.org**

Corporation for National and Community Service

The Corporation is the federal agency that administers national service and volunteerism programs, including AmeriCorps, VISTA (Volunteers in Service to America), Learn and Serve America, Foster Grandparents Program, and the Retired and Senior Volunteer Program (RSVP). It also provides the Community Guide to Helping America's Youth, a Web-based guide with up-to-date research on youth development and effective programs.
Website: **www.nationalservice.gov**

Girl Scouts of the USA

Chartered by Congress in 1950, Girl Scouts is helping today's girls become tomorrow's leaders. Girl Scouts of the USA today numbers more than 300 local Girl Scout councils or offices; 236,000 troops or groups; 986,000 adult volunteers; and countless corporate, government, and individual supporters.
Website: **www.girlscouts.org**

Girls Inc.

Girls Incorporated is a national nonprofit youth organization dedicated to inspiring all girls to be strong, smart, and bold. With roots dating to 1864, Girls Inc. has provided vital educational programs to millions of American girls, particularly those in high-risk, underserved areas. Today, innovative programs help girls confront societal pressures and prepare them to lead successful, independent, and fulfilling lives.
Website: **www.girlsinc.org**

Hands On Network

Hands On Network is a growing network of more than one million volunteers changing communities inside and outside the United States through meaningful volunteer action. Hands On Network is currently made up of 58 national and international volunteer organizations that create and manage nearly 50,000 projects a year, from building wheelchair ramps in San Francisco and teaching reading in Atlanta to rebuilding homes and lives in the Gulf Coast communities.
Website: **www.handsonnetwork.org**

Jobs for America's Graduates

Jobs for America's Graduates (JAG) is a school-to-career program implemented in 700 high schools, alternative schools, community colleges, and middle schools through 29 state affiliates across the country. JAG's mission is to keep young people in school through graduation and provide work-based learning experiences that will lead to career advancement opportunities or to enroll in a postsecondary institution that leads to a rewarding career.

Website: **www.jag.org**

Jobs for the Future

Jobs for the Future (JFF) believes that all young people should have a quality high school and postsecondary education, and that all adults should have the skills needed to hold jobs that pay enough to support a family. As a nonprofit research, consulting, and advocacy organization, JFF works to strengthen our society by creating educational and economic opportunity for those who need it most. Through partnerships with states and communities, national and local foundations, and other organizations, JFF accelerates opportunities for people to advance in education and careers through research, analysis, and policy development; practical, on-the-ground projects; and advocacy, communications, and peer learning.

Website: **www.jff.org**

Knowledge Is Power Program (KIPP)

KIPP is a national network of free, open-enrollment, college-preparatory public schools in underresourced communities throughout the United States. There are currently 52 locally run KIPP schools in 16 states and Washington, D.C., which are serving more than 12,000 students. KIPP schools have been widely recognized for putting underserved students on the path to college.

Website: **www.kipp.org**

MENTOR/National Mentoring Partnership

MENTOR/National Mentoring Partnership works to expand the world of quality mentoring. MENTOR believes that with the help and guidance of an adult mentor, each child can discover how to unlock and achieve his or her potential. Widely acknowledged as the nation's premier advocate and resource for the expansion of mentoring initiatives nationwide, MENTOR works with a strong network of state and local mentoring partnerships to leverage resources and provide the support and tools that mentoring organizations need to effectively serve young people in their communities.

Website: **www.mentoring.org**

National 4-H Council

The mission of the National 4-H Council is to advance the 4-H youth development movement to build a world in which youth and adults learn, grow, and work together as catalysts for positive change. The National 4-H Council provides grants, establishes programs/initiatives, designs and publishes curriculum and reference materials, and creates linkages fostering innovation and shared learning to advance the 4-H youth development movement.

Website: **www.fourhcouncil.edu**

National Alliance for Public Charter Schools

The National Alliance for Public Charter Schools develops sound, coherent policies that support high-quality public education options for families who need them the most. Key priorities include lifting arbitrary "caps" on charter growth, closing the finance gap between charters and other public schools, and updating the federal Charter Schools Program to spur a new era of charter achievement.

Website: **www.publiccharters.org**

The National Association of Charter School Authorizers (NACSA)

NACSA is a professional organization of authorizers and other education leaders who work to achieve quality public charter schools. Fifteen years of chartering has resulted in thousands of quality charter schools. Authorizers protect the public interest as these entrepreneurial schools come into being. Authorizers include state and local boards of education; colleges and universities; special-purpose boards; municipal bodies; and nonprofits. These are the entities charged by law to approve, oversee, and evaluate the performance of public charter schools. NACSA developed principles and standards that define professional practice for quality authorizing across America.

Website: **www.qualitycharters.org**

National Collaboration for Youth

The National Collaboration for Youth (NCY), a 30-year-old organization, is a coalition of 50 member organizations that have a significant interest in youth development. NCY members collectively serve more than 40 million young people; employ over 100,000 paid staff; utilize more than 6 million volunteers; and have a physical presence in virtually every community in America.

Website: **www.collab4youth.org**

National Dropout Prevention Center/Network

Since 1987, the National Dropout Prevention Center/Network (NDPC/N) has worked to improve opportunities for all young people to fully develop the academic, social, work, and healthy-life skills needed to graduate from high school and lead productive lives. By promoting awareness of successful programs and policies related to dropout prevention, the work of the NDPC/N and its members has made an impact on education from the local to the national level.

Website: **www.dropoutprevention.org**

National Parent Teacher Association

The mission of the Parent Teacher Association is to support and speak on behalf of children and youth in the schools, in the community, and before governmental bodies and other organizations that make decisions affecting children; to assist parents in developing the skills they need to raise and protect their children; and to encourage parent and public involvement in the public schools of this nation.

Website: **www.pta.org**

New Leaders for New Schools

New Leaders for New Schools is a movement dedicated to promoting high levels of academic achievement for every child. It promotes high

academic achievement by attracting, preparing, and supporting the next generation of outstanding leaders for our nation's urban public schools.
Website: **www.nlns.org**

Peace Games

Peace Games empowers students to create their own safe classrooms and communities by forming partnerships with elementary schools, families, and young-adult volunteers. Peace Games believes that this goal is best achieved by building the capacity of schools and community groups to implement holistic peace- and justice-education programs.
Website: **www.peacegames.org**

Points of Light Foundation

The Points of Light Foundation & Volunteer Center National Network engages and mobilizes millions of volunteers who are helping solve serious social problems in thousands of communities. Through a variety of programs and services, including 300 local Volunteer Centers, the Foundation and VCNN encourage people from all walks of life—businesses, nonprofits, faith-based organizations, low-income communities, families, youth, and older adults—to volunteer.
Website: **www.pointsoflight.org**

Public Allies

Since 1992, Public Allies has built a powerful model for identifying, training, and supporting talented and diverse young adults to lead positive community change. Young people ages 18 to 30 serve in full-time apprenticeships creating, improving, and expanding services at local nonprofit organizations; and they participate in a rigorous leadership development program that combines weekly training, coaching, team projects, and reflection.
Website: **www.publicallies.org**

Stand Up Campaign

Developed by The Broad Foundation and the Bill & Melinda Gates Foundation, Stand Up is a nonpartisan national campaign to raise awareness about the education crisis and to transform education in America. The campaign will engage the nation in debate about education and demand that all children in every state are inspired to learn, are given the support they need to succeed academically, and are prepared for life. Stand Up provides data broken out by state, a parent tool kit and a community action tool kit, and periodic live online forums to exchange information about issues and solutions to the dropout crisis.
Website: **www.standup.org**

Teach For America

Teach For America is the national corps of outstanding recent college graduates of all academic majors who commit two years to teach in urban and rural public schools and become leaders in the effort to expand educational opportunity. TFA's mission is to enlist our nation's most promising future leaders in the movement to eliminate educational inequality. TFA serves 25 urban and rural regions, supports 4,400 current corps members, engages 12,000 alumni, and serves 375,000 students annually (and 2.5 million students since inception).
Website: **www.teachforamerica.org**

United Way

United Way is a national network of more than 1,300 locally governed organizations that work to create lasting positive changes in communities and people's lives. Building on more than a century of service as the nation's preeminent community-based fund-raiser, United Way engages the community to identify the underlying causes of the most significant local issues, develops strategies and pulls together financial and human resources to address them, and measures the results.
Website: **www.unitedway.org**

YMCA

YMCAs are at the heart of community life across the country: 42 million families and 72 million households are located within three miles of a YMCA. The nation's 2,617 YMCAs work to meet the health and human-service needs of 20.2 million men, women, and children in 10,000 communities in the United States, supported by 561,909 volunteers, who are central to the YMCA mission.

Website: **www.ymca.net**

YouthBuild USA

The mission of YouthBuild USA is to unleash the intelligence and positive energy of low-income youth to rebuild their communities and their lives. YouthBuild addresses core issues facing low-income communities: housing, education, employment, crime prevention, and leadership development. Young people ages 16 to 24 work toward their GED or high school diploma, learn job skills, serve their communities by building affordable housing, and transform their own lives and roles in society.

Website: **www.youthbuild.org**

Youth Service America (YSA)

YSA is a resource center that partners with thousands of organizations committed to increasing the quality and quantity of volunteer opportunities for young people ages 5 to 25 to serve locally, nationally, and globally. Founded in 1986, YSA's mission is to strengthen the effectiveness, sustainability, and scale of the youth-service and service-learning fields.

Website: **www.ysa.org**

YWCA

The YWCA, whose mission is to eliminate racism and empower women, is the oldest and largest multicultural women's organization in the world, including more than 25 million members in 122 countries, with 2.6 million members and participants in 300 local associations in the United States. It provides safe places for women and girls, builds strong women leaders, and advocates for women's rights and civil rights in Congress.

Website: **www.ywca.org**

■ ■ ■ ■ ■

APPENDIX 4

Research on
Asset-Based
Approaches

The America's Promise Alliance, whose mission is to help deliver the "Five Promises" (based on the Five Basics of Communities In Schools) to children across the nation, is one of several organizations providing useful summaries of current research on asset-based approaches to improving outcomes for young people in school.

The group's Website (**www.americaspromise.org**) describes findings from four research projects:

1. The Search Institute's 2006 study of 40 developmental assets among youth in 2,000 U.S. cities

2. University-based research (including the well-regarded Hawkins and Catalano work) on risk and resiliency among youth

3. The National Academy of Science's 2002 report, "Community Programs to Promote Youth Development"

4. A meta-study in Child Trends' *American Teens Series* that summarizes the results of more than 1,000 research studies

The research reveals a consistent positive correlation between developmental assets such as the Five Promises/Basics and success in school and in life—and a consistent negative correlation between lack of these assets and being at a clear disadvantage compared to better-equipped peers.

The Search Institute's study, for instance, finds that young people with at least 31 of 40 developmental assets "consistently engage in fewer risk behaviors and have more indicators of thriving (such as doing well in school, helping others, and overcoming adversity) than young people with fewer assets." The 40 assets include categories such as family support, other adult relationships, a caring school climate, service to others, safety, youth programs, and a host of social and psychological competencies.[1]

The *American Teens Series* meta-study's emphasis on relationships as key to teens' well-being and its rejection of "silver bullet" solutions are both particularly congruent with the CIS approach to building assets. "Parent-child interactions and bonding greatly influence adolescents' choices and attitudes," the authors write. They also say:

> Peer relationships—including positive ties among teens— are important; and siblings, teachers, and mentors can provide additional support to young people. Significantly, research indicates that supportive relationships seem to trump lectures that simply tell teens "to do" or "not to do" something as a strategy to enhance adolescent development. Program developers and policy makers should view adolescents as whole people, not just as students, patients, or delinquents, and not expect a "silver bullet" solution to improve teens' lives.[2]

Based on its overview of this research, America's Promise is clear that:

. . . unless they have a critical mass of key developmental resources in their lives—four or five Promises—children are far less likely to achieve academic success, avoid violence and become involved in their communities. . . . Children who experience at least four of the five Promises are significantly more likely to be successful, as measured by four indicators: social competence, frequency of volunteering, avoiding violence, and earning mostly A's in school.[3]

Communities In Schools practitioners have repeatedly found that their own experiences with young people reinforce this research, and the CIS movement confidently offers an asset-based model—the Five Basics—as a vital tool to combat the dropout epidemic.

■ ■ ■ ■ ■

ENDNOTES

Introduction

1. *The Silent Epidemic: Perspectives of High School Dropouts,* Civic Enterprises in association with Peter D. Hart Research Associates. Bridgeland; DiIulio, Jr.; and Morison, the Bill & Melinda Gates Foundation, March 2006.

2. Civic Enterprises Website, **www.civicenterprises.net**, accessed March 29, 2007.

3. *Rethinking High School Graduation Rates and Trends,* Mishel and Roy, Economic Policy Institute, April 2006.

4. Bridgeland et al.

5. Statistics taken from Bridgeland et al. and from *Diplomas Count 2006,* Editorial Projects in Education (EPE) Research Center, 2006.

Chapter 2

1. Milloy, *Washington Post,* July 26, 2006.

Chapter 3

1. Rhodes, "School Based Mentoring," MENTOR Website, **www.mentoring.org**, accessed March 15, 2007.

2. National Coalition for the Homeless Website, **www.nationalhomeless.org**, accessed May 17, 2007.

3. Afterschool Alliance Website, **www.afterschoolalliance.org**, accessed March 15, 2007.

4. MENTOR Website, **www.mentoring.org**, accessed March 15, 2007.

5. National Summit on America's Silent Epidemic Website, **www.silentepidemic.org**, accessed May 22, 2007.

Chapter 4

1. Horne, *Breach of Faith: Hurricane Katrina and the Near Death of a Great American City*, Random House, 2006.

Chapter 5

1. Quoted in Collins, *Good to Great*, HarperBusiness, 2001.

2. Assessment Office, Charlotte-Mecklenburg School District.

Chapter 6

1. U.S. Department of Education Website, **www.ed.gov/nclb/ overview/intro/execsumm.html**, accessed March 29, 2007.

Chapter 8

1. Broder, *Washington Post,* July 10, 1977.

2. Ashoka Website, **www.ashoka.org**, accessed May 21, 2007.

3. National Center for Education Statistics, U.S. Department of Education, **www.nces.ed.gov**, accessed March 15, 2007.

4. Communities In Schools, Inc., *Addressing America's Dropout Crisis: 2005–2006 Results from the CIS Network*, 2007.

Chapter 9

1. *Time* magazine Website, **www.time.com/time/magazine/ article/0,9171,1617527,00.html**, accessed May 21, 2007.

2. New York City Public Schools' Office of Youth Development

Website, **http://schools.nyc.gov/Offices/DYD/OYD/default.htm**, accessed March 15, 2007.

3. US Charter Schools Website, **www.uscharterschools.org**, accessed May 21, 2007.

Appendix 4

1. *Keeping America's Promises to Children and Youth,* Benson, Scales, Hamilton, and Sesma, Search Institute, 2006.

2. *American Teens Series,* Moore and Zaff, Child Trends, 2003.

3. America's Promise Website, **www.americaspromise.org**, accessed March 14, 2007.

■ ■ ■ ■ ■

IN RECOGNITION

The Last Dropout tells many stories that are part of the growth of the Communities In Schools movement, but it is *not* a complete history. Such a book would be twice as long—and it would be filled with twice as many incredible, compassionate individuals, all of whom played unique roles over the past 30 years.

Time and again as I drafted this book, I had to remind myself that it would be impossible to mention everyone who deserved my gratitude for the way they "walked their talk" for children. Some of these people—**James M. Allwin, Robert H. B. Baldwin, Cynthia Briggs, Burt Chamberlin, Anne Cox Chambers, Ray Chambers, Dr. Alonzo Crim, Martha Gale, Lois Gracey, Linda Harrill, Jim Hill, George Johnson, Dave Lewis, Harv Oostdyk, Dean Overman, Nellie Reyes,** and **Julian Robertson**—are named at key points in the story you've just read; their contributions are much greater than I can fully tell here. But in addition, I want to recognize a number of individuals who didn't find their way into these pages, but who nonetheless were absolutely crucial to whatever successes I've documented.

Clark and **Edith Jones** came into my life when they were young people living in the housing project next door to me at 215 Madison in New York City. Clark and Edith became street leaders, helped us run resident apartments for homeless kids, and went on to help start Communities In Schools in Atlanta and grow it nationally. They're an important part of my own spiritual growth and wonderful godparents to my daughter, Lani.

My friendship with **Reid Carpenter** began when I was 20 and has remained a lifetime commitment to share our spiritual journey and give kids hope and a future. Reid helped launch Communities In Schools in Pittsburgh and throughout Pennsylvania, and I'm honored to serve on the board of his Leadership Foundation.

Herb Alpert and **Jerry Moss** stepped forward when we really needed them and told me: "We're with you for life." And that has proved true. They're part of my extended family, real brothers who have given so much and opened so many doors for us in the music industry.

Patty Pflum helped launch Communities In Schools in Atlanta, and in 30 years she has never faltered in her amazing commitment to children. She was the first person we officially hired when we became a national organization, and we never made a better choice.

Robert Arias, Jill Binder, Doug Denise, Alyce Hill, Andrea McAleenan, Cordell Richardson, and **Al Ward** helped design and replicate Communities In Schools in dozens of new communities and states. Their role as regional directors represented a critical transition from the early days of the CIS movement to its eventual adoption of a state-level strategy for growth.

Jonathan G. Powers stepped in as CIS's executive director at one of the most difficult and delicate moments in the organization's history. His trustworthiness, compassion, and expertise were a blessing to us; and he has continued to share his skills as a key member of our national board of directors. I'm also grateful for the positive contributions of our other executive directors over the years: **Doug Johnston, Dr. Walter J. Leonard, Janet Longmore,** and **Dr. Marilyn W. Smith.**

Mark Emblidge was for many years the head of our Entertainment Industry's Foundation for CIS, where he worked tirelessly to win friends for our work. Mark went on to lead the CIS state office in Virginia, setting new standards of accomplishment there.

Nicholas C. Forstmann's untimely death in 2001 at the age of 54 took from us one of CIS's greatest friends and leaders. Nick served on the board of directors for 15 years, 3 of them as board chair. His generosity and acumen will never be forgotten.

Jackie Robinson was a crucial part of our Street Academy work in New York, especially at Lower East Side Prep. He later helped launch CIS in Washington, D.C., and served as head of field operations at the CIS national office.

Willoughby Walling, Charles Tisdale, and **Jane Hansen** taught me the ways of Washington as they managed the relationship between our little proto-CIS office and Jimmy Carter's White House.

Maurice Weir, whom I first met when he was still a teenager, became a "warrior for CIS" and played a vital role in our work in the nation's capital.

Howard Samuels, one of CIS's founding board members, helped keep our young organization alive and growing through difficult times.

My heartfelt appreciation goes out to all these wonderful people and to many others who have gone unnamed—the teachers, principals, families, service providers, members of the faith and business communities, and volunteers who together form a community of caring adults on behalf of our nation's children.

■　■　■　■　■

ACKNOWLEDGMENTS

This book draws on the collective wisdom of so many individuals who have helped shape my life and set the course for the Communities In Schools movement. A few deserve special acknowledgment for their invaluable help.

John Morris has long been the anonymous voice of Communities In Schools. His exceptional gift for words is complemented by his strong faith and unwavering commitment to getting the story right. His light shines through every page in this book.

Sally DeLuca kept me focused and supported from the first word. Without her deep insights about, and passion for, our work with young people, and without her extraordinary editorial and management skills, this project would never have crossed the finish line.

Neil Shorthouse, my colleague and friend for 40 years, has shared my journey with me in more ways than I can possibly say. The writing of this book was no exception. Thank you, Neil—I couldn't have asked God for a better partner, or a smarter reader.

Dan Cardinali's wisdom, leadership, and commitment to children are reflected on so many pages of this book. His generation will write an exciting new chapter in the Communities In Schools story.

I also extend my heartfelt appreciation to **Allison Hertz** for her great spirit, patience, and organizational wizardry; **Jillian Manus** for being the perfect agent, full of enthusiasm and creativity; **Jerry Breslauer,** my longtime board member and friend, for always being there through the hard times, and being the one who pushed hardest for me to get this book written; **Sean Milliken** and **Kathryn Fisher** for perceptive feedback on early drafts; **Jill Kramer** and **Jessica Kelley** at Hay House for their enthusiasm and meticulous editing; **Deborah Veney Robinson** for her energy and ingenuity in getting this book to the public; and **Gwen Pegram** for the joy and tenacity she brought, in the midst of the chaos of finishing this manuscript.

Lastly, the book would have been nothing without the generous contributions of time and energy in interviews and conversations with **Reginald Beaty, Judy Frick, Mike Hayes, Paul Houston, Cynthia Marshall, William "Blinky" Rodriguez,** and **Susan Siegel.** Many, many thanks, too, to our other original "brain trust" members: **Eva Askew-Houser, Peter Bankson, Cynthia Briggs,** and **Mort Stanfield.**

■ ■ ■ ■ ■

ABOUT THE AUTHOR

Bill Milliken has been a tireless advocate for disenfranchised youth and one of the foremost pioneers in the movement to connect schools with community resources to help troubled students graduate and succeed in life. In 1977, he and others developed a model organization, now known as Communities In Schools, for which he served more than 25 years as national president and currently is vice chairman of the board.

Bill has advised U.S. Presidents of both parties and has received numerous awards, including the Edward A. Smith Award for Excellence in Nonprofit Leadership, the Champion for Children Award from the American Association of School Administrators, the National Caring Award from the Caring Institute, the Temple Award for Creative Altruism from the Institute of Noetic Sciences, and an honorary doctorate in humane letters from Bard College. He is the author of two previous books, *So Long, Sweet Jesus* and *Tough Love.*

Contact: **founder@cisnet.org**

■ ■ ■ ■ ■

We hope you enjoyed this Hay House book.
If you'd like to receive a free catalog featuring additional
Hay House books and products, or if you'd like information about the
Hay Foundation, please contact:

Hay House, Inc.
P.O. Box 5100
Carlsbad, CA 92018-5100

**(760) 431-7695 or (800) 654-5126
(760) 431-6948 (fax) or (800) 650-5115 (fax)
www.hayhouse.com® • www.hayfoundation.org**

■ ■ ■ ■ ■

Published and distributed in Australia by: Hay House Australia Pty. Ltd., 18/36
Ralph St., Alexandria NSW 2015 • *Phone:* 612-9669-4299 • *Fax:* 612-9669-4144 •
www.hayhouse.com.au

Published and distributed in the United Kingdom by: Hay House UK, Ltd., 292B
Kensal Rd., London W10 5BE • *Phone:* 44-20-8962-1230 • *Fax:* 44-20-8962-1239 •
www.hayhouse.co.uk

Published and distributed in the Republic of South Africa by: Hay House SA
(Pty), Ltd., P.O. Box 990, Witkoppen 2068 • *Phone/Fax:* 27-11-467-8904 • orders@
psdprom.co.za • www.hayhouse.co.za

Published in India by: Hay House Publishers India, Muskaan Complex, Plot No.
3, B-2, Vasant Kunj, New Delhi 110 070 • *Phone:* 91-11-4176-1620 • *Fax:* 91-11-
4176-1630 • www.hayhouse.co.in

Distributed in Canada by: Raincoast, 9050 Shaughnessy St., Vancouver, B.C. V6P
6E5 • *Phone:* (604) 323-7100 • *Fax:* (604) 323-2600 • www.raincoast.com

■ ■ ■ ■ ■

Tune in to **HayHouseRadio.com**® for the best in inspirational talk radio
featuring top Hay House authors! And, sign up via the Hay House USA Website to
receive the Hay House online newsletter and stay informed about what's going on with
your favorite authors. You'll receive bimonthly announcements about Discounts and
Offers, Special Events, Product Highlights, Free Excerpts, Giveaways, and more!
www.hayhouse.com®